Marx, Engels, and Marxisms

Series Editors
Marcello Musto
York University
Toronto, ON, Canada

Terrell Carver
University of Bristol
Bristol, UK

The Marx renaissance is underway on a global scale. Wherever the critique of capitalism re-emerges, there is an intellectual and political demand for new, critical engagements with Marxism. The peer-reviewed series Marx, Engels and Marxisms (edited by Marcello Musto & Terrell Carver, with Babak Amini, Francesca Antonini, Paula Rauhala & Kohei Saito as Assistant Editors) publishes monographs, edited volumes, critical editions, reprints of old texts, as well as translations of books already published in other languages. Our volumes come from a wide range of political perspectives, subject matters, academic disciplines and geographical areas, producing an eclectic and informative collection that appeals to a diverse and international audience. Our main areas of focus include: the oeuvre of Marx and Engels, Marxist authors and traditions of the 19th and 20th centuries, labour and social movements, Marxist analyses of contemporary issues, and reception of Marxism in the world.

Thomas Kemple

Marx's Wager

Das Kapital and Classical Sociology

palgrave
macmillan

Thomas Kemple
Department of Sociology
University of British Columbia
Vancouver, BC, Canada

ISSN 2524-7123 ISSN 2524-7131 (electronic)
Marx, Engels, and Marxisms
ISBN 978-3-031-08064-7 ISBN 978-3-031-08065-4 (eBook)
https://doi.org/10.1007/978-3-031-08065-4

This Palgrave Macmillan imprint is published by the registered company Springer Nature Switzerland AG.
The registered company address is: Gewerbestrasse 11, 6330 Cham, Switzerland

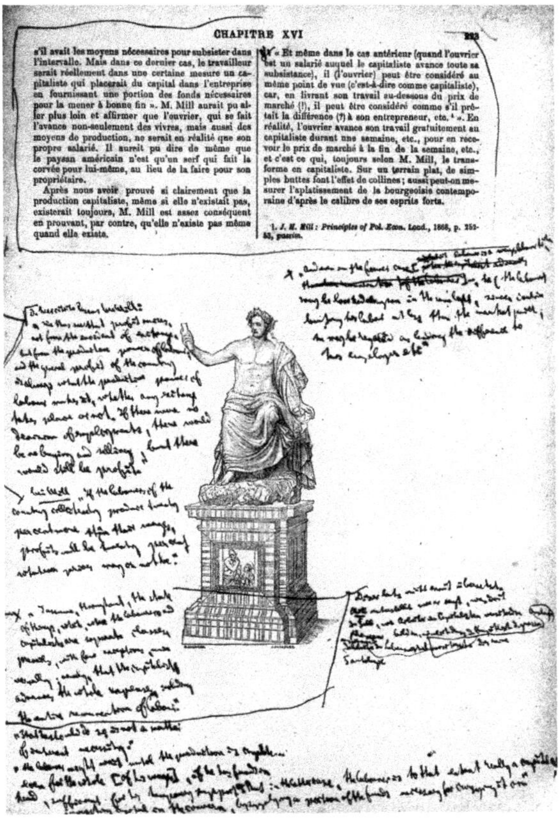

CHAPITRE XVI 223

s'il avait les moyens nécessaires pour subsister dans l'intervalle. Mais dans ce dernier cas, le travailleur serait réellement dans une certaine mesure un capitaliste qui placerait du capital dans l'entreprise en fournissant une portion des fonds nécessaires pour la mener à bonne fin ». M. Mill aurait pu aller plus loin et affirmer que l'ouvrier, qui se fait l'avance non-seulement des vivres, mais aussi des moyens de production, ne serait en réalité que son propre salarié. Il aurait pu dire de même que le paysan américain n'est qu'un serf qui fait la corvée pour lui-même, au lieu de la faire pour son propriétaire.

Après nous avoir prouvé si clairement que la production capitaliste, même si elle n'existait pas, existerait toujours, M. Mill est assez conséquent en prouvant, par contre, qu'elle n'existe pas même quand elle existe.

« Et même dans le cas antérieur (quand l'ouvrier est un salarié auquel le capitaliste avance toute sa subsistance), il (l'ouvrier) peut être considéré au même point de vue (c'est-à-dire comme capitaliste), car, en livrant son travail au-dessous du prix de marché (!), il peut être considéré comme s'il prêtait la différence (?) à son entrepreneur, etc.[1] ». En réalité, l'ouvrier avance son travail gratuitement au capitaliste durant une semaine, etc., pour en recevoir le prix de marché à la fin de la semaine, etc., et c'est ce qui, toujours selon M. Mill, le transforme en capitaliste. Sur un terrain plat, de simples buttes font l'effet de collines ; aussi peut-on mesurer l'aplatissement de la bourgeoisie contemporaine d'après le calibre de ses esprits forts.

1. *J. M. Mill : Principles of Pol. Econ. Lond.*, 1868, p. 252-53, *passim*.

Page 222 of the French version of *Capital*, with Marx's annotations and corrections in English and French. (Source: Karl Marx, *Le Capital*. Traduction de M. J. Roy, entièrement révisée par l'auteur. *Marx Engels Gesamtausgabe* II/7 Apparat. Berlin: Dietz Verlag. Page 746. Reproduced with permission from IMES Amsterdam)

Preface and Acknowledgements

Each year in my social theory classes I present students with a mock quiz on Karl Marx (1818–1883) and Marxism, starting with this question:

> Which of the following expressions did Marx use in his published writings?
> (A) dialectical materialism
> (B) historical materialism
> (C) commodity fetishism
> (D) capitalism
> (E) all of the above
> (F) none of the above.

Only a few students ever choose the correct answer (F), and most seem surprised that the other options all come from Marx's contemporaries or later commentators, including Friedrich Engels (1820–1895), who worked tirelessly in the last years of the nineteenth century to consolidate his friend and collaborator's legacy as a scholar and political writer. Many students are particularly astonished to learn that the term 'capitalism' was not in Marx's vocabulary, at least in the sense we use it today to refer to a variegated socio-economic system that arose from multiple cultural-economic sources. Although Marx is now known as the foremost critical theorist of capitalism, I explain that he used phrases like 'capitalist mode of production', 'bourgeois society', and on a few occasions '*capitalisme*' (in French) to refer to 'a group or class of capitalists' in contrast to 'wage-labourers' (*salariat*) (e.g. Marx 1989: 535; C: 763). Later classic sociologists, including Max Weber (1864–1920) and Georg Simmel (1858–1918), would discuss 'capitalism' (*Kapitalismus*) in the sense we use it today, while Emile Durkheim (1858–1917) prefers the term 'industrial society' (*société industrielle*). My point with this exercise is less to expose students' ignorance than to highlight the contrast, often ignored today, between what Marx wrote and thought and what often passes under the name of 'Marxism' in sociology and in public discussion. I also want to emphasize how most classical sociologists writing a generation *after* Marx were often responding to the emerging influence of his writings and the socialist movements of their own day. This book is my attempt to highlight the importance of these distinctions for social theory and political practice in their time and in ours.

Among the statements Marx actually did publish, and which profoundly affected the subsequent development of sociology and political science, was his summary of what he called 'the general result' and 'guiding thread' of his academic studies. In the Preface to *A Contribution to the Critique of Political Economy* published in 1859 he writes:

> The totality of [...] relations of production makes up the economic structure of society, the real foundation on which arises a legal and political superstructure and to which correspond definite forms of social consciousness. The mode of production of material life conditions the general process of social, political, and intellectual life. It is not the consciousness of human beings that determines their existence, but rather their social existence that determines their consciousness. (CW 29: 263)

Framed by a kind of 'curriculum vitae' where Marx tries to establish his scientific credentials by listing out his scholarly publications, this passage from the so-called 1859 Preface employs a topological metaphor for the whole of society consisting of a superstructure (*Überbau*), made up of legal and political institutions and ways of thinking, resting atop material relations that form an economic structure (*Struktur*) and social foundation (Lopez 2003: 51–2). This socio-economic base materializes or conditions (*bedingt*) cultural ideas and values just as social existence (*Sein*) shapes and determines (*bestimmt*) various forms of consciousness (*Bewußtsein*). Classical sociologists and social theorists in our own day would later struggle with these sentences in trying to reformulate 'historical materialism' (Engels's phrase, not Marx's), often arguing that religious, cultural, cognitive, moral, and metaphysical values are in some ways even more foundational to the rise of industrial capitalist society. Leaving aside the question of whether Marx himself was fully committed to this scheme in 1859, I argue that he does not always follow this 'guiding thread' when weaving the text of *Capital*. In fact, by pursuing a wide range of topics, problems, and issues beyond strictly economic concerns, he creates his own sociology in the process.[1]

Today capitalist forces and relations of production and consumption have taken on a paradoxical and painful character that can be characterized as both neo-liberal and neo-feudal. By reading how *Capital* was (or was not) taken up by the classical sociologists, I am also concerned with how this book addresses the capitalist accumulation processes of our own time. As I write these lines our world is still at grips with the SARS-COVID 19 pandemic, and signs are already evident that a new kind of 'corona capitalism' or 'command capital' is emerging in its wake. Many observers have been quick to treat these developments not just as exposing and accelerating the inner contradictions of capital but also as a sign of our capacity to overcome them (Mallett 2020; Foster et al. 2021; Humphreys 2020; Wallace et al. 2020). An old meme from 'The skeletal hatter', re-circulated on social media a few days after the World Health Organization declared the pandemic in March 2020, jokes about what many were wondering after the financial crash of 2008:

[1] In a footnote to Chapter 1 of *Capital*, Marx quotes these now famous words from the 1859 Preface to defend himself against a negative reviewer in a 'German-American publication', who misconstrues him to mean that material interests are *always* preponderant in *all* historical periods. Marx replies with a snide reminder that the Middle Ages could not live off Catholicism or Athens and Rome off politics any more than Don Quixote could survive for long on the illusions of knight errantry (C: 175–6n35). In other words, the social life of any epoch cannot be sustained by its ruling ideas or beliefs alone, but ultimately by its dominant mode of production, including property regimes and technological infrastructures, productive relations and productive forces. In Appendix A, I explain why a focus on the first volume of *Capital* should lead us to qualify or criticize such simplifications of Marx's primary theses. Contemporary readers should also pay some attention to his posthumously published notebooks, such as the *Economic and Philosophical Manuscripts* and the *Grundrisse*, the unfinished drafts of the other three volumes of *Capital*, and the writings he is best known for, especially *The Communist Manifesto* which he co-authored with Engels, and his articles on America and British colonialism (Kemple 1995, 2000). Like Marx's many asides in *Capital*, here and in the other footnotes to this book—33 in total (three in this Preface plus six in each of the five chapters), mirroring the 33 chapters of *Capital*—I trace the path of my own intellectual development in arriving at the arguments presented here, such as the Faustian thread that runs through my previous writings (Kemple 1995: 30–43, 2014: 45–59, 2018: 172–8, 2019).

> Weird how the stock markets are plunging so much when no infrastructure has been destroyed and no natural resources have been depleted. Almost like all the value comes from people's labour. I wonder if anyone's written anything about this? (@DrStedx)

The punch line is a mock-up of the cover of the first English translation of *Capital*, now with a new title: '*I F*****g Warned You Dude, I Told You Bro: A Critical Analysis of Capitalist Production*, By Karl Marx'. Besides challenging assumptions about 'essential workers', 'free markets', and 'supply chains', the pandemic has exposed ecological and biological vulnerabilities on a global scale in ways that would have been as obvious to Marx as they are to us. In the posthumously published Volume 3 of *Capital* (written before Volume 1), he provides a telling anecdote about the 'colossal wastage' of capital: 'In London, for instance, one can do nothing better with the excrement produced by 4 ½ million human beings than to contaminate the Thames, at monstrous expense' (CW 37: 103). Writing these lines in the early 1860s, Marx could recall the Great Stink of the summer of 1858 when he was living in Soho and writing drafts of the *Contribution* in the British Library. The human waste and industrial effluent dumped into the river over many years had led to a cholera outbreak and forced officials to redesign the ageing sewer system, and yet they continued to neglect the need to recycle sewage into ecologically sustainable agriculture. This event demonstrated the importance to him of drainage, transportation, urban planning, and civil engineering in maintaining the physical and cultural infrastructure of the capitalist economy, as well as of any socialist alternative.

Capital is a book of many layers and complex parts, mixing philosophy with history, social science with literature. My approach to this text and its reception among the classical sociologists highlights its literary qualities along with its narrative structure. Thus, I pay special attention to the model Marx followed from his favourite German writer, Johann Wolfgang von Goethe (1749–1832). My interests are as much pedantic and aesthetic as they are ethical and analytical, since all these features of the work inform Marx's commitment to social change, political reform, and revolutionary action. He was deeply concerned with how to use empirically rigorous and scientifically valid knowledge of the capitalist mode of production in the service of struggles for a more human and just world. Marx shares this commitment with later classical sociologists in their efforts to translate social theory into political practice and to transform scholarship into action. I call this literary aspect of Marx's work 'Faustian', after the title character of Goethe's great tragic epic drama of modernity. Sceptical of the antiquated spiritualist worldview, frustrated with his books, and exhausted with learning, the ageing Faust succumbs to the temptation to strike a bargain with satanic powers by submitting to a pact with Mephistopheles, the devil's advocate and earthly representative. I argue that the classical sociologists follow Marx's lead in acknowledging their own complicity with diabolical social, political, and economic forces in their efforts to be socially relevant and politically influential, or at least persuasive, enlightening, and entertaining to a reading public. Like Marx, many classical sociologists could recall scenes and passages from Goethe's famous play by heart, sometimes reciting or paraphrasing lines at strategic places in their work. Marx himself tends to treat the bourgeois economists as Faust does Mephistopheles, that is, as a guide to the earthly experiences and infernal worlds of capitalist society. Occasionally, the classical sociologists also explicitly cite or tacitly draw on this story to dramatize the issues of their own day, such as the unintended consequences of the Protestant Reformation (Weber), the infinite desires spurred on by the industrial order (Durkheim), and the divided subjectivities of the money economy (Simmel). As I try to show, Marx himself plays the role of Mephistopheles for the next generation of Faustian sociologists, tempting them to compromise their scholarly studies by cultivating socialist sympathies and by channelling their scientific ambitions towards social change.[2]

In *Capital* Marx ultimately resists the temptations of his own Mephistophelean guides, the political economists, and like Faust he chooses a tragic path of perpetual striving which ultimately leads to his salvation. Rather than submit to the diabolical pact (*Pakt*) that would lure him away from his studies, Marx comes up with his own version of the

[2] As Marx hints in his frequent allusions to fictional works (including Don Quixote invoked in the previous footnote), narrative models and literary flourishes are not merely ornamental but rather essential articulations of his critical aims and scientific ambitions. For this reason, we must attend not just to *reading Marx writing* insofar as we must also engage in the work of *writing Marx reading* (Barbour 2012: 100; Kemple 1995). Despite the obvious rhetorical character of *Capital*, only a few scholars have considered how he reads other writers or addressed his use of linguistic tropes in relation to his conceptual arguments (among them Hyman 1962; Ludovico 1971; Neocleous 2003; Roberts 2017; Stallybrass 1998; Whyte 2017; Wolff 1988). Despite the literary sophistication that Fredric Jameson (2011) develops in other writings, he mostly ignores these textual and rhetorical features of *Capital* in order to focus on problems of philosophical representation. In Appendix B, I outline the literary structure of *Capital* with respect to the grand narrative of the Faust story.

wager (*Wette*) that Faust makes with himself in the form of a promise to continue struggling and learning, even at the cost of immense suffering to himself and others. Before signing his soul away to Mephistopheles, Faust too pledges to resist the urge to rest on his achievements or to dwell on the beauty of any single moment, no matter how charming, enlightening, seductive, or pleasurable. Instead, he resolves to continue thinking, feeling, striving, and acting in the world to end of his days:

Werd ich beruhigt je mich auf ein Faulbett legen	Should I ever take ease upon my leisure,
So sei es gleich um mich getan!	May that same moment mark my end! (F: 1692–3)

What I call 'Marx's wager' in the title of this book is a more severe version of Faust's, since it entails patient understanding ***and*** vigorous action, an audacious imagination ***and*** disciplined attention to reality (Eagleton 1990: 170; Fracchia 2022: 16). Like Goethe's resolve in dedicating his life to the completion of his masterpiece as the supreme expression of his life, Marx never wavers in his commitment to produce a work that maps the possible directions for human history and that also calls for social change.[3] For Marx, the scholarly aspect of this wager lies in the risk of miscommunication and misunderstanding, while the political aspect lies in the danger of defeat and discontent. Like many of the classical and contemporary sociologists I discuss in this book, I too have been inspired by Faust's restless strivings. However, my model is less Goethe's life-long desire to transform his life into a work of art than Marx's tireless efforts to create a literary representation of the capitalist word that might also contribute to its transformation.

[3] 'Marx's wager' is also a biographical reference to Marx's notorious delays over many years in completing volume one of *Capital*. In a letter from July 1865, Engels reminds his friend of their bet to send the manuscript to the publisher by the end of the summer: 'The ultimate and final date [*Ultimatissimal-Termin*] for completion was 1 September, and the price, you remember, is 12 bottles of wine' (CW 42: 168; and in Wolff 1988: 6). In his reply, Marx concedes, in effect, that he will deliver no wine before its time, since his method prohibits him from going to print before all the parts lie before him: 'the advantage of my writings is that they are an artistic whole' (CW 42: 173). I argue that *Capital, Volume 1* is scientifically systematic as well as aesthetically complete, even though as a political project it had to remain unfinished within the lifetime of its author. In Appendix C, I situate the classical sociologists that concern me here not in Faust's study but alongside Marx in the Reading Room of the British Museum.

Although I cannot fully account for all the debts that have accumulated over the years, I will start by thanking Babak Amini, a former undergraduate student, recent PhD from the London School of Economics, and current assistant editor of the Marx and Marxism(s) series who persuaded me over a few beers in Vancouver that I should submit the proposal that became this book. The editors and anonymous reviewers at Palgrave Macmillan gave me the encouragement and advice I needed to complete it during a tumultuous time. I am grateful to countless students, friends, and colleagues, among whom I shall name only a few (in alphabetical order): Moneeza Badat (the artist behind Figure 3.1), Gilles Beaudin, Sylvia Berryman, Terrell Carver, David Chacon, Leora Courtney-Wolfman, Wolf Draegestein, Mark Featherstone, Billy Flynn, Nick Gane, Heather Holroyd, Ulas Ince, Robert Jungmann, Simon Lafontaine, Bryan Leung, Jastej Luddu, Renisa Mawani, Fred Neufeld, Dean Ray, Tristan Nkoghe (who helped with the index), Scot Richie (the artist behind Figure 2.1), Olli Pyyhtinen, Sanjeev Routray, Ryan Stillwagon, Agnes Vashegyi, Ana Vivaldi, Rafa Wainer, Paul Woodhouse, and Yun Han Yap. My father Donald J. Kemple (1934–2022) listened patiently to versions of several chapters and offered his wise reflections and good humoured remarks over dinners and wine. This book is dedicated to my partner Stephen Guy-Bray, who shows me daily that I do not need to choose between beauty and truth, or between happiness and hard work.

I hope that these reflections on the world of the nineteenth century will hold a mirror—however convoluted—up to the life we live today and are struggling to realize for future generations. I ask readers to approach my efforts as Marx imagined *Capital*: despite the unfamiliar names, foreign words, and scholarly references, it is 'a story about you'—'*De te fabula narratur!*' (C: 90; quoting Horace's *Satires*). And like Marx, who takes the advice that the classical poet Virgil gives to the fourteenth-century Italian poet Dante in his Preface to *Capital*, I ask you to follow me on my path through *Capital*, although in the end you must 'go on your way, and let the people talk': '*Segui il tuo corso, e lascia dir le genti*' (C: 93, quoting Dante's *Purgatorio*). Despite Faust's wager, I hope that together we might learn as we strive while enjoying the beauty we find in each of us:

Verweile doch, du bist so schön.	Tarry a while, you are so lovely. (F: 1670)

My own wager (hypothesis) in this book is that *Faust* is one of the best guides to *Capital*, and that *Capital* is among our best guides to classical sociology and contemporary critical theory.

N.B.: I often modify existing English translations, drawing on German or French editions readily available online or from print sources. References to *Faust* are by line number as indicated in both English and German editions.

Works Cited and Consulted

Abbreviations Used

C—Marx, Karl (1976). *Capital: A Critique of Political Economy, Volume 1.* Ben Fowkes trans. Ernest Mandel intro. London: Penguin Books.

CW—*The Collected Works of Karl Marx and Friedrich Engels 1844–1895.* 47 Volumes. New York: International Publishers. (Electronic Edition, Charlottesville, Virginia).

DL—Durkheim, Emile (2004). *The Division of Labor in Society.* W. D. Wells trans. Lewis Coser intro. New York: The Free Press.

F—Goethe, Johann Wolfgang von (1986). *Faust: Eine Tragödie.* Erster und Zweiter Teile. Stuttgart: Philipp Reclam Jun.

Goethe, Johann Wolfgang von (1976). *Faust: A Tragedy.* Walter Arndt trans., Cyrus Hamlin ed. New York: W. W. Norton & Company.

PE—Weber, Max (2009). *The Protestant Ethic and the Spirit of Capitalism, with Other Writings on the Rise of the West.* Fourth edition. Stephen Kalberg trans., intro. Oxford: Oxford University Press.

PM—Simmel, Georg (2004). *The Philosophy of Money.* Thomas Bottomore, David Frisby trans. London: Routledge.

Eagleton, Terry (1990). *The Ideology of the Aesthetic.* Oxford, UK: Blackwell.

Foster, John Bellamy, R. Jamil Jonna, Brett Clark (2021). 'The Contagion of Capital: Financialized Capitalism, COVID-19, and the Great Divide'. *Monthly Review* 72 (8): https://monthlyreview.org/2021/01/01/the-contagion-of-capital/?fbclid=IwAR1f9Iw1uL7FFrAsew1rAuw00me-0yoXmKEJsaL7Einl0PL9Mp486g-Sqpo

Fracchia, Joseph (2022). *Bodies and Artifacts: Historical Materialism as Corporeal Semiotics*, Volumes I and II. Leiden, NL and Boston, MA: Brill Academic Publishers.

Humphreys, Jordan (2020). 'Conventional Capitalism is Dying': COVID-19, Recession, and the Return of the State'. *Marxist Left Review* 18: https://marxistleftreview.org/articles/conventional-capitalism-is-dying-covid-19-recession-and-the-return-of-the-state/

Lopez, José (2003). Society and its Metaphors: Language, Social Theory, and Social Structure. London: Continuum.

Mallett, Kandist (2020). 'The Coronavirus Pandemic Demonstrates the Failures of Capitalism'. *Teen Vogue*, March 24: https://www.teenvogue.com/story/coronavirus-pandemic-failures-capitalism/amp?__twitter_impression=true&fbclid=IwAR3_bBS0b7Gioq2LOD5ZuCy0kcHvEvd29UP4kvWW-GVpulXmkK_QFAx8R5gg

Marx, Karl (1989). *Le Capital*. M. J. Roy trans., entièrement révisée par l'auteur. *Marx Engels Gesamtausgabe* II/7 and Apparat. Berlin: Dietz Verlag.

Wallace, Robert, Alex Liebman, Louis Fernando Chaves, Rodrick Wallace (2020). 'COVID-19 and Circuits of Capital'. *Monthly Review* 72 (1): https://monthlyreview.org/2020/03/27/covid-19-and-circuits-of-capital/?fbclid=IwAR2IVdc_SvHnH9R6jdF5W3ycZUnZpgOm1JTtZ_LBOhdilUsQyNKyhy7bouI#en29backlink

Titles Published

1. Terrell Carver & Daniel Blank, *A Political History of the Editions of Marx and Engels's "German Ideology" Manuscripts*, 2014.
2. Terrell Carver & Daniel Blank, *Marx and Engels's "German Ideology" Manuscripts: Presentation and Analysis of the "Feuerbach chapter,"* 2014.
3. Alfonso Maurizio Iacono, *The History and Theory of Fetishism*, 2015.
4. Paresh Chattopadhyay, *Marx's Associated Mode of Production: A Critique of Marxism*, 2016.
5. Domenico Losurdo, *Class Struggle: A Political and Philosophical History*, 2016.
6. Frederick Harry Pitts, *Critiquing Capitalism Today: New Ways to Read Marx*, 2017.
7. Ranabir Samaddar, *Karl Marx and the Postcolonial Age*, 2017.
8. George Comninel, *Alienation and Emancipation in the Work of Karl Marx*, 2018.
9. Jean-Numa Ducange & Razmig Keucheyan (Eds.), *The End of the Democratic State: Nicos Poulantzas, a Marxism for the 21st Century*, 2018.
10. Robert X. Ware, *Marx on Emancipation and Socialist Goals: Retrieving Marx for the Future*, 2018.
11. Xavier LaFrance & Charles Post (Eds.), *Case Studies in the Origins of Capitalism*, 2018.
12. John Gregson, *Marxism, Ethics, and Politics: The Work of Alasdair MacIntyre*, 2018.

13. Vladimir Puzone & Luis Felipe Miguel (Eds.), *The Brazilian Left in the 21st Century: Conflict and Conciliation in Peripheral Capitalism*, 2019.
14. James Muldoon & Gaard Kets (Eds.), *The German Revolution and Political Theory*, 2019.
15. Michael Brie, *Rediscovering Lenin: Dialectics of Revolution and Metaphysics of Domination*, 2019.
16. August H. Nimtz, *Marxism versus Liberalism: Comparative Real-Time Political Analysis*, 2019.
17. Gustavo Moura de Cavalcanti Mello and Mauricio de Souza Sabadini (Eds.), *Financial Speculation and Fictitious Profits: A Marxist Analysis*, 2019.
18. Shaibal Gupta, Marcello Musto & Babak Amini (Eds), *Karl Marx's Life, Ideas, and Influences: A Critical Examination on the Bicentenary*, 2019.
19. Igor Shoikhedbrod, *Revisiting Marx's Critique of Liberalism: Rethinking Justice, Legality, and Rights*, 2019.
20. Juan Pablo Rodríguez, *Resisting Neoliberal Capitalism in Chile: The Possibility of Social Critique*, 2019.
21. Kaan Kangal, *Friedrich Engels and the Dialectics of Nature*, 2020.
22. Victor Wallis, *Socialist Practice: Histories and Theories*, 2020.
23. Alfonso Maurizio Iacono, *The Bourgeois and the Savage: A Marxian Critique of the Image of the Isolated Individual in Defoe, Turgot and Smith*, 2020.
24. Terrell Carver, *Engels Before Marx*, 2020.
25. Jean-Numa Ducange, *Jules Guesde: The Birth of Socialism and Marxism in France*, 2020.
26. Antonio Oliva, Ivan Novara & Angel Oliva (Eds.), *Marx and Contemporary Critical Theory: The Philosophy of Real Abstraction*, 2020.
27. Francesco Biagi, *Henri Lefebvre's Critical Theory of Space*, 2020.
28. Stefano Petrucciani, *The Ideas of Karl Marx: A Critical Introduction*, 2020.
29. Terrell Carver, *The Life and Thought of Friedrich Engels, 30th Anniversary Edition*, 2020.
30. Giuseppe Vacca, *Alternative Modernities: Antonio Gramsci's Twentieth Century*, 2020.

31. Kevin B. Anderson, Kieran Durkin & Heather Brown (Eds.), *Raya Dunayevskaya's Intersectional Marxism: Race, Gender, and the Dialectics of Liberation*, 2020.
32. Marco Di Maggio, *The Rise and Fall of Communist Parties in France and Italy*, 2020.
33. Farhang Rajaee, *Presence and the Political*, 2021.
34. Ryuji Sasaki, *A New Introduction to Karl Marx: New Materialism, Critique of Political Economy, and the Concept of Metabolism*, 2021.
35. Kohei Saito (Ed.), *Reexamining Engels's Legacy in the 21st Century*, 2021.
36. Paresh Chattopadhyay, *Socialism in Marx's Capital: Towards a De-alienated World*, 2021.
37. Marcello Musto, *Karl Marx's Writings on Alienation*, 2021.
38. Michael Brie & Jörn Schütrumpf, *Rosa Luxemburg: A Revolutionary Marxist at the Limits of Marxism*, 2021.
39. Stefano Petrucciani, *Theodor W. Adorno's Philosophy, Society, and Aesthetics*, 2021.
40. Miguel Vedda, *Siegfried Kracauer, or, The Allegories of Improvisation: Critical Studies*, 2021.
41. Ronaldo Munck, *Rethinking Development: Marxist Perspectives*, 2021.
42. Jean-Numa Ducange & Elisa Marcobelli (Eds.), *Selected Writings of Jean Jaurès: On Socialism, Pacifism and Marxism*, 2021.
43. Elisa Marcobelli, *Internationalism Toward Diplomatic Crisis: The Second International and French, German and Italian Socialists*, 2021.
44. James Steinhoff, *Automation and Autonomy: Labour, Capital and Machines in the Artificial Intelligence Industry*, 2021.
45. Juan Dal Maso, *Hegemony and Class Struggle: Trotsky, Gramsci and Marxism*, 2021.
46. Gianfranco Ragona & Monica Quirico, *Frontier Socialism: Self-organisation and Anti-capitalism*, 2021.
47. Tsuyoshi Yuki, *Socialism, Markets and the Critique of Money: The Theory of "Labour Notes,"* 2021.
48. Gustavo Moura de Cavalcanti Mello & Henrique Pereira Braga (Eds.), *Wealth and Poverty in Contemporary Brazilian Capitalism*, 2021.
49. Paolo Favilli, *Historiography and Marxism: Innovations in Mid-Century Italy*, 2021.

50. Levy del Aguila Marchena, *Communism, Political Power and Personal Freedom in Marx*, 2021.
51. V Geetha, *Bhimrao Ramji Ambedkar and the Question of Socialism in India*, 2021.
52. Satoshi Matsui, *Normative Theories of Liberalism and Socialism: Marxist Analysis of Values*, 2022.
53. Kei Ehara (Ed.), *Japanese Discourse on the Marxian Theory of Finance*, 2022.
54. Achim Szepanski, *Financial Capital in the 21st Century*, 2022.
55. Stephen Maher, *Corporate Capitalism and the Integral State: General Electric and a Century of American Power*, 2022.

Titles Forthcoming

Vesa Oittinen, *Marx's Russian Moment*

Kolja Lindner, *Marx, Marxism and the Question of Eurocentrism*

Adriana Petra, *Intellectuals and Communist Culture: Itineraries, Problems and Debates in Post-war Argentina*

George C. Comninel, *The Feudal Foundations of Modern Europe*

Spencer A. Leonard, *Marx, the India Question, and the Crisis of Cosmopolitanism*

Joe Collins, *Applying Marx's Capital to the 21st century*

Jeong Seongjin, *Korean Capitalism in the 21st Century: Marxist Analysis and Alternatives*

Marcello Mustè, *Marxism and Philosophy of Praxis: An Italian Perspective from Labriola to Gramsci*

Shannon Brincat, *Dialectical Dialogues in Contemporary World Politics: A Meeting of Traditions in Global Comparative Philosophy*

Francesca Antonini, *Reassessing Marx's Eighteenth Brumaire: Dictatorship, State, and Revolution*

Xavier Vigna, *A Political History of Factories in France: The Workers' Insubordination of 1968*

Attila Melegh, *Anti-Migrant Populism in Eastern Europe and Hungary: A Marxist Analysis*

Marie-Cecile Bouju, *A Political History of the Publishing Houses of the French Communist Party*

Peter McMylor, Graeme Kirkpatrick & Simin Fadaee (Eds.), *Marxism, Religion, and Emancipatory Politics*

Mauro Buccheri, *Radical Humanism for the Left: The Quest for Meaning in Late Capitalism*
Rémy Herrera, *Confronting Mainstream Economics to Overcome Capitalism*
Tamás Krausz, Eszter Bartha (Eds.), *Socialist Experiences in Eastern Europe: A Hungarian Perspective*
Martin Cortés, *Marxism, Time and Politics: On the Autonomy of the Political*
João Antonio de Paula, Huga da Gama Cerqueira, Eduardo da Motta e Albuquer & Leonardo de Deus, *Marxian Economics for the 21st Century: Revaluating Marx's Critique of Political Economy*
Zhi Li, *The Concept of the Individual in the Thought of Karl Marx*
Lelio Demichelis, *Marx, Alienation and Techno-capitalism*
Dong-Min Rieu, *A Mathematical Approach to Marxian Value Theory: Time, Money, and Labor Productivity*
Salvatore Prinzi, *Representation, Expression, and Institution: The Philosophy of Merleau-Ponty and Castoriadis*
Agon Hamza, *Slavoj Žižek and the Reconstruction of Marxism*
Éric Aunoble, *French Views on the Russian Revolution*
Terrell Carver, Smail Rapic (Eds.), *Friedrich Engels for the 21st Century: Perspectives and Problems*
Patrizia Dogliani, *A Political History of the International Union of Socialist Youth*
Alexandros Chrysis, *The Marx of Communism: Setting Limits in the Realm of Communism*
Paul Raekstad, *Karl Marx's Realist Critique of Capitalism: Freedom, Alienation, and Socialism*
Alexis Cukier, *Democratic Work: Radical Democracy and the Future of Labour*
Christoph Henning, *Theories of Alienation: From Rousseau to the Present*
Daniel Egan, *Capitalism, War, and Revolution: A Marxist Analysis*
Genevieve Ritchie, Sara Carpenter & Shahrzad Mojab (Eds.), *Marxism and Migration*
Emanuela Conversano, *Capital from Afar: Anthropology and Critique of Political Economy in the Late Marx*
Marcello Musto, *Rethinking Alternatives with Marx*
Vincenzo Mele, *City and Modernity in George Simmel and Walter Benjamin: Fragments of Metropolis*
David Norman Smith, *Self-Emancipation: Marx's Unfinished Theory of the Working Class*

José Ricardo Villanueva Lira, *Marxism and the Origins of International Relations*
Bertel Nygaard, *Marxism, Labor Movements, and Historiography*
Fabio Perocco (Ed.), *Racism in and for the Welfare State*
Marcos Del Roio, *Gramsci and the Emancipation of the Subaltern Classes*
Marcelo Badaró, *The Working Class from Marx to Our Times*
Tomonaga Tairako, *A New Perspective on Marx's Philosophy and Political Economy*
Matthias Bohlender, Anna-Sophie Schönfelder, & Matthias Spekker, *Truth and Revolution in Marx's Critique of Society*
Mauricio Vieira Martins, *Marx, Spinoza and Darwin on Philosophy: Against Religious Perspectives of Transcendence*
Jean Vigreux, Roger Martelli, & Serge Wolikow, *One Hundred Years of History of the French Communist Party*
Aditya Nigam, *Border-Marxisms and Historical Materialism*
Fred Moseley, *Marx's Theory of Value in Chapter 1 of* Capital*: A Critique of Heinrich's Value-Form Interpretation*
Armando Boito, *The State, Politics, and Social Classes: Theory and History*
Anjan Chakrabarti & Anup Dhar, *World of the Third and Hegemonic Capital: Between Marx and Freud*
Hira Singh, *Annihilation of Caste in India: Ambedkar, Ghandi, and Marx*
Salvatore Engel-Di Mauro, *An Introduction to Ecosocialism*

Praise for *Marx's Wager*

"*Marx's Wager* explores the interconnections between the various classical sociological thinkers by focusing on their relations (direct and indirect) to the work of Karl Marx. In the process we are offered fascinating new insights into Marx, together with new ways of looking at figures as various as Herbert Spencer, Auguste Comte, Harriet Martineau, Emile Durkheim, Georg Simmel, Max Weber, Thorstein Veblen, W.E.B. Du Bois, Charlotte Perkins Gilman, and Sigmund Freud. The result is an intellectual feast for sociologists."

—John Bellamy Foster, *Professor of Sociology, University of Oregon*, author of *The Return of Nature: Socialism and Ecology*

"In *Marx's Wager*, Thomas Kemple explores the dense and thorny bramble where the classic sociological tradition wrestled with Marx's critique of political economy even as it tried to escape from his socialist conclusions. A book replete with keen observations and insights, this is also a profound meditation on what it means to really engage with the modern world, to study its forces and dynamics in the hope that one might, in some measure, transform it."

—William Clare Roberts, *Associate Professor of Political Science, McGill University*, author of *Marx's Inferno: The Political Theory of Marx's Capital*

"What a treasure of insight awaits readers who open this fine book! With a light touch and a lapidary style, Thomas Kemple offers a master class in Marx's *Capital*, which he views through a double lens—on the one hand, the literary masterpieces from which Marx drew inspiration, and second, the classical sociology which drew inspiration from Marx and *Capital*. Wearing his erudition lightly, Kemple weaves a tapestry in which Marx appears alongside Goethe, Dante, Durkheim, Weber, Simmel, and a cornucopia of others. Subtleties of Marx's analysis are matched with corresponding subtleties in the works of his successors, and it becomes clear that, clichés to the contrary notwithstanding, all of the major classical sociologists contributed to the project he inaugurated—the effort to understand capital in the light of what Kemple calls Marx's "surplus-value theory of labour-power." That effort, in the age of globalization, remains as relevant as ever, and Thomas Kemple is a sure-footed guide to the classical literatures that, I am convinced, remain central to our insight into this subject."

—David N. Smith, *Professor of Sociology, University of Kansas*, author of *Marx's Capital: An Illustrated Introduction*

"This book takes its reader on a Faustian journey, with Marx's *Capital*—one of the most profound works in social theory ever written, yet largely underappreciated or misrepresented—at the center of its own wager. An exemplary work of interpretive sociology, the book animates encounters with some of the most influential early sociologists through brilliantly constructed juxtapositions and creative syntheses. The journey is as thrilling as it is thought provoking."

—Babak Amini, *Visiting Research Fellow in Sociology at the London School of Economics*, co-editor of the forthcoming *Routledge Handbook of Marx's Capital: A Global History of Translation.*

"Provides some very creative readings of Marx in relation to social theory for the twenty-first century."

—Kevin B. Anderson, *Professor of Sociology, University of California at Santa Barbara*, author of *Marx at the Margins*

Contents

List of Figures

CHAPTER 1

Introduction: A Colossal Collection of Commodities—Marx *Contra* Sociology?

Abstract Marx and Engels are situated among the first generation of classical sociologists writing in the nineteenth century, including Herbert Spencer, Harriett Martineau, Auguste Comte, and Alexis de Tocqueville. Despite Marx's dismissal of their work, he implicitly adapts some of their key insights in *Capital.* A generation later, Emile Durkheim, Max Weber, and Georg Simmel approached Marx's ideas less through a careful or systematic reading of *Capital* than through shorter works like *The Communist Manifesto* and popular writings by Engels. This chapter is framed in terms of Marx's discussion of commodity exchange in Parts I and II of *Capital* and concludes with a consideration of his commitment to revolutionary action and critical enlightenment in the *Economic and Philosophical Manuscripts of 1844*, where he brings Hegel's dialectical philosophy together with Goethe's epic poetry to develop his own approach to the political economy of capital and the sociology of work.

Keywords Commodity • Spencer • Martineau • Comte • Tocqueville

Capital begins by invoking the deceptively simple image of a dazzling display of the modern temptations presented by capitalist commerce:

T. Kemple, *Marx's Wager*, Marx, Engels, and Marxisms,
https://doi.org/10.1007/978-3-031-08065-4_1

> The wealth of societies in which the capitalist mode of production rules appears as a 'an immense accumulation of commodities', the individual commodity as its elementary form. (C: 125)

As Marx announces in the Preface to the first edition, *Capital* is a 'continuation' of his *Contribution to the Critique of Political Economy* published eight years earlier (C: 89). It is not surprising then that this dramatic opening line simply re-cites the curtain-raiser of the earlier work (C: 125n1, quoting CW 29: 269). The immense mass of merchandise produced and consumed in capitalist societies—this colossal collection of commodities (*ungeheure Warensammlung*)—recalls the seductive window displays of exotic goods from all over the world in the shops of the great commercial centres of Europe, as vividly depicted in the *Critique*:

> The busiest streets of London are crowded with shops whose showcases display all the riches of the world, Indian shawls, American revolvers, Chinese porcelain, Parisian corsets, furs from Russia and spices from the tropics, but all these worldly things bear odious white paper labels with Arabic numerals and then laconic symbols £ s. d. [pound shillings and pence]. This is how commodities are presented in circulation. (CW 29: 324)

All that unifies this cheerful arrangement of luxurious, worldly (*weltlustige*), desirable (*lustige*) things are the non-descript price tags on each item. To discover how such a motely collection (*Sammlung*) of things might constitute an 'accumulation' that increases systematically through its own inner logic, Marx starts out with a micrological examination of its elementary form (*Elementarform*)—the commodity.[1]

[1] As Marx writes in a footnote, a growing miscellany of antiquities had been piling up around him in the British Museum for over a century. Most of these artefacts were looted from colonies of the British Empire. At the same time they offer ample evidence of pre-capitalist ingenuity and cooperative work regimes:

> The ancient Assyrian, Egyptian and similar collections in London and other European capitals allow us to witness those co-operative labour processes with our own eyes. (C: 452n19; see Appendix C)

The materials in the Reading Room where Marx worked and those which were housed in the Museum are themselves a 'colossal collection' of books, articles, documents, and artifacts, just as the text of *Capital* is a kind of colossal collection of texts arranged and presented for readers from different classes, competences, and cultures. Theoretical insights and worldly wisdom appear beside political arguments and moral appeals, scientific and literary references are presented next to statistics and reports. Despite the apparent chaos, *Capital* is also a *systematic* work organized around a guiding thesis—what in the following chapter I call the 'surplus-value theory of labour-power'—as well as a rigorous contribution to the leading social science of the day—political economy.

Among the intended readers of *Capital* are scholars in political economy, the leading social science of nineteenth-century Europe. At the same time, he addresses liberal middle-class reformers and sympathetic government officials, including factory inspectors whose reports are quoted extensively, along with socialist activists and the educated working classes with their 'great capacity for theory' (C: 95). Appealing to such a vast and diverse readership requires a complex method of writing or mode of presentation (*Darstellungsweise*), he points out (C: 102). As Robert Paul Wolff argues, 'at one instant he is a polemicist writing to the moment. At the next, he is a pedant, calling down authorities in six languages from twenty centuries confirm his etymological tracings and analytical speculations' (Wolff 1988: 13). In his dual role as polemicist and pedant, Marx is at the same time a political actor provoking both critical thought and social change through the power of the written word.

Insofar as Marx is a reader and writer of texts as well as a producer and consumer of ideas, he is like the ageing scholar Faust. The legendary character of Johann Wolfgang von Goethe's great drama recites his *curriculum vitae* on a sleepless night as he stands by his desk surrounded by his books. He is exhausted with his studies and despairs over his own inaction and ignorance:

Habe nun, ach! Philosophie, *Juristerei und Medizin,* *Und leider auch Theologie!* *Studiert, mit heißem Bemühn.*	I have pursued, alas, philosophy, Jurisprudence, and medicine And help me God, theology, With fervent zeal through thick and thin,
Da steh ich nun, ich *armer Tor!* *Und bin so klug als wie zuvor.*	And here, poor fool, I stand once more, No wiser than I was before. (F: 355–9)

On the one hand, Marx shares Faust's dilemma in acknowledging that he both knows too much and feels his incompetence too intensely. Marx too has reached the limits of understanding while sensing the urge for restless activity and the need to broaden his horizons. As he remarks in the famous 11th Thesis on Feuerbach:

Die Philosophen haben nur die Welt	The philosophers have only interpreted
verschieden interpretiert;	the world in various ways;
es kommt darauf an sie zu verändern.	the point however is to change it (CW 5: 8)

On the other hand, unlike Faust who abandons his study to experience the world, Marx combines solitary study and collaborative scholarship with participation in collective action. He is committed to bringing the *vita contemplativa* together with the *vita activa*.

This introductory chapter critically examines the common characterization of *Capital* strictly as a work of economic theory with only meagre sociological insights, or simply as a call to revolution lacking a developed class analysis (Wright 1997). A focus on the abstract arguments of Parts I and II among many readers of *Capital* is partly to blame for the neglect of the broad scope and subtle complexity of the whole text, not to mention its philosophical subtleties and political implications (Althusser and Balibar 1970; Cleaver 1979). Marx's own dismissive remarks about other scholars can also be misleading, including those who have later been acknowledged as sociological founders (and to be sure, 'sociology' in his day did not yet exist as an specialized academic discipline). For example, he was highly critical of Herbert Spencer (1820–1903), a giant of early sociology, and other contributors to the *Westminster Review*, such as Harriett Martineau (1802–1876), who has since been dubbed 'the first woman sociologist' (Hoecker-Drysdale 1992). He also attacked the early sociological ideas of Auguste Comte (1798–1857) and only casually took up the writings on civil society by Alexis de Tocqueville (1805–1859), another forerunner of modern sociological thought. Despite these missed encounters, Marx's career-long collaboration with Friedrich Engels (1820–1895) grounds his critique of political economy in the wide-ranging ethnographic insights, empirical data, and socio-cultural observations that have since come to distinguish the sociological imagination. As Marx boasts in his preface to his friend's popular pamphlet, *Socialism: Utopian and Scientific* (1880), he does 'full justice in *Capital* to Engels' *Condition of the Working Class in England*' (CW 24: 335). I also consider how the relative neglect of *Capital* in social science today stems in part from the generation of classical sociologists writing in the decades after Marx and Engels. Emile Durkheim (1858–1917), Max Weber (1864–1920), and Georg Simmel (1858–1918) tend to approach *Capital* less through careful interpretation, sustained study, or systematic engagement than from the perspective of *The Communist Manifesto*. Their approach to Marx's published writings is typically framed by the socialist movements of their day and through the lens of what came to be known as 'historical materialism', a term Engels later popularized but which Marx himself never used in his published writings. For these reasons, I argue that the question—'Marx *contra* sociology?'—remains an open one not just for writers in the formative age of classical sociology but also for those who still share many of their guiding assumptions today.

I

The first major challenge for any reader of *Capital* lies in its opening pages, which begin not with vivid descriptions of the sufferings of flesh-and-blood workers, or even of the wonders of capitalist commerce, but with a dry description of the 'cell-form' of the capitalist mode of production—the commodity (C: 90, 125). As Marx acknowledges in the Preface to the first edition of 1867, his focus is more on abstract relationships and roles than on actual persons and situations: 'Individuals are dealt with here only in so far as they are personifications of economic categories, the bearers [*Träger*] of particular class-relations and interests' (C: 92). Against the expectations of both an activist audience and a scholarly readership, he starts by examining how an abstract *thing*—the commodity—satisfies human needs or is traded for something else (C: 125–6).[2] He leaves aside

[2] As Wolfgang Fritz Haug has pointed out, interpreters and translators of *Capital* tend to elide the subtle way Marx finesses the relationship between the 'use-value of the commodity's body [*Gebrauchswert der Warenkörper*]', on the one hand, and its 'ghostly objectivity [*gespenstige Gegenständlichkeit*]' as exchange-value, on the other (Haug 2017: 67). *Use-values* may be material as well as imaginary; they may be corporeal but also semiotic and notional, and they are therefore not to be treated crudely as mere 'objects of use' in any instrumental, materialist, or utilitarian sense: 'whether they spring from the stomach or the from fancy makes no difference', Marx notes on the first page of *Capital* (C: 125). *Exchange-value*, by contrast, is initially defined by mass and measure, by ratios and relationships, and thus has a certain abstract, conceptual, or ideal existence: 'exchange-value appears first of all as a quantitative relation, the proportion in which use-values of one kind exchange for use-values of another kind' (C: 126). Neither aspect of the commodity is reducible to 'value' as such, he notes: 'The common factor represented [*was sich … darstellt*] in the exchange relation, or in the exchange-value of the commodity, is therefore its value' (C: 128). As Simmel and other commentators later elaborate, the socio-cultural, non-monetary, moral, and immaterial character of value is built into both use-value and exchange-value, and is not simply added on to them as objects of sharing and selling (Smith 2017; Spivak 1987: 158; Wilson 2004: 159–60). As Marx notes in the early pages of *Capital*, 'a thing can be a use-value without being a value', here acknowledging that the capitalist system necessarily draws upon zones of non-commodified values and processes of de-commodification (C: 131; Fraser 2014: 66).

for the moment any detailed account of the individuals or groups who produce, use, exchange, consume, or profit from such things. The 'thing-power' of the commodity, he seems to suggest, has a curious ability 'to animate, to act, to produce effects dramatic and subtle' (Bennett 2010: 6). The commodity conceals not just the splendours of the modern age but also the key to worker exploitation in factories. Its value holds the secret to the expropriation of peasants from the land, the displacement of people from the country to the city, and their migration across the oceans.

Unlike the works of the later classical sociologists, *Capital* does not open by observing the shift from traditional to modern societies, the ravages of social inequality, or the personal experiences of modern life. Even less does it attempt to solve such classic economic puzzles as the wealth of nations, the principles of taxation, or the mechanisms of price-formation. Rather, the introductory discussion is organized somewhat oddly around the trope of metamorphosis (*Verwandlung*) and specifically the transformation of *useful goods* into *exchangeable commodities*. After a long list of such things—iron, paper, watches, corn, sugar, coffee, boot-polish, silk, gold, and diamonds—Marx settles on the homely examples of coats and linen, familiar products of the ordinary work of tailoring and weaving (C: 131–63). Following the thread of these use-values from production through circulation to consumption, he spins a simple tale of their 'form of appearance' as ordinary commodities exchanged for other commodities, such as wheat, bibles, and brandy. A certain amount of wheat might be bartered for a certain amount of linen ('the simple, isolated, or accidental form of value'). Insofar as each item can be traded for a bible, a bottle of brandy, or some other good ('the total or expanded form of value'), then it follows that each of them may be treated as equivalent to a single good, such as a coat ('the general form of value') or a certain quantity of gold functioning as the universal equivalent ('the money form of value'). The difference between the 'general value-form' and the 'money value-form' is thus more a matter of degree than of kind: 'we may speak of the coat-value of the linen when its value is expressed in coats' (C: 155), and likewise 'gold [*Gold*] confronts the other commodities as money [*Geld*] only because it previously confronted them as a commodity' (C: 162). Despite the trivial appearance of a commodity such as a simple coat, Marx's analysis 'brings out that it is a very strange thing, abounding in metaphysical subtleties and theological niceties' (C: 163). From this angle, the coat can seem a bit queer, an intricate thing (*ein vertracktes Ding*) in that it may serve as the equivalent of other things ('the fetish-character of the commodity'). It might even strike one as an absurdity (*Verrücktheit*) that something so simple as can be generally exchangeable and grandly thought of as the 'universal incarnation' of value (C: 169).

Marx's elaborate examination of how an ordinary commodity (C) like linen can be exchanged for another simple commodity (C') of equal or more value, such as a coat (C—C'), is both deliberately and deceptively complicated. So too is his discussion of how a third commodity, such as gold, may be 'monetized' as their equivalent and used as a medium of exchange between them (C—M—C'). To flesh out this analysis, which playfully 'flirts with the mode of expression' peculiar to the great idealist philosopher G. W. F. Hegel, as he confesses in the Postface to the second edition of 1873 (C: 103), he imagines how the *owners* of commodities and money (*Warenbesitzer* and *Geldbesitzer*) facilitate this exchange in practice by mutually acknowledging their respective roles in practice as personifications of exchange-value:

> Commodities cannot themselves go to market and perform exchanges in their own right. We must, therefore, have recourse to their guardians [...] who recognize each other as owners of private property. (C: 178)

Taking the examples of the wheat-farmer, the linen-weaver, the Bible-pusher, the brandy-distiller, and the coat-tailor, Marx pictures each passing a two-pound note to the other in a chain of transactions motivated by physical need, fantastical desire, or monetary gain. This extended process of buying in order to sell—particularly buying cheap in order to sell dear (M—C—M', 'the general formula of capital')—is simply a formal expression for the accursed greed for gold (*auri sacra fames*) which has been so garishly depicted in classical literature, and which is familiar to anyone as the logic of commercial exchange or 'merchants capital'. It is at this point that Marx's sociological imagination takes over from his philosophical arguments and critical analyses of the categories of political economy as he begins to flesh out the actual human and social worlds that constitute these abstract transactions.

Marx was wary of presenting this banal point about the pursuit of profit in the guise of a scientific code. Advising Engels on how to pitch his review of *Capital*, he expresses a concern that many may only grasp at the technical formulas and skim over their underlying logic:

> It appears to me that you are on the wrong track with your fear of presenting such simple formulas as M—C—M, etc. to the English review philistines. On the contrary. If you were forced, as I am, to read the economic articles of Messrs Lalor, Herbert Spencer, Macleod, etc., in *The Westminster Review*, etc., you would see that all of them are fed up with the economic trivialities — and know their readers are fed up, too—so they try to give their scribblings some flavour through *pseudophilosophical or pseudoscientific slang* [English -- TK]. The pseudocharacter in no way makes the writing (content = 0) easy to understand. On the contrary. The trick lies in so mystifying the reader and causing him to rack his brain, that he may finally be relieved to discover that these *hard words* [Engl.] are only fancy dress for *loci communes.* (CW 43: 38–9)

The allusion to Herbert Spencer in this letter form 1868 stands out to us today as a rare nod to the polymathic scholar now considered a pioneer of sociology and a monumental figure in the heroic age of the discipline. Spencer's pathbreaking essay 'The Social Organism' published in *The Westminster Review* in 1861 laid the groundwork for his *Principles of Sociology* which appeared in a series of volumes from 1876 to 1896 (Spencer 1972: 53–70). In *Capital* Marx admonishes contributors to the *Review* for dismissing his argument that a commodity may serve as a standard of value for other commodities, as in the case of the 'coat-value of linen' noted above (C: 155). Against Spencer's belief in free trade as somehow natural and necessary, Marx examines the coercive character of exchange and the unequal nature of commercial transactions. And in contrast to Spencer's account of the historical evolution from military to industrial society, he describes the surplus workers of the present day as forming a kind of industrial army under the command of capital. Notwithstanding these differences, both Marx and Spencer (like Durkheim following him, as I show in the next chapter) freely employ biological metaphors to describe how 'the social metabolism' is mediated through commodities, and Marx himself examines how capital is defined by its 'organic composition'.

Despite Marx's scathing attack on 'the English review philistines' who dress up commonplaces (*loci communes*) in technical jargon ('hard words', as he writes in English), in its own way *Capital* blends mathematical rigour with ribald humour, abstract equations with rhetorical exaggerations. Another regular contributor to *The Westminster Review*, Harriet Martineau, is also now recognized as a founder of sociology, indeed as the first woman sociologist. In contrast to Spencer who wraps difficult points in fancy dress, Martineau presents complex ideas through plain fictions. In a draft chapter of *Capital*, Marx scorns the 'impertinent and superficial rubbish that one finds doled out with self-important complacency by [...] the nursery stories of a Mother Martineau' (C: 999). Elsewhere in Chapter 25, 'The General Law of Capitalist Accumulation', he sarcastically quotes from Martineau's 1832 story, 'A Manchester Strike', while critiquing the 'laws of surplus population':

> After political economy has thus declared that the constant production of a relative surplus population of workers is a necessity of capitalist accumulation, she [i.e. political economy—TK] very aptly adopts the shape of an old maid and puts into the mouth of her ideal capitalist the following words addressed to the 'redundant' workers who have been thrown out onto the streets by their own creation of additional capital: 'We manufacturers do what we can for you, whilst we are increasing that capital on which you are to subsist, and you must do the rest by accommodating your numbers to the means of subsistence'. (C: 787–8; quoting Martineau 2004: 196–7)

Martineau's *Illustrations of Political Economy*, where this story appears, is presented as a contribution to liberal social thought in advocating for the rights of workers to receive a just proportion of the wage fund. In this story, Martineau's aim is to teach her reform-minded readers a lesson about Thomas Malthus's notorious theory of population, which she didactically summarizes in a list of 'principles' at the end (Martineau 2004: 215–6). In the scene Marx quotes from, a Mr. Wentworth addresses workers in a public meeting to debate over whether to hold a strike to increase their miserable wages and improve their deplorable working conditions. By depicting poverty as a problem that can be corrected through the adjustment of market mechanisms, the story effectively repackages 'tragedy as error' rather than presenting social problems as effects of industrial processes or even as socially unjust (Freedgood 1995: 35). By suggesting that class conflicts may be harmonized by being brought into conformity with natural law rather than inflamed through strike action, the story demonstrates the futility of both state legislation and social revolution. To emphasize the ideological purpose of the tale's lesson, Marx conflates both the political economist (Malthus) and the author of the story (Martineau, who never married) with one of its characters (in fact, the speech is by a union organizer, not a manufacturer). As if to present a counter-narrative of the trials and tribulations of the conflict between capital and labour, at the end of this chapter Marx nevertheless presents his own 'Illustrations of the General Law of Capitalist Accumulation' in the form of an extended series of gruesome vignettes on proletarian suffering and struggle in England and Ireland (C: 802–70).

Martineau's posthumous reputation today as a sociological forerunner, liberal reformer, and feminist intellectual is largely based on her widely read *Society in America*, published in 1837, and the accompanying methodological treatise, *How to Observe Morals and Manners,* which appeared following year. In her own day, she was also known for her free translation in 1853 of Auguste Comte's courses in positive philosophy, which spell out the grand vision of the new science of 'sociology' that inspired Spencer. In a letter to Engels the year before *Capital* appeared, Marx admits to 'studying Comte as a sideline, because the English and the French make such a fuss over the fellow', and goes on to praise Comte's expertise in mathematics and physics while judging Hegel 'infinitely greater as a whole' (CW 42: 291–2). This assessment is qualified in Marx's Postface to the second edition of *Capital*, where he mocks the followers of Comte in the *Revue Positiviste* for accusing him of providing a 'critical analysis of actual facts, instead of writing recipes (Comtist ones?) for the cook-shops of the future' (C: 99). In *Capital*, he dismisses Comte for idealizing the old aristocracy as 'judge and general' while ignoring its new role in directing, leading, superintending, and adjusting land and labour in the interests of capital: 'Hence Auguste Comte and his school might just as well have shown that feudal lords are an eternal necessity, in the same way as they have done in the case of the lords of capital' (C: 451n18). On the contrary, he argues, both capitalist farmers and agricultural wage-workers are increasingly 'incorporated into capital [...] as members of a working organism', and their collective labour now 'appears as a power of capital possessed by nature' (C: 451). In Marx's view, Comte and his pupils are not simply defenders of the old feudal order but also enforcers of the emerging disciplinary regime of industry, as Michel Foucault notes in citing these passages from *Capital*, echoing that Marx's historical sense of the dynamic interplay of prevailing ideas and institutional orders:

'surveillance thus becomes a decisive economic operator both as an internal part of the production machinery and as a specific mechanism of disciplinary power' (Foucault 1977: 175). Despite Comte's sociological vision of an emancipated modern polity of women, workers, and intellectuals, in the end his 'recipes' serve merely as apologies for the capitalist status quo (Comte 1975: 378; Kemple 2017).

Martineau's *Society in America* now stands with Alexis de Tocqueville's *Democracy in America* as pioneering ethnographies of the racial, gendered, and class tensions of the republican post-colony, and thus as canonical reference points of classical sociology (Kemple 2011). Tocqueville's collaboration with Gustav de Beaumont, his travel companion in his voyage to the United States in 1831, caught the young Marx's attention as evidence of the persistence of religiosity in the modern world. In a polemical article, 'On the Jewish Question', Marx quotes Beaumont to highlight a thesis Max Weber would later develop in his essays on how members of the Protestant sects justify capitalist enterprise: 'In the US a person without religion cannot be honest' (CW 3: 151, quoting Beamont; see PE: 185–204). A year later in the *The Holy Family*, Marx's first jointly authored work with Engels, he cites Tocqueville's report with Beaumont on the penitentiary system in the United States. Here he presents a sarcastic sketch of 'the new penal theory' in America which combines the 'legal punishment' of imprisonment with the 'theological torture' of solitary confinement (CW 4: 186). Referring to official debates in France which dispute the effectiveness of these methods, Marx counters that that solitary confinement does not in fact eliminate criminality but leads rather to insanity, leaving only deportation to the colonies as a last resort. As Foucault notes, Tocqueville and Beaumont's report was among many of the period that make up the 'prolix technology of the prison' in blending rehabilitation, reform, and incarceration: 'The prison has always formed part of an active field in which projects, improvements, experiments, theoretical statements, personal evidence and investigations have proliferated' (Foucault 1977: 234–5). In Part VIII of *Capital*, Marx documents the emergence of this regime of discipline and punishment from the 'bloody legislation against the expropriated' in the formative years of capitalism which criminalized vagrants, landless peasants, and other unproductive workers through repressive laws and aggressive police action (C: 896–904).[3]

Marx largely rejects the sociologists of his day not just for their thin theoretical claims but also for their weak empirical arguments and their accommodationist political views. He appreciates the scholarly ambition of Spencer but not his pseudoscientific verbiage; he admires the encyclopaedic breadth of Comte but not his romantic nostalgia for the feudal order; he adapts some of Martineau's style of presenting political economic illustrations but rejects her moralizing lessons; and he engages with Tocqueville's ideas on post-revolutionary civil societies but dismisses his apologies for the capitalist status quo. In Marx's view, these writers do not adequately address the material conditions of capitalist production, and so overlook how the reality of exploitation is often concealed by the promise of equality, thereby ignoring how the ideals of collective freedom are constrained within the realities of private property. Marx's sociology of the

[3] Marx was familiar with Tocqueville's later work on the history of the French Revolution, which he reads as an account of 'original accumulation' through the partial expropriation of the peasantry by landed proprietors. In a chapter of *Capital, Volume 3,* 'The Genesis of Capitalist Ground Rent', he alludes to *The Old Regime and the French Revolution* (1856) where Tocqueville discusses the system of sharecropping in which tenant farmers (*métayers*) provide labour and operating capital to landowners in exchange for land and livestock. Marx characterizes this semi-feudal system as a transitional stage leading to the pure form of capitalist rent: 'On the one hand, the sharecropper, whether he employs his own or another's labour, is to lay claim to a portion of the product not in his capacity as labourer, but as possessor of part of the instruments of labour, as his own capitalist. On the other hand, the landlord claims his share not exclusively on the basis of his landownership, but also as lender of capital (cf. Buret, Tocqueville, Sismondi)' (CW 37: 789). Tocqueville himself comments on the social and cultural impact of this system: 'Though they were free and, in a small way, landowners, they were left in a state of ignorance and often destitution worse than that of the serfs, their forefathers. In an age of industrial progress they had no share in it; in an age of enlightenment they remained backward and uneducated' (de Tocqueville 1955: 133). As a Legitimist writing for likeminded liberal aristocrats, Tocqueville appeals to the charitable sentiments of neighbouring wealthy landowners to support oppressed tenants in a way that would have been seen by Marx as inadequate, though admirable. Marx's comments, which anticipate the famous 'trinity formula' discussed in the final section of volume 3 of *Capital*, should be placed within this larger historical and sociological argument: 'The owners merely of labour power, owners of capital, and landowners, whose respective sources of income are wages, profit and ground rent, in other words, wage labourers, capitalists and landowners, constitute the three big classes of modern society based upon the capitalist mode of production' (CW 37: 870). As Marx acknowledges in the 1859 Preface, he first turned his attention to economic questions and to the class conflicts these questions illuminate in his first published articles on the division of landed property and the thefts of wood among peasants in the Rhine Province (CW 29: 262).

capitalist mode of production thus begins not from these early social scientists but from the sober study of the industrial labour process and the sorrowful tale of proletarian suffering described in *The Condition of the Working Class in England* (1845) by his friend Friedrich Engels. Here is the point where his empirical and theoretical analysis most emphatically emerges as a moral and political critique.

II

In the closing lines of Part II of *Capital* Marx stages a kind of sociological theatre by dramatically turning his attention away from the commodity-owners and money-owners described in the previous sections, who act in the sunny sphere of the market, in order to focus on the more sombre characters who operate in the dark dungeon of the factory:

> In taking leave of this sphere of simple circulation or the exchange of commodities [...], a certain change takes place in the physiognomy of our *dramatis personae*. He who was previously the money-owner now strides out in front as a capitalist; the owner of labour-power follows as his worker. The one smirks self-importantly and is intent on business; the other is timid and holds back, like someone who has brought his own hide to market and now has nothing to expect but—a hiding. (C: 280)

As the worker submits to the punitive measures of the capitalist, the story of the coat which Marx began to tell in the first chapter comes to a conclusion in a violent scene of naked exploitation: the owner of labour-power (*Arbeitskraftbesitzer*) has nothing more to trade with the owner of money (*Geldbesitzer*) than his own skin or hide (*Haut*), or rather, the labour-time he can offer to earn back the equivalent value of the coat he has lost. In Peter Stallybrass's formulation, '*Capital* was Marx's attempt to give the coat back to its owner', that is, to trace the chain of 'free and equal' exchanges back to the exploitative scene of its production (Stallybrass 1998: 187).

The dramatic scene-change at the end of Part II of *Capital* leads readers into the dark recesses of the production process examined in the rest of the book. On the previous page Marx describes this dreary world as a hidden abode (*verborgene Stätte*) where the secret of profit making will finally be revealed: 'Let us therefore, in company with the owner of money and the owner of labour-power, leave this noisy sphere, where everything takes place on the surface and in full view of everyone, and follow them into the hidden abode of production, on whose threshold there hangs the notice "No admittance except on business"' (C: 279–80). Marx's parodic self-portrait as a writer guiding his readers into a concealed enclave recalls Dante's *Inferno*, where the Italian poet is led through the circles of hell by his classical hero, Virgil.[4] Marx is inviting his readers to follow him as he too is conducted by 'our friend Moneybags' (the cartoon character invoked in the first English translation) who himself leads the cowering worker onto the infernal floor of the factory (Fraser 2014; Smith and Evans 2012; Wolff 1988).

Besides Dante, another model for Marx is certainly Goethe's *Faust*, with the capitalist money-owner cast in the role of Mephistopheles and the worker playing the role of Faust. But where the capitalist only gives the worker a whipping (and a wage), Mephistopheles fulfils his end of their infernal bargain by magically sweeping Faust away under his coat to his

[4] In *Marx's Inferno*, William Clare Roberts makes a compelling case that *Capital, Volume 1* is ingeniously designed to follow the famous first part of Dante's poetic masterpiece. Just as the *Inferno* is divided into 33 cantos, so the French edition of *Capital* (the last version Marx revised and supervised to print) is divided into 33 chapters, with Marx acting in the role of Virgil leading the proletariat and their socialist comrades into the capitalist underworld. To guide his descent (*katabasis*) through the hell-fires of the factory, Marx treats the dismal science of political economy as a kind of map for how capital works *and* for what is wrong with it (Roberts 2017: 24–8, 40–4). The combination of literary bravado and scientific sincerity is made necessary by Marx's multiple aims in *Capital*: 'binding exchange to exploitation, contracts to conquest, prices to poverty, development to despotism' (Roberts 2017: 292). In effect, Marx adopts a double authorial voice to address a dual readership of scholars and socialists. Roberts's argument may be taken a step further, insofar as Marx seems to have had all three canticles of Dante's *Divine Comedy* in mind as a model for his critique of political economy: the 1859 Preface concludes with a quotation from the *Inferno* to describe our entry through the gates of science; the Preface to the first edition of *Capital* ends with a quotation from the *Purgatorio* to encourage readers to climb the steep slopes of political economy; and Part I of volume 1 cites a passage from the *Paradiso* to describe how heavenly values somehow lurk about in the material form of hard cash (CW 29: 265; C: 93, 198). As he suggests in the Preface to the French edition, the 'road to science' eventually leads up 'steep slopes' on the way to its 'luminous summits', like the pilgrim in Dante's poem who descends into hell before ascending to purgatory and paradise (C: 104). In the tradition of the great works of Aeschylus, Cervantes, Dante, and Goethe that Marx repeatedly returned to, *Capital* is a tragic story of loss and suffering that turns on a singular relationship between odd couples and strange pairings, as well as a human comedy anticipating a triumphant conclusion and a happy ending (Prawer 1976).

fabulous 'new career' (F: 2051–73), an epic journey that will take them through 'the small world then the great [*Die kleine, dann die große Welt*]' (F: 2051–2). As I show in the following chapters, most of Marx's allusions to Goethe's masterpiece project the voice of Mephistopheles into the character of the political economists he criticizes or lampoons, while the workers and their socialist allies or theoreticians typically speak in the voice of Faust (Prawer 1976: 320–7). Finding the social science of his day lacking, Marx reaches for literary inspiration as a way of highlighting the momentous significance of this dramatic turning point in his argument.

Notably, the empirical writings of Marx's friend Engels present him with a crucial social scientific supplement to these fictional models, especially the 'Outline for a Critique of Political Economy' (1844), which Marx credits as the first work to examine the formation and augmentation of value as a 'law' and thus as a key precedent for his own insights (C: 168). In the long Chapter 10 of *Capital*, 'The Working Day', he acknowledges the prescience of *The Condition of the Working Class in England* for its exemplary treatment of England as 'the classic representative of capitalist production', and as a model for Marx's critical use of empirical observations and official statistics:

> How well Engels understood the spirit of the capitalist mode of production is shown by the Factory Reports, Reports on Mines, etc. which have appeared since 1845, and how wonderfully he painted the circumstances in detail is seen in the most superficial comparison of his work with the official reports of the Children's Employment Commission, published 18 to 20 years later (1863–7). (C: 349n15)

Engels's sharp ethnographic eye and keen attention to detail in the factory inspection reports are especially evident in the second long Chapter 15 of *Capital*, 'Machinery and Large-Scale Industry', as in Marx's allusion to Engels's description of the factory hand whose muscles are exhausted as his mind atrophies. The employer strikes a kind of Faustian bargain with the worker through a wage contract that is formally free yet legally coerced: 'the courts say to the working man: "You were your own master, no one forced you to agree to such a contract if you did not wish to; but now, when you have freely entered into it, you must be bound by it"' (C: 448–50, quoting CW 4: 467). In effect, Engels plays Mephistopheles to Marx's Faust by guiding him into the hidden abode of the capitalist inferno, each of them treating the diabolical discourse of political economy as a guide-book to this underworld even as they also trace a possible path out of it.

Though Marx is the sole author of *Capital, Volume 1*, many of its core insights are evident in his collaborative joint-work with Engels. As Marx's first reader and trusted critic, Engels's scholarly expertise, political savvy, and stylistic flair mark virtually every page, and *The Communist Manifesto* which they wrote together sets the rhetorical tone and revolutionary tenor of *Capital*. In the dramatic account of heavy machinery in Chapter 25, for instance, Marx adds a footnote quoting the climactic lyrical passage of the *Manifesto* on the unprecedented revolutionary role played by the bourgeoisie. The technical foundations of large-scale industry require constant variations in the production process, rapid shifts in functions between sectors, and the flexible adaptability of workers in all directions:

> The bourgeoisie cannot exist without constantly revolutionizing the instruments of production, thereby the relations of production, and hence social relations in their entirety. [...] All firmly rusted relations, with their retinue of ancient and venerable prejudices and opinions, are swept away, all newly formed ones become antiquated before they can ossify. All that is established and stable evaporates, all that is holy is profaned, and people are at last compelled to confront with sober eyes their situation in life and their mutual relationships. (C: 617n29, quoting CM: 64–5)

The old world with its feudal (*ständishe*) hierarchies and fixed (*stehende*) traditions is vanishing before our eyes, Marx and Engels proclaim, while 'all that is solid melts into air [*Alles Ständische und Stehende verdampft*]'; or as I have rendered this famous phrase, 'everything established and stable evaporates', like the fossil fuels that power the steam-engines of the factory, the train, and the ship (in the French version: '*tout ce qui paraissait solide et fixe s'évapore'*; Marx 1989: 423n319). Among Marx's aims in *Capital* is to deepen and expand on this poetic motif with a wealth of theoretical insights, a variety of empirical details, and a repertoire of rhetorical flourishes. Likewise, the gothic imagery of the opening lines of *The Manifesto*—'A specter is stalking Europe, the specter of communism'—haunts the later work from beginning to end and the *Manifesto*'s final exhortation to revolution—'Proletarians of all lands, unite!'—is eerily echoed in the concluding call of *Capital*—'The expropriators are expropriated' (CM: 61, 94; C: 929; Carver 1998: 9–14).

Gripping passages from the *Manifesto* like the one Marx cites in *Capital* have posed a formidable intellectual challenge and set a high literary

Fig. 1.1 The Marx-Engels machine (the four-part structure of *The Communist Manifesto*)

standard for later generations of social scientists. The *Manifesto* as a whole has served as a kind of template for the theatrical, legal, pedagogical, and political applications of critical social theory that have circulated among activists and scholars ever since (Kemple 2000; Martin 2015). Figure 1.1 presents this argument by depicting the text's four main sections as icons or applications (apps) of the *Manifesto*'s key theoretical claims. Just as Marx plays on these themes (memes) in *Capital*, they are taken up in various ways in the work of later writers as well. Above all, the first and most widely cited first section of *The Manifesto* dramatizes the history of class struggles, with the bourgeoisie taking a leading revolutionary role (*eine revolutionäre Rolle*) only to be overtaken by the proletarians who sound the knell of its downfall (what I call the theatrical app). Since this story cannot stand on its own as an adequate account of history, Marx and

Engels go on to stage a kind of courtroom scene in the second section where they defend their fellow communists against the accusations and objections of sceptics and opponents (the legal app). The notorious 'summation' of the ten-point plan for the seizure of power in the conclusion of these arguments, which has attracted so much attention from the critics of socialism, is then given more subtle intellectual justification in the following section, where they deliver a series of lessons on the strengths and weaknesses of socialist and communist literature (the pedagogical app). After deploying the rhetoric of the theatre, the courtroom, and the classroom, Marx and Engels end by turning their attention to the struggle on the streets, the fighting in the factories, and the disputes among movement leaders, especially their allies in oppositional parties operating across national borders (the political app). In *Capital*, Marx carefully redeploys this textual 'machine' through a critique of political economy, an analysis of legislative reforms, an assessment of the theory and practice of socialism, and a sociological investigation of factory work.[5]

More than any other text by Marx and Engels, *The Communist Manifesto* has served as the platform on which later scholars, including Simmel, Durkheim, and Weber, came to understand the social scientific pretentions of 'Marxism' and the political aspirations of 'socialism'. When Simmel, in his influential 1903 essay 'Metropolises and Mental Life [*Die Großstädte und das Geistesleben*]', describes how the money economy levels all qualities to the 'common denominator' of 'exchange value' and

[5] I present the collaboration between Marx and Engels—the ME-Machine—in the anachronistic figure of an i-Phone partly as a provocation for us to imagine how the insights of the *Manifesto* and *Capital* can be applied to the new media marketing strategies of today's capitalist tech companies (Daub 2020). In Heideggerian terms, a hand-held device like a cellphone (or a manifesto) is 'ready-to-hand' (*zuhanden*) when we thoughtlessly carry it around or when it recedes into the background of everyday life, but it becomes 'present-to-hand' (*vorhanden*) when we use it to communicate or recall something; when we lose, damage, repair, or replace it; or when we reflect on it 'thematically' as a technology of communication or an instrument of revolution (Nemorin 2018: 105–6; 187). The latest advances in brain-mining and attention-capture intensify what Marx calls the 'original accumulation' of land and labour by commodifying intelligence and emotion as well: 'As capital produces workers, mass media businesses produce audiences and deliver them to advertisers. This process of socio-political, cultural and economic interconnectivity comprises […] an assemblage with neuro-marketing as the agent of predictive intelligence offering scientifically grounded strategies to maximize advertising effectiveness' (Nemorin 2018: 162, 205–11). In short, the *Manifesto* may offer us a kind of prototype for thinking about how communications technologies of many kinds can be seized upon and deployed for other ends.

reduces all distinctions to the question of 'how much', he is echoing a key claim in the *Manifesto*: bourgeois society 'has left remaining no other nexus between man and man than naked interest, than callous "cash payment"' (Simmel 1997: 176; CM: 64). And when Simmel writes of 'the money equivalent of personal values' in the *Philosophy of Money*, he is expanding on the *Manifesto*'s sardonic characterization of the physician, the lawyer, the priest, the poet, and the man of science as mere 'paid wage-labourers' (PM: 357–432; CM: 64). In many ways, Simmel's public persona as a teacher and his compassion for the plight of the poor in his native Berlin exemplify the pedagogical programme of the *Manifesto* as well: 'the bourgeoisie itself [...] supplies the proletariat with its own elements of education, that is to say, with weapons usable against itself' (CM: 71). And yet his way of examining the newfound individual freedoms of the metropolis, which he calls 'the seat of money economy', largely ignores Marx and Engels's concern with how those freedoms have been built upon 'that single, unconscionable freedom—Free Trade', and for the most part Simmel leaves aside any consideration of the deeper sources of this newfound emancipation in 'naked, shameless, direct brutal exploitation' (CM: 64).

Simmel does not explicitly allude to the *Manifesto*, while Durkheim in a 1897 review of a book that includes a French translation of the text in an appendix more directly presents the *Manifesto* as a concise formulation of 'the dogma of economic materialism'. This dogma assumes that 'the living source of social evolution is the state of industrial technology at each moment in history' (Durkheim 1978: 123–4). Paraphrasing the passage in the *Manifesto* on how 'the organisation of the proletarians into a class [...] compels legislative recognition of particular interests of the workers', Durkheim presents the bourgeois legal system as an expression and defence of ruling class interests, along with science, art, and politics (Durkheim 1978: 125; CM: 71). While he endorses Marx's suggestion that social life is largely created by 'profound causes which escape awareness', on the whole, he argues, the *Manifesto* is at best a political document of historical significance and at worst a set of unproven hypotheses without intellectual merit. Anticipating the core theme of his later writings, Durkheim insists that religion cannot be reduced to economics, but that on the contrary the economy more likely depends on religion (Durkheim 1978: 129–30).

In contrast to Simmel and Durkheim, Weber engages even more closely with the *Manifesto* in his 1918 lecture 'Socialism', delivered to an audience of Austrian army officers in response to the Russian Revolution the year before. *The Communist Manifesto* lays the foundation for the socialist programmes of the social democratic parties, he argues, and is at the same time 'a scholarly achievement of the highest order' (Weber 1994: 287). As a prophetic rather than a moralizing work, it projects the 'dictatorship of the proletariat' (a phrase not actually used in the *Manifesto*) as a transitional stage to an unspecified 'free association' of individuals. The text predicts the downfall of the bourgeoisie as 'a law of nature' (also not a phrase that can be found in the *Manifesto*) and prophesies revolution as 'inevitable' (in a factual sense and not just as an imperative). Weber rejects what he claims are three 'crucial theses' invoked in the *Manifesto* in support of this prophecy: the 'theory of immisersation', which states that the ruling classes cannot guarantee even bare subsistence to wage-workers and the permanently unemployed; the 'elimination of competition', which leads to unsustainable monopolies and the tenuous rule of finance capital; and finally, 'periodic crises' of overproduction and bankruptcy, which become increasingly destructive and must end in system collapse (Weber 1994: 289–91). In Weber's view, these theses are untenable not just because they express a romanticism of the general strike and an unrealistic view of revolution, but also because they have since been invalidated by 'the dictatorship of the official' in both private enterprise and public bureaucracy (Weber 1994: 298). In fact, however, none of these theses are explicitly developed in the *Manifesto*, and if anything, they further substantiate its assertion that 'modern state power is but a committee for managing the common affairs of the whole bourgeoisie' (CM: 64). Following Marx and Engels in broad outline, Weber examines the contradictions as well as the countervailing tendencies that supress and undermine state-managed capitalism in the long run.

Simmel, Durkheim, and Weber are typical among classical sociologists in treating *The Communist Manifesto* as a statement of the core theses of 'historical materialism' and of the political programme of 'socialism'. At the same time, they follow the lead of Marx and Engels in translating the slogan of the French Revolution—'Liberty! Equality! Fraternity!' into a set of research questions concerning the limits of personal freedom, legal equality, and collective action in the modern world. In their own way they take up the challenge Marx poses at the end of Part II of *Capital* to explore the underlying social foundations of capitalist institutions and the cultural underpinnings of the work process, as if in reply to Marx's wry joke about the political economists:

> The sphere of circulation or commodity exchange, within whose boundaries the sale and purchase of labour-power goes on, is in fact a very Eden of the innate rights of man. It is the exclusive realm of Freedom, Equality, Property and Bentham. Freedom!, because both buyer and seller of a commodity, say of labour-power, are determined only by their own free will. They contract as free persons, who are born equal before the law. Their contract is the final result in which their will finds a common legal expression. Equality!, because they relate to each other as simple owners of commodities, and exchange equivalent for equivalent. Property!, because each disposes only of what is his own. And Bentham!, because each looks only to himself. (C: 280)

In the chapters that follow I consider how these classical sociologists of the next generation find their own path into the hidden abodes of the capitalist world system behind the allure of consumer choice, beneath the power of the wage contract, and beyond the façade of self-interest. Following Marx in his descent from the market into the factory, these classical sociologists explore the emancipating culture of money economy (Simmel), the equalizing asceticism of the work ethic (Weber), and the collective sentiments of social solidarity (Durkheim) both inside and beyond the conventional workplace.

* * *

Fired up by Engels's investigations into the condition of the working classes, Marx would probably have treated these later sociologists with the same scepticism and scorn as he did the sociologists of this own day. In *Hegel Contra Sociology* Gillian Rose approaches a similar issue from another direction, arguing that the classical sociologists in the generation after Marx were stalled in a pre-Marxian waystation between Kant and Hegel and never quite attained the critical insights of either thinker. Where Durkheim produced 'an "empirical" sociology of values (moral facts)' that emphasized the prior construction of social structures, Weber developed 'an "empirical" sociology of validities (legitimate orders)' that emphasized individual agency (Rose 2009: 23). Likewise, she argues that Simmel's sociology is at most a precursor to neo-Kantian Marxism insofar as it selectively generalizes Marx's theory of commodity fetishism as 'the tragedy of culture' (Rose 2009: 26–39). Even Marx 'returned to a pre-Hegelian position by reading Hegel non-speculatively and by reviving the dichotomies that Hegel had sought to expose as rooted in bourgeois social relations', such as the separation of ideology and reality (Rose 2009: 223). In leaving aside any notion of subjectivity and self-formation and by treating individuals only as 'bearers of economic functions', Marx's sociology lacks any sustained attention or commitment to 'transformative activity, property relations, law and the corresponding media of representation' (Rose 2009: 229). Like the classical sociologists who came after him, he bypasses Hegel's insight into the essential unity of theory and practice and thereby severs the bond between knowledge and action.

Against the grain of this argument, I begin by acknowledging the performative character of *Capital* as both a scholarly text and a political work, and thus I distinguish between *Marx*'s critical analysis of capital and *Marxism* as a practice directed to the possibility of change. In fact, Marx's own version of Marxism entailed a sustained engagement with Hegel's dialectic of desire, work, and recognition (O'Neill 2020: 193–6). In the Postface to the second edition of *Capital*, he famously defends himself against critics who charge him with 'Hegelian sophistry' and claims instead to have turned Hegel's idealist method back on its feet 'in order to discover the rational kernel within the mystical shell' (C: 102–3). In a similar vein, Engels's Preface to the fourth edition of 1890 notes how Marx draws on his 1844 notebooks, the so-called *Economic and Philosophical Manuscripts*, which engage with Hegel in a less casual and more systematic way. In the final pages of these notebooks Marx praises Hegel's negative dialectics as the impetus and inspiration for his own approach to the sociology of work and the political economy of capital:

> The outstanding achievement of Hegel's *Phenomenology* and of its final outcome, the dialectic of negativity as the moving and generating principle, is thus first that Hegel conceives the self-creation of the human as a process, conceives objectification as loss of the object, as alienation and the overcoming [*Aufhebung*] of this alienation; that he thus grasps the essence of *labour* and comprehends the objective human—true because real—as the result of the human being's *own labour*. (CW 3: 332–3)

Here in a nutshell is where Marx's critique of German idealism finds common ground with his critique of political economy. Following Hegel he directs his focus to the human capacity for self and social transformation through work not just in the narrow sense of alienated labour on behalf of another (*Entäusserung* and *Enfremdung*) but also in its larger meaning as the mutual making and unmaking of human subjects and more-than-human objects (*Vergegenständlichung* and *Entgenständlichung*). Despite the abstraction, one-sidedness, and errors in Hegel's philosophical account of the story of domination and servitude (the so-called master-slave dialectic), Marx discovers that 'Hegel's standpoint is that of political economy', and as I would add, of the sociology of global capitalism (CW: 323; Habib 2017).[6]

Like Goethe's *Faust*, Marx's *Capital* is an 'incommensurable production' composed out of multiple literary forms, including satire, polemic, drama, and epic, and fashioned together into a systematic work of scholarly prose in philosophy, sociology, economics, political science, and history (Lukács 1968: 157–94). In a passage from the *Economic and Philosophical Manuscripts* that exemplifies this fusion of genres, Marx treats a speech by Mephistopheles in the 'Study Scene' of *Faust* as a dramatization of the diabolical temptations of money and private property:

Was Henker! Freilich Händ und Füße	Bah! Hands and feet belong to you,
Und Kopf und Hintern, die sind dein;	And head and arse too, if you please,
Doch alles, was ich frech genieße	But what I freely taste and view,
Ist das drum weniger mein?	Is that less mine than these?
Wenn ich sechst Hengste zahlen kann,	If I can pay for half-a-dozen horses,
Sind ihre Kräfte nicht die meine?	Have I not bought their sixfold thew?
	(CW 3: 323, quoting F: 1820–5)

[6] Marx appreciates the activist and materialist strain in Hegel's work, despite its abstractness and idealism. In the chapter of the *Phenomenology of Spirit* on 'the actualization of rational self-consciousness through its own activity', Hegel cites a monologue by Mephistopheles in Goethe's *Faust* to express the necessity of engaging with the practical world rather than simply speculating on the universe of ideas. After the scene in which the earth sprit (*Erdgeist*) enters into Faust's rational mind as he despairs over the futility of his studies, Mephistopheles invokes the diabolic drive of this spirit and beckons Faust to indulge in the voluptuous pleasures of pure individuality:

Es verachte Vernunft und Wissenschaft,	It spurns reason and science,
Des Menschen allerhöchste Gaben, [...]	Man's most supreme gift, [...]
Es hat dem Teufel sich ergeben,	It has given itself over to the devil,
Und muß zugrunde gehn!	And still must needs perish!
	(Hegel 1977: 207–8, paraphrasing F: 1851–2, 1866–7)

Like the scholar Faust ceding to the worldly temptations of Mephistopheles, Hegel and Marx embrace the desire to experience the creative life not simply as a rational and intelligent undertaking but also as an imaginative and passionate project that engages with the material world, even at the risk of destruction and death.

Mephistopheles's cynical view of the body as self-possession suggests that its parts—hands, feet, head, and ass—can be transformed into alienable objects of exchange and exploitation. By extension, the powers of nature too can be appropriated and exploited to enhance human capacities and other-than-human powers. Goethe's poetic intuition into what may be counted and paid for (*zahlen*) prompts Marx's theoretical analysis of the logic of value through the 'metamorphoses' of commodities into money and of money into capital. Money appears as a magic power enthroned as the supreme commodity, the ultimate object of possession, and the extension of human powers in which each individual may appear to own everything, do anything, and have access to everyone, and yet be estranged from oneself and others. In *Capital* Marx will expand on this notion of transformation through the metaphor of the metamorphosis of values by describing the physical form of the commodity as the 'social chrysalis state of human labour', and the money-owner as a 'capitalist in larval form' (C: 159, 269; Berman 1988: 111–5). Mephistopheles' infernal vision of total possession, of universal prostitution, materializes through the monstrous metamorphosis of capital in which not only land and labour but also language and life itself are commodified.

N.B.: I often modify existing English translations, drawing on German or French editions readily available online or from print sources. References to *Faust* are by line number as indicated in both English and German editions.

Works Cited and Consulted

Abbreviations Used

C—Marx, Karl (1976). *Capital: A Critique of Political Economy, Volume 1.* Ben Fowkes trans. Ernest Mandel intro. London: Penguin Books.

CW—*The Collected Works of Karl Marx and Friedrich Engels 1844–1895.* 47 Volumes. New York: International Publishers. (Electronic Edition, Charlottesville, Virginia).

DL—Durkheim, Emile (2004). *The Division of Labor in Society.* W. D. Wells trans. Lewis Coser intro. New York: The Free Press.

F—Goethe, Johann Wolfgang von (1986). *Faust: Eine Tragödie.* Erster und Zweiter Teile. Stuttgart: Philipp Reclam Jun.

Goethe, Johann Wolfgang von (1976). *Faust: A Tragedy.* Walter Arndt trans., Cyrus Hamlin ed. New York: W. W. Norton & Company.

PE—Weber, Max (2009). *The Protestant Ethic and the Spirit of Capitalism, with Other Writings on the Rise of the West*. Fourth edition. Stephen Kalberg trans., intro. Oxford: Oxford University Press.

PM—Simmel, Georg (2004). *The Philosophy of Money*. Thomas Bottomore, David Frisby trans. London: Routledge.

Althusser, Louis and Étienne Balibar (1970). *Reading Capital*. Ben Brewster trans. London: New Left Books.

Bennett, Jane (2010). *Vibrant Matter: A Political Ecology of Things*. Durham, SC: Duke University Press.

Berman, Marshall (1988) *All that is Solid Melts into Air: The Experience of Modernity*. New York: Penguin Books.

Carver, Terrell (1998). *The Postmodern Marx*. University Park, PA: Penn State University Press.

Cleaver, Harry (1979). *Reading Capital Politically*. Brighton, UK: The Harvester Press.

Comte, Auguste (1975). *Auguste Comte and Positivism: The Essential Writings*. G. Lenzer ed. New York: Harper and Rowe.

Daub, Adrian (2020). *What Tech Calls Thinking*. New York: Ferrar, Strauss, and Giroux.

Durkheim, Emile (1978). *On Institutional Analysis*. Mark Traugott ed., trans. Chicago, IL: University of Chicago Press.

Foucault, Michel (1977). *Discipline and Punish: The Birth of the Prison*. A. Sheridan trans. New York: Random House.

Fraser, Nancy (2014). 'Behind Marx's Hidden Abode: For an Expanded Conception of Capitalism'. *New Left Review* 86: 55–72.

Freedgood, Elaine (1995). 'Banishing Panic: Harriet Martineau and the Popularization of Political Economy'. *Victorian Studies* 39 (1): 33–53.

Habib, A. R. (2017). *Hegel and Empire: From Postcolonialism to Globalism*, Basingstoke, UK: Palgrave Macmillan.

Haug, Wolfgang Fritz (2017). 'On the Need for a New English Translation of Marx's *Capital*'. *Socialism and Democracy* 31 (1): 60–86.

Hegel, G. W. F. (1977). *Phenomenology of Spirit*. A. V. Miller trans. Oxford, UK: Oxford University Press.

Hoecker-Drysdale, Susan (1992). *Harriett Martineau: First Woman Sociologist*. New York: Berg.

Kemple, Thomas (2017). 'Comte's Civic Comedy: Secular Religion and Modern Morality in the Age of Classical Sociology.' In *Anthem Companion to Auguste Comte*. A. Wernick ed. London, New York, Delhi: Anthem Press. Pp. 159–174.

Kemple, Thomas (2011). 'The Spatial Sense of Empire: Encountering Strangers with Simmel, Tocqueville and Martineau'. *Journal of Classical Sociology* 11(4): 340–355.

Kemple, Thomas (2000). 'Post-Marx: Temporal Rhetoric and Textual Action in *The Communist Manifesto*'. *Rethinking Marxism* 12(2) 2000: 44–60.

Lukács, Georg (1968). *Goethe and his Age*. R. Anchor trans. London: Merlin Press.
Martin, James (2015). 'The Rhetoric of the *Manifesto*'. In *The Cambridge Companion to the Communist Manifesto*. T. Carver ed. Cambridge, UK: Cambridge University Press, pp. 50–66.
Martineau, Harriett (2004). *Illustrations of Political Economy: Selected Tales*. D. A. Logan ed. Peterborough, ON: Broadview Press.
Nemorin, Selena (2018). *Biosurveillance in New Media Marketing: World, Discourse, Representation*. Basingstoke, UK: Palgrave Macmillan
O'Neill, John (2020). *Writing the Body Politic: A John O'Neill Reader*. M. Featherstone, T. Kemple eds. London: Routledge.
Prawer, S. S. (1976). *Karl Marx and World Literature*. Oxford, UK: Oxford University Press.
Roberts, William Clare (2017). *Marx's Inferno: The Political Theory of Capital*. Princeton University Press.
Rose, Gillian (1981/2009). *Hegel Contra Sociology*. London: Verso Books.
Simmel, Georg (1997). *Simmel on Culture*. D. Frisby, M. Featherstone eds. London: SAGE Publications.
Smith, David N. (2017). 'Sharing Not Selling: Marx Against Value'. *Continental Thought & Theory* 1(4): 653–95.
Smith, David N., Phil Evans (2012). *Marx's Capital Illustrated*. Chicago: Haymarket Books.
Spencer, Herbert (1972). *On Social Evolution*. J. D. Y. Peel ed. Chicago: University of Chicago Press.
Spivak, Gayatri Chakravorty (1987). 'Scattered Speculations on the Question of Value'. In *In Other Words*. London: Methuen, pp. 154–75.
Stallybrass, Peter (1998). 'Marx's Coat'. In *Border Fetishisms: Material Objects in Unstable Spaces*. P. Spyer ed. London: Routledge. Pp. 183–207.
de Tocqueville, Alexis (1955) *The Old Regime and the French Revolution*. S. Gilbert trans. Garden City, NY: Doubleday & Co.
Weber, Max (1994). *Political Writings*. P. Lassman, R. Speirs trans, eds. Cambridge, UK: Cambridge University Press.
Wilson, H. T. (2004). *The Vocation of Reason: Studies in Critical Theory and Social Science in the Age of Max Weber*. T. Kemple ed. Leiden: Brill.
Wolff, Robert Paul (1988). *Moneybags Must Be So Lucky: On the Literary Structure of Capital*. Amherst: The University of Massachusetts Press.
Wright, Eric Olin (1997). *Class Counts: Comparative Studies in Class Analysis*. Cambridge, UK: Cambridge University Press.

CHAPTER 2

Sensuously Suprasensuous Things: *Capital* and Social Solidarity

Abstract Throughout his career Durkheim grapples with the challenge of socialist politics and the 'theory of historical materialism', on one occasion with reference to the discussion in *Capital* of the struggle for a normal working day. His cure for the pathologies of industrial society, including strikes, commercial crises, and overwork, centres on a broad understanding of the moral, sentimental, and practical bases of social solidarity. What Marx calls the thing-like or 'fetishistic' character of commodified social relations is likewise extended by Durkheim in what he calls the external and coercive character of 'social facts'. Each writer takes up these themes while alluding to the celebrated love story in Goethe's play where Faust seduces Gretchen into a romance that ends in her tragic death and ultimate redemption, a story which serves for them as a warning about the destructive and seductive powers of the industrial order of capital.

Keywords Labour-power • Durkheim • Religion • Surplus-value • Vampire

Marx makes a lot out of his claim that 'As exchange-values, all commodities are merely definite quantities of *congealed labour-time*', noting in *Capital* that he had already developed this crucial point in *A Contribution to the Critique of Political Economy* (C: 130; CW 29: 272). The idea that in order to be traded, goods must first somehow be *made* and that their

T. Kemple, *Marx's Wager*, Marx, Engels, and Marxisms,
https://doi.org/10.1007/978-3-031-08065-4_2

production takes *time* is common among classical political economists from John Locke to David Ricardo in their attempts to explain price and wage fluctuations and to address the moral problem of the source of profit in unequal exchanges. In Marx's day this argument was also taken up by prominent socialists such as Pierre-Joseph Proudhon and John Bray in their efforts to secure a more just distribution of wealth between workers and employers. Even the specification that labour-time is 'socially necessary'—depending on the skills, resources, and technologies employed—is not Marx's invention. From his first sole-authored book *The Poverty of Philosophy* to the unfinished volumes of *Capital*, he would criticize many of the assumptions attributed to what has since been called his 'labour theory of value', a phrase Max himself does not use. What he does claim to be his own original idea is that the labour contained in commodities has a 'dual character', both in creating use-values and when expressed as value (C: 132; CW 29: 283–4). Diane Elson has therefore called Marx's analysis of how value represents labour, and how value-forms change over time and in space, 'the value theory of labour' (Elson 1979: 139; Roberts 2017: 74–82; Harvey 2018: 9). More precisely, Marx focuses on how the 'capacity to labour' may itself be consumed as a use-value in producing exchange-value, and how this 'labour-power' generates not just 'value' but 'more value' (surplus-value) under certain conditions of production and exchange. His original insight can therefore more accurately be called a *surplus-value theory of labour-power*, as Marx himself implies early on Part III of the French edition of *Capital*, the last version published in his lifetime. There he explicitly contrasts 'the production of use-values' not just with the production of exchange-values or the 'valorisation process' as such, but more precisely with the 'production of surplus-value' (Marx 1989: 145, 153; C: 293). Parts I–III of *Capital* (Chapters 1–11) are his attempt to elaborate on this theory and illustrate it empirically.

Marx assumes that under the prevailing capitalist mode of production, labour and other activities traditionally undertaken in isolation have become both more specialized and more interdependent: 'In a society of commodity producers, this qualitative difference between the useful forms of labour which are carried on independently and privately by individual producers develops into a complex system, a social division of labour' (C: 133). A generation later, Emile Durkheim will elaborate on the thesis that in an industrial society 'private labour manifests itself as an element of the total social labour' (C: 165). The French title of Durkheim's breakthrough book, *De la division du travail social* (literally, *On the Division of Social Labour*), published in 1893 and reissued in 1902, offers a clue to how he takes up Marx's problematic in *Capital*. Despite the title in English, Durkheim is only residually concerned with the division of labour *in society*, that is, with how work becomes divided up and coordinated between various socio-economic sectors. Even less is he interested in the division of labour *in manufacturing and industry*, topics Marx examines in Chapter 14 of *Capital* and elsewhere (C: 470–80). Rather, Durkheim devotes his career to studying *social solidarity* as the underlying basis not just of the division of labour in the capitalist economy but in every aspect of modern life.

This chapter considers how Durkheim grappled with the challenge of socialist politics and the 'theory of historical materialism', in part through a brief encounter with *Capital*. His solution to the conceptual and practical problems of industrial society centres on a broad understanding of the moral, sentimental, and practical basis of social order. I begin by showing how *The Division of Labour* takes up Marx's analysis (in Parts III and IV of *Capital*) of the exploitation of labour-power (*la force de travail*), which is compelled to submit to the forces of capital. Following Marx, he argues that the 'abnormal' forms of the division of labour—including strikes, commercial crises, and overwork—do not simply have a mechanical foundation or economic cause but ultimately emerge from social-cultural and 'religious' sources with profound moral implications and political consequences. In a similar vein, Marx argues that commodities are 'sensuously suprasensuous or social things' that seem to resist and tempt us, as if they have a will of their own. What he calls the 'fetishistic' character of commodified social relations can therefore be understood as a particular instance of what Durkheim calls the external and coercive character of thing-like 'social facts' in general.[1] Curiously, both Marx and Durkheim

[1] Durkheim's more general argument is that *desire* and *power* lie at the foundation of all social life. Marx's humorous remark in the opening lines of Chapter 2 of *Capital* on the coercive character of commodity exchanges can serve as an illustration:

> Commodities are things, and therefore lack the power to resist man. If they are unwilling, he can use force; in other words, he can take possession of them [*Si elles manquent de bonne volonté, il peut employer la force, en d'autres termes s'en emparer*]. (C: 178; Marx 1989: 63–4)

This playful characterization of the apparently wilful character of commodities adapts the wording of one of Goethe's most famous poems, 'The Earl King', which Franz Schubert turned into a popular song in the early 1800s. A young boy dies at the hands of a fairy king who lures him away from his father and then seizes him by force:

take up these themes while alluding to the celebrated love story in Goethe's play where Faust seduces Gretchen into a romance that ends in her tragic death and ultimate redemption. The so-called Gretchen tragedy is emblematic for them of the modern drive to conquer 'the small world, then the great' (F: 2052), and thus serves as a warning about the destructive and seductive powers of the industrial order of capital.

I

Durkheim marks a 'dividing line' in his own intellectual development around 1895 with what he calls a 'revelation' about the social basis of religion, which he came to see as the source of the elementary forms of all social and cultural life (Alexander 1989: 138–43). The significance of this breakthrough, when he first came to see an alternative to 'Marxism', is still evident in the conclusion of his last book published in 1912, *The Elementary Forms of Religious Life*:

> But the last thing to do is to see this theory of religion as merely a refurbishment of historical materialism. [...] I do indeed take it to be obvious that social life depends on and bears the mark of its material base, just as the mental life of the individual depends on the brain and indeed on the whole body. But collective consciousness is something other than a mere epiphenomenon of its morphological base, just as individual consciousness is something other than a mere product of the nervous system. If collective consciousness is to appear, a *sui generis* synthesis of individual consciousnesses must occur. (Durkheim 1995: 426)

In other words, individual feelings, ideas, and images combine and interact with one another in ways that manifest their own forces of attraction and repulsion and follow distinct laws of division and proliferation. Mental

'*Ich liebe dich, mich reizt deine schöne Gestalt;*	I love thee, I'm charmed by thy beauty, dear boy!
Und bist du nicht willig, so brauch' ich Gewalt.'	And if thou'rt unwilling, then force I'll employ.' (Goethe 1983: 86)

Just as in Goethe's poem the boy's face is an alluring sight for the Earl King, who in turn tempts the child with a beautiful image of his daughter, so commodities for Marx seem to display a deadly charm that appeals to our desire while eluding our power to possess them.

life does indeed have a material basis, Durkheim concedes, but collective life also has its own uniquely emergent properties manifested in self-generating representations (a point Marx himself had made earlier in *The 18th Brumaire of Louis Bonaparte*; CW 11: 103–4). In *The Division of Labour*, Durkheim calls the objective reality of collective life *social solidarity*, which he examines in part by expanding on Marx's understanding of how labour-power takes on a life of its own.

In the opening pages of Part III of *Capital*, Marx briefly revises his unpublished youthful meditations on what is distinctive about the human work of objectification (*Vergegenständlichung*): 'Labour is, first of all, a process between man and nature by which man, through his own actions, mediates, regulates, and controls the metabolism between himself and nature' (C: 283; Burkett 2014; Jarvikoski 1996). Through the work process (*Arbeitsprozess*) human beings exchange material properties with the natural world through the metabolism (*Stoffwechselprozess*) between human and other-than-human beings. The culturally distinct and historically specific ways in which these processes take place constitute the 'mode of production' by which socio-natural relations and socio-technical forces combine over time and on multiple scales. A 'socially necessary' use-value in one spatio-temporal context, such as corn in pre-colonial South American, is produced and understood differently in another time and place, such as modern-day North America. In Durkheim's terms, such needs and wants are culturally defined by beliefs and practices that characterize different forms of social solidarity.

Throughout *Capital* Marx is concerned with how this metabolic process between human and natural worlds is commodified under the capitalist mode of production where land and labour are bought and sold as exchange-values, such as when plots of land are sectioned off as real estate or a worker's skills are hired out for wages. The alienation or estrangement (*Entfremdung*) of labour under capitalist conditions entails the sale and purchase of labour-power (*Arbeitskraft*), 'those mental and physical capabilities existing in the embodied living personality of a human being', the value of which is not just physically limited but also historically and morally determined (C: 270, 274). Marx conceives this general human capacity or work force (*force de travail*) broadly to include the manual, mental, and emotional labour-power set in motion to produce use-values—physical, imagined, material, or symbolic. Labour takes on a 'dual character' when it produces not just use-values but exchange-values as well, and whether or not it mainly takes the form of hand-work, head-work, or heart-work.[2] Marx describes valorization (*Verwertungsprozess*) as the process through which living labour produces commodities out of materials and instruments which are themselves already commodities. When labour-power and the material conditions of production are themselves bought and sold as commodities, he calls them 'variable capital' and 'constant capital', respectively, which together make up the 'organic composition' of capital (C: 317, 762). Extending Marx's idea that capital is more than the sum of its parts, Durkheim calls the social bonds underlying the industrial division of labour 'organic solidarity', implying that social organization itself can take on a life of its own (DL: 88–104).

Durkheim treats legal rules broadly as 'visible symbols' of the otherwise imperceptible social attachments that underlie the material conditions of organized life and render them morally coherent (DL: 24). Legal sanctions express not just the class interests that drive economic activity, as Marxists and historical materialists might claim, but also deeper moral values and

[2] Engels draws on his knowledge of English to clarify this two-fold character in a footnote to the fourth edition of *Capital*: 'Labour which creates use-values and is qualitatively determined is called "work" as opposed to "labour"; labour which creates value and is only measured quantitatively is called "labour", as opposed to work' (C: 138n16). In everyday speech, for example, we might contrast unpaid 'housework' by family members with paid 'domestic labour' by servants, although in other contexts English usage does not correspond to Engels's distinction (as translator Ben Fowkes points out in an addendum to Engels's remark). In a key footnote of *The Managed Heart*, Arlie Hochschild draws out the sociological implications of this terminological distinction in professional and private settings: 'I use the term *emotional labor* to mean the management of feeling to create publicly observable facial and bodily display; emotional labor is sold for a wage and therefore has *exchange-value*. I use the synonymous terms *emotion work* or *emotion management* to refer to those same acts done is a private context where they have *use-value*' (Hochschild 2012: 7). Whether or not 'work' can be terminologically set apart from 'labour', at least in theory as Hannah Arendt has argued, Marx's main point is that the commodification of labour-power is constitutive of value (Arendt 1958: 85–90, 130–1). He notes that this thesis is only implicit in the writings of William Petty, the founder of political economy in the seventeenth century, and of Benjamin Franklin, in the eighteenth century (C: 142n18; Max Weber later takes up Franklin's maxim 'Time is Money' as a precedent-setting principle of modern capitalist work processes). He also points out that Thomas Hobbes was the first to allude to this two-fold nature of labour-power in the *Leviathan*: '"The value or worth of a man, is as of all other things, his price—that is to say, so much as would be given for the use of his power"' (C: 274n5, quoting Hobbes 1968: 151). Marx's 1865 lectures in English on 'Value, Price, and Profit' stress the significance of this analytical distinction: 'What the working man sells is not directly his *Labour*, but his *Labouring Power*, the temporary disposal of which he makes over to the capitalist' (CW 20: 128).

feelings that are more or less shared by everyone: 'The totality of beliefs and sentiments common to the average members of a society forms a determinate system with a life of its own [which] can be termed the collective or common consciousness' (DL: 39). For instance, criminal law and the corresponding repressive measures that expiate criminal elements, such as the *lex talionis* ('eye for an eye') of the Pentateuch, reinforce extremely strong states of the collective consciousness (DL: 94). By contrast, administrative, civil, and business law tends to be enforced through so-called restitutive sanctions, such as factory legislation or traffic fines, which aim to restore the status quo between individuals or groups. Where repressive sanctions may compel conformity during an existential crisis, restitutive sanctions are generally more widely applied to transactions in daily and institutional life. Each kind of law manifests the inherently dual nature of human beings as both individual and social: 'Two consciousnesses exist within us: the one comprises only states that are personal to each one of us, characteristic of us as individuals, whilst the other comprises the states that are common to the whole society' (DL: 61). In the Preface to the second edition of *The Division of Labour*, Durkheim expresses this duality in terms of 'the relationship between individual personality and social solidarity' and formulates his research question in terms of how a person in modern societies can be 'both *more individual* and *more socially integrated*' (DL: xxx). In the *Elementary Forms* he ventures even further to assert that 'the collective consciousness is the consciousness of consciousnesses' (Durkheim 1995: 445). Inverting Descartes's *cogito* with his own *sumus*, he seems to suggest that 'we are, therefore we think' insofar as collective existence is the precondition for individual thought.

In contrast to Durkheim's general programmatic statements, Marx focuses more narrowly on the role of factory legislation in regulating working conditions while appealing to moral sensibilities that may inspire further reforms, if not revolution. In the monumental Chapter 10 of *Capital*, he presents gripping descriptions of the varying effects of English laws on limiting the maximum length of working day and the minimum age or sex of workers, ostensibly protecting their health, safety, and welfare while upholding the interests of capital. Government laws can only be applied within natural limits (*Schranke*) that are ultimately absolute, such as the material resources an employer has access to, the 24 hours in a day, or the exhaustion and death of the working body: 'The length of the working day therefore fluctuates within boundaries both physical and social, but these limiting conditions are of a very elastic nature, and allow a tremendous amount of latitude' (C: 341). In the final sections of Chapter 10, Marx traces the history of 'the struggle for a normal working day' up to nineteenth-century efforts to reduce child labour and establish a ten-hour workday (C: 375–416). Durkheim addresses these issues in broad strokes in the final book of *The Division Labour* on 'Abnormal Forms' against the background of the increasingly acute industrial and commercial crises in late nineteenth-century Europe (DL: 292). The lack of regulatory norms governing the economy ('the anomic division of labour') may lead some groups to reassert inherited privileges of work and wealth, or else fuel hostilities between capital and labour ('the forced division of labour'). Powerful employers may exercise coercive power over workers in factories by requiring them to work long hours for low wages or throwing them into the ranks of the unemployed. In a normal and healthy society, by contrast, 'labour only divides up spontaneously if society is constituted in such a way that social inequalities express precisely natural inequalities' (DL: 311). By treating the division of labour as a quasi-natural phenomenon, Durkheim provides a diagnosis of the pathologies of industrial society, but without prescribing a cure for them.

Although class conflicts and economic crises are familiar themes in Marx's writings, Durkheim only explicitly refers to *Capital* when discussing what he vaguely calls 'another abnormal form'. Overspecialization and overwork restrict individual activity in pathological ways, resulting in an unhealthy waste of human resources and the morbid dissolution of social order. Strike actions and repressive laws only exacerbate the lack of coordination between economic functions which might otherwise be rendered spontaneous, harmonious, and efficient on their own:

> [T]he division of labour itself tends of its own accord to render functions more sustained [...], the main reasons for which have been set out by economists as follows:
>
> (1) When tasks are not divided up one is constantly disturbed, passing from one occupation to another. The division of labour economizes all this time; according to Karl Marx's expression, it contracts the pores of the [working] day.
>
> (2) Functional activity increases with skill, the ability of the worker, which the division of labour develops; there is less time used up in vacillation and trial and error. (DL: 323)

In Durkheim's view, worker solidarity dissolves or becomes sporadic through the compulsion to overwork or when the division of labour grows slack and unproductive under the excessively competitive regime of large-scale industry. When tasks become overspecialized, workers cannot develop their skills to the fullest, their natural talents atrophy, and industrial enterprises become disorganized and stagnant.

Durkheim is referring here to the second massive chapter of *Capital*, 'Machinery and Large-Scale Industry', where Marx extends his historical narrative of the working day to account for how factory legislation may provide an inducement for technological innovations. Despite the potential for new and improved machinery to alleviate the drudgery of work and to economize on labour-time, the actual effect of these laws has been to accelerate the work process and intensify pressure on the worker to produce more in less time:

> The enormous impulse that this [compulsory shortening of work hours] gives to the development of the system of machinery and the economy of costs also constrains the worker, through a heightened tension, to exert more activity in the same time period, to fill up the pores of his day [*à resserrer les pores de sa journée*] and thereby to condense the work to a degree that he could not have done otherwise. (C: 534; Marx 1989: 351)

By increasing the regularity, continuity, and uniformity of the labour process, capital requires the strictest discipline that squeezes the very pores of the working day: 'The denser hour of the 10-hour working day contains more labour, i.e. expended labour-power, than the more porous hour of the 12-hour working day' (C: 534). Whereas earlier Marx describes how 'circulation sweats money from every pore', here the worker literally sweats under the requirement to work harder (C: 208). Large-scale industry is increasingly organized and regulated in the interests of efficiency, forming a kind of 'organic relation' determined by a 'fixed mathematical ratio' between the volume of workers and the tools employed in each function (C: 465). The division of labour within manufacturing and industry thus propels the division of labour in society as production and trade become more interdependent, town and country more separate, and populations more connected through transportation and communication networks (C: 472). In the famous phrase of the *Manifesto* (repurposed in *Capital*), the worker becomes 'an appendage of the machine' as the hands, stomach, nervous and circulatory systems of the workforce along with the intellectual potentialities (*geistige Potenzen*) of the sciences are pressed into the service of capital (C: 482; CM: 68).

Durkheim's diagnosis of the 'abnormal forms' of the division of labour would eventually lead him to consider a treatment for alleviating their symptoms. He takes up this task in his lecture courses of the 1890s on 'professional ethics and civic morals', in the conclusion to *Suicide*, and again in the Preface to the second edition of *The Division of Labour* in 1902. These prescriptions are prefigured in the chapter of *The Division of Labour* on 'Contractual Solidarity', where he expresses considerable scepticism over whether legal contracts can effectively impose social cohesion through political coercion and economic force. Rather, social solidarity is only sustainable when contracts emerge spontaneously from reciprocal regulations, mutual exchanges, social cooperation, and intersecting networks of obligations and entitlements (Follert 2019). When economic activities become increasingly specialized and unruly, state intervention and political controls can no longer adequately govern social life or render personal relations morally coherent (DL: xxxv). Here Durkheim echoes *Capital* in considering how the slogans of equality and solidarity for workers often amount to the right to be equally exploited, and how the principles of free competition are frequently imposed on individual capitalists as a 'coercive law' (C: 381).[3] Not the state but only the occupational groups, he concludes, have the moral authority and expert knowledge needed for working out disciplinary codes to govern

[3] Marx does not mince words in satirizing the sadism of capital's way of justifying the cruelties of industry: 'Its answer the outcry about the physical and mental degradation, the premature death, the torture of over-work, is this: Should that pain trouble us since it increases our pleasure (profit)?' (C: 381). Marx's wording here—*Sollte diese Qual uns quälen / Da sie unsre Lust vermehrt?*—is adapted from Goethe's *West-Eastern Diwan*, a poem cycle that envisions the global harmony of Orient and Occident through cross-cultural exchanges and the spread of cosmopolitan world literature. In Marx's shocking editorial for *New York Daily Tribune*, 'The British Rule in India' (1853), he makes very different use of these lines to justify the social revolution of an imagined Orient stagnating in its own past. English steam and science may serve as 'the unconscious tool of history' by destroying the inert village-system, he argues, which has served for too long as the foundation for a brutal 'Oriental despotism' (Said 1978: 153–4). Where the 1853 editorial employs the collective abstraction of Goethe's Romantic Orientalism to bolster an argument for global revolution, in *Capital* Marx expresses compassion for the suffering of the working masses who provide pleasure and profit to those who employ and exploit them.

themselves and to create social order out of economic anomie. Social solidarity must emerge from within each trade and profession if states are to work together in managing economic crises, moderating class conflicts, and alleviating overwork: 'The general health of the body social is at stake' (DL: lv). Rather than imposing order from above, professional groups and trade unions provide leverage for reviving and upgrading the corporations, collegial bodies, and craft guilds of the Middle Ages while taking on public functions accountable to the modern democratic state (DL: xxvii).

II

Durkheim's religious revelation of the 1890s would eventually inspire him to expand on and reformulate these curative measures for regenerating the collective consciousness not just within occupational groups but across the full range of civil institutions. In *The Elementary Forms* he develops an essentially secular conceptualization of religion, arguing that the modern state, secondary associations, and kinship groups foster repeatable routines and replicable representations that reinforce the sacred bonds of social life:

> There can be no society that does not experience the need at regular intervals to maintain and strengthen the collective feelings and ideas that provide its coherence and its distinct individuality. This moral remaking can only be achieved through meetings, assemblies, and congregations in which the individuals, pressing close to one another, reaffirm their common sentiments. (Durkheim 1995: 429)

Collective representations and regular assemblies endow moral forces with solidity and render social currents cohesive. Without these occasional iterations of social solidarity, the volatility of modern life would disrupt into the pathologies of egoism (excessive individuation and weak social attachments) and anomie (excessive freedom and waning moral regulations).

Durkheim thus treats religion in an expansive way as the elementary source of social life itself, with 'Church' understood as the prototype for all social institutions: 'A religion is a unified system of beliefs and practices relative to sacred things—that is to say, things set apart, forbidden—beliefs and practices which unite into one and the same moral community called a Church all those who adhere to them' (Durkheim

1995: 44). The vitality of all collectives, not just organized 'religions' in the narrow sense, is sustained by shared ways of thinking, feeling, and acting that form a unified system (*système solidaire*). Modern life is distinguished from its predecessors not in rejecting religious faith and pious reverence, but by its 'worship of the dignity of the human person, which [...] has already accumulated its superstitions' (DL: 122). The dignity of the person is paradoxically set apart (*séparée*) from all other sacred beliefs as a *collective value* while at the same time 'the collective consciousness is reduced to the cult of the individual' (DL: 122). Any violation of this 'religion of humanity' through suicide or any other sacrilege against individual persons or private property is strictly forbidden (*interdite*) (Durkheim 1957: 334, 337). In modern industrial societies, faith in the divine is replaced by a belief in worldly justice as our most revered social bond, and science based on evidence rather than superstition animates the transcendent spirit of social life (DL: 340; Durkheim 1995: 431).

To bring the apparently clashing perspectives of Marx and Durkheim into focus, I present an historical anachronism of my own in the image of 'The Cathedral of Capital' (Fig. 2.1).

Durkheim conceives the elementary forms of religious life on the model of a social assembly (*ekklesia* in Greek, the root of the French word for church, *église*) that gathers periodically to reaffirm the common bonds and collective values of natural, human, and other-than-human worlds. The 'secular' world, in the etymological sense of rituals repeated through the ages, is not cut off from but rather folded into the sacred through institutionalized practices that sustain social integration and strengthen interpersonal attachments. By extension, the church may or may not be materialized in an edifice (*kurakon* in Greek, *Kirche* in German) that distinguishes the members of a moral community and fixes them in place. The profane world, in the etymological sense of what is outside or 'before the temple' (*pro-fanum*), is not simply opposed to sacred prescriptions but manifested in the mundane world through moral regulations symbolized in collective and individual representations. Modern conditions of collective life thus do not erase the separation between sacred and profane as much as they redefine and consecrate this separation in the figure of the person whose body and soul must not be violated, even at the risk of destroying social solidarity in the individualizing pathologies of egoism and anomie.

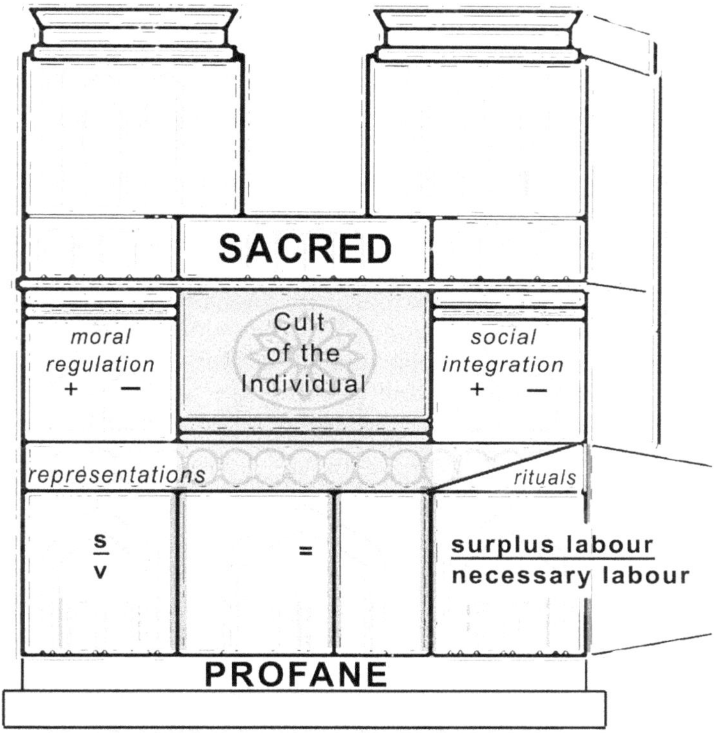

Fig. 2.1 The Cathedral of Capital (Marx and Durkheim on social labour and collective conscioiusness)

As Marx and Engels proclaim in the *Manifesto,* the bourgeoisie 'has worked wonders of a different order than Egyptian pyramids, Roman aqueducts, and Gothic cathedrals; it has conducted expeditions of a different order than all the diasporas of peoples and crusades' (CM: 64). Rather than simply demolishing these monumental wonders of antiquity, this 'different order' of capital reinvents the ancient pyramids, aqueducts, and medieval cathedrals so that 'everything is holy is profaned', and upgrades these wonders of the world to meet the needs of a new age, inducing mass migrations and explorations on an unprecedented scale in the process (CM: 65). Where the Gothic cathedral required the cooperation of extensive teams of workers, artisans, technicians, and visionaries to build a structure of belief out of a mass of materials, under the rule of capital 'the civilized horrors of over-work are grafted onto the barbaric horrors of slavery, serfdom, etc.' (C: 345). As Marx notes in the chapter on the working day, where forced surplus labour (the *corvée*) in the medieval system 'is accurately marked off from the necessary labour', the extra work done to meet the needs of wage-labour is largely indistinguishable from the needs of capital accumulation (C: 346). He defines this new work regime first in mathematical terms as the ratio of the surplus value (s) appropriated by capital over the variable capital (v) employed in its production, and then again in sociological terms as the proportion of surplus labour to necessary labour that workers are subjected to within the course of an ordinary working day:

> Both ratios [...] express the same thing in different ways; in the one case in the form of objectified labour, in the other in the form of living, fluid labour. The rate of surplus-value is therefore an exact expression of the degree of exploitation by capital, or of the worker by the capitalist. (C: 326)

Perhaps predictably, in recent years the 'cathedral' has become a common way of referring to how finance and information capital hide unremunerated work behind a façade of faith in numbers (Finn 2017: 6–10). The unwaged serfs and sovereign lords of European feudalism suggest a compelling analogy for the extreme inequalities and entrenched hierarchies of the virtual platforms and rent regimes that drive today's digital capitalism (Dean 2020). Entering the portals of these cathedrals of capital, commerce, and computing still entails the cooperation of manual trades and the division of labour between crafts, manufactories, and industries, but they also compel the massive extraction of unpaid eye-work and the micro-exploitation of unremunerated digital labour.

If in Marx's view the commodity is the elementary form (*Elementarform*) or basic building block of the edifice of capital, then we should not be surprised that this simple and straightforward thing turns out to be complex and confounding when looked at more closely (C: 125). Packed into each commodity are the values of the materials and instruments and of the surplus and necessary labour employed in producing it. The puzzling concluding section of Chapter 1 of *Capital*, 'The Fetish-character of the Commodity and its Secret', presents Marx's mad method of tracing these manifest and latent dimensions of capitalist society: 'A commodity appears at first sight as an extremely obvious, trivial thing. But its analysis brings out that it is a very queer thing [*ein vertracktes Ding*], abounding in metaphysical subtleties and theological niceties' (C: 162). Despite his playful way with words, Marx's more serious point is that in theory if not in practice there is no direct line from the production of a commodity to its sale; no easy path from purchase to consumption; and no immediate fit between supply and demand. At each stage the production, circulation, and distribution of use-values skew the circulation of exchange-values in the direction of human needs, and the drive towards expanding reproduction and accumulation is dragged down by the lure of desires. Just as the circuits of commodities are frequently disrupted by recycling or repairing, the circuits of profit may be delayed by the tempo of the seasons, the rhythm of bodies, or the pace of the clock.

In Marx's concise formulation of this problematic, 'the definite social relation between human beings assumes here for them the fantastic form of a relation between things' (C: 165). Finding an apt analogy in the 'misty realm of religion', he inverts the charge made by Europeans against African 'primitives' who made their carved figures into 'a cult of the fetish-gods' by accusing political economists of engaging in their own kind of irrational fetish-worship, thereby forgetting the socially necessary labour that goes in to the production of commodities (Kemple 1995: 178–9). Use-values become exchange-values by representing 'social labour in the abstract', and the products of labour are exchanged as commodities through their metamorphosis into 'sensuously suprasensuous or social things' (C: 163, 165: Marx 1989: 53; Khatib 2017: 56–9). The magnitudes of value embodied in commodities are constantly fluctuating and 'vary continually, independently of the will and foresight of the producers, in whose eyes their actual movement takes the form of a movement of things, a movement that leads them far more than they are able to direct it [*mouvement qui les mène bien loin qui'ils puissent les diriger*]' (C: 167–8; Marx 1989: 56; Roberts 2017). Rather than veiling the material conditions concealed behind these movements, what Marx calls the fetish-character of commodities—the mystery of money and merchandise—acknowledges an open secret, namely that the metabolism among human and more-than-human beings is always and everywhere intricately involved in their production and consumption.[4]

The odd phrase describing commodities as 'sensuously suprasensuous or social things' (*sinnlich übersinnliche oder gesesellschaftliche Dinge*) obliquely echoes a line in Goethe's *Faust* where Mephistopheles warns his protégé against himself being duped in the act of seduction:

[4] The French translation of *Capital* substantially expands on and reworks this discussion of 'the fetish-character of the commodity'. A key sentence in the French, which is missing from all four German editions but included the English translation of 1887, articulates this play of appearance and reality: 'The religious world is but the reflection of the real world [*Le monde religieux n'est que le reflet du monde réel*]' (CW: 90; Marx 1989: 59; C: 172 follows Engels's 1890 edition and so omits this sentence). Marx's well-known comment that religion 'is the opium of the people' arguably prefigures these later remarks not by crudely unmasking religion as mere ideology, collective delusion, or false consciousness but rather by exposing the material conditions that make the religious world both meaningful and necessary (Baehr 2019: 3, 50–5). The notorious assertion from 'A Contribution to a Critique of Hegel's *Philosophy of Right*: Introduction', which the 25-year-old Marx published in the sole issue of the *Franco-German Yearbook that he himself edited*, concludes a series of dialectical statements:

> [1] *Religious* suffering is at one and the same time [i] the *expression* of real suffering and [ii] a *protest* against real suffering. [2] Religion is [i] the sigh of the oppressed creature, [ii] the heart of a heartless world, and [iii] the spirit of spiritless conditions. [3] It is the *opium* of the people. (CW 3: 175; numbers in square brackets are my own)

Generations of social theorists and Marxist revolutionaries have cited this striking metaphor while discarding the preceding statements, thereby ignoring their place within his critique of political philosophy as well as the implied historical context of British imperialism (the first Opium War having ended a year and half earlier). Here, Marx both deploys and critiques Hegel's dialectical method of reasoning by asserting that religious beliefs are the expression of actual conditions of misery, distress, and poverty (*Elend*), which they negate through protests that appeal to the heart and soul (*Gemüt und Geist*) of people resisting these conditions. The negation of this negation is not the direct abolition of religion, but rather the transformation of an impoverished state of affairs that induces such cries for redemption and a longing for intoxication or escape. The young Marx here employs the rhetoric of an activist-revolutionary writing in solidarity with 'the people' (politicized as 'the proletariat' in the concluding paragraphs) rather than in the guise of a philosopher-critic looking down on them. Like Durkheim in his later writings, in *Capital* Marx explicitly acknowledges how the world of religion expresses practical truths and reflects material realities, noting how religious beliefs are social products and cultural symptoms that give meaning to human existence, reasons for social action, and recognition of the human in the more-than-human.

Du übersinnlicher sinnlicher Freier!	Oh you supersensously sensuous squire!
Ein Mägdelein nasführet dich.	A lassie has you by the nose!
	(F: 3524–5)

In this most famous part of the Faust story, the scholar newly freed from the confines of his study becomes infatuated with Gretchen, an impressionable young girl who is dazzled by her suitor's generous gifts, noble manners, and apparent wealth. Gretchen's tragic fate is sealed when she meets Faust on the street in front of the cathedral, where earlier the ringing of the bells had evoked his youthful memories and awakened his desires. The love union between two people from such different stations in life represents the necessary passing of the old world and the emergence of the new, as Georg Lukács points out: 'The seduction of young bourgeois girls by aristocrats and the resultant tragedies understandably form an important part of this still insufficiently developed revolt against feudal domination' (Lukács 1968: 218). A turning point in the larger epic, this love story dramatizes not just the disruptive force of class antagonisms but also the conflicting desires of men and women. By invoking this episode in his analysis of the fetish-character of commodities, Marx implicitly alludes to the destruction of these smaller and older worlds by the creative and commodified mega-forces of capital.

Where Mephistopheles accuses his master of losing his senses (*übersinnlich sinnlich*), Marx skews the meaning of this charge by characterizing sensual things as themselves somehow beyond sense and sensibility (*sinnlich übersinnlich*), in a way both falling and not falling under the sway of the senses (*'qui tombent et ne tombent pas sous les sens'* in the French version). These apparently minor musings get to the heart of the respective projects of Marx and Goethe and arguably speak to Durkheim's programme for sociology as well. Durkheim's mature theory of religion considers how human collectives treat things as social facts, such as when land, animals, stars, and other classes of things are integrated into classes of human beings within kinship relationships and as objects of science (Durkheim and Mauss 1963: 82–3). In effect, this insight radicalizes and reverses 'the first and most basic' of his *Rules of Sociological Method* (1895) '*to consider social facts as things*' (Durkheim 1982: 60). In the 1901 Preface to the Second Edition, he clarifies how this methodological principle simply acknowledges 'the objective reality of social facts' rather than reifying human subjectivity or reducing social relationships to things (Durkheim 1982: 46). Social facts (*faits sociaux*) are *constraining* with respect to the will of individuals and *abstract* with respect to their particular manifestations: '*A social fact is any way of acting, whether fixed or not, capable of exerting over the individual an external constraint; or: which is general over the whole of a given society whilst having an existence of its own, independent of its individual manifestations*' (Durkheim 1982: 59). Durkheim therefore generalizes Marx's intuition concerning the 'sensuously suprasensuous or social' world of commodities to encompass the manifold ways that thinking, feeling, and acting make social life itself possible and durable. A commodity is both an intricate thing and an elementary form of capitalist societies, as well as a social fact, in Durkheim's sense, with its own constraining properties and having an independent existence of its own.

Curiously, Durkheim himself finds inspiration for his claim on behalf of the science of sociology in the so-called Gretchen tragedy. In *Suicide* (1897), published two years after the *Rules of Sociological Method*, he takes up the decision to end one's own life, that quintessential individual act of personal will, as the ultimate test of his thesis that social life has an objective reality of its own. In death the human body becomes a mere unthinking, unfeeling, and inert thing even as the lifeless corpse remains a social fact and a cultural concern for others. The most lyrical passages in Durkheim's study express how a sudden loss of regulatory controls on individuals induces higher rates of suicide as in crises of poverty and in periods of sudden abundance. In times of moral and material collapse, an unending abyss opens beneath individuals who lose the familiar ground orienting their lives, while in boom times the lack of a restraining force opens an infinite space of desires above them. At each extreme, 'the state of de-regulation or anomie is thus further heightened by passions being less disciplined, precisely when they need more disciplining' (Durkheim 1957: 253). Surprisingly, here is where Durkheim alludes to Faust's very personal predicament with Gretchen. On the one hand, the regulation of sexual relations through monogamous marriage generally offers some degree of protection or 'coefficient of preservation' against the catastrophes of widowhood or divorce which induce a kind of 'domestic anomie'. On the other hand, in stark contrast to the situation of a single and relatively poor woman like Gretchen, an unmarried and wealthy bachelor like Faust can form attachments whenever and wherever he wishes so that his perpetually unfulfilled desires push him to aspire to everything but be satisfied with nothing:

> When one is no longer checked, one becomes unable to check one's self. Beyond experienced pleasures one senses and desires others; if one happens

almost to have exhausted the range of what is possible, one dreams of the impossible, one thirsts for the non-existent. How can the feelings not be exacerbated by such unending pursuit? (Durkheim 1957: 271)

Durkheim describes the 'trail of weariness and disillusionment' that condemns the single man-of-means to a life of constant change and subjects him to a disorienting state of disturbance, agitation, and discontent to the point where he questions his very existence. In the footnote to this passage Durkheim refers to 'the monologue of Faust in Goethe's work', presumably the 'Forest and Cave' scene which forms a pivotal interlude in Faust's romance with Gretchen.[5]

Although Faust's cosmic broodings on the meaning of life and death in this scene are not explicitly about suicide, they exemplify Durkheim's conception of anomie as an insatiable thirst for the infinite:

So tauml ich von Begierde zu Genuß,	Thus I reel from desire to fulfillment,
Und im Genuß verschmacht ich nach Begierde.	And in fulfilment languish for desire.
	(F: 3249–50)

This momentous episode marks a classic turning point (*peripeteia*) in the drama as a whole where Faust expresses doubts about ruining the life of a

[5] Durkheim's thesis concerning the social types and cultural causes of suicide is poignantly illustrated in Faust's early dialogue with Mephistopheles in the study scene where he questions the meaning of life and death:

Und so ist mir das Dasein eine Last,	Existence seems a burden to detest,
Der Tod erwünscht, das Leben mir verhaßt.	Death to be wished for, life a hateful jest.
	(F: 1570–1)

Faust's dilemma at this moment is concerned less with how to manage the infinite desires presented to him by the pact with the devil, which has yet to be signed, than with the feelings of isolation and disillusionment that now make his very existence unbearable. His meditations on his own mortality (his suicidal ideations) have their social sources less in the unregulated passions that induce a personal state of anomie than in the lack of social attachments and excessive individualism that Durkheim calls 'egoistic', and which he treats as the symptom of a more general 'collective asthenia, or social malaise' (Durkheim 1957: 214). While these moods or motives may feel similar for the individual, they derive from different social milieus and cultural environments: '[egoism] has its main location in the intellectual occupations, the world of thought; [anomie] in the industrial and commercial world' (Durkheim 1957: 258). The stages in Faust's journey as he progresses from scholar to lover to colonizer give these suicidogenic types the 'personal stamp' of his unique temperament and special circumstances (Durkheim 1957: 277).

young woman and yet begins to cede to his epic desire for self-fulfilment and social development, which means that Gretchen and her 'little world' must be sacrificed (Lukács 1968: 170, 201, 208). Rather than indulging in his wonder for the natural world and the sensual pleasures of life, Faust eventually comes to embrace his destiny to realize his personal potential and attain a universal social existence. Putting aside his reservations, he ultimately rejects the idea of settling down to marriage and submitting to the confines of domesticity and resolves instead to continue on with his adventurous lifecourse (*Lebenslauf*) with Mephistopheles at any cost.[6]

Writing in the early decades of the industrial revolution and the expansion of the world market, Goethe envisions the character of Faust under Mephistopheles's diabolic guidance as a kind of proto-capitalist and entrepreneur who is driven to conquer old worlds (including the Holy Roman Empire and even Hellenic Greece in Acts 3 and 4 of Part II) and build new ones (a system of dams and dikes to reclaim land from the sea in Act 5). Faust therefore prefigures not just the cultural chaos and economic crises that Durkheim views as the primary source of the modern malaise he calls anomie but also the rapacious exploitation of labour, land, and life that Marx examines in such excruciating detail in *Capital*. In the early pages of the chapter

[6]While Faust spars with Mephistopheles in the forest over his lover's demise and his own destiny, Gretchen is working alone at the spinning wheel in her cramped quarters. In one of the most well-known passages of the play, later set to music by Schubert, she pines away for the life of peace and love that her suitor represents for her.

Wo ich ihn nicht hab,	When he is fled,
Ist mir das Grab,	My soul is dead,
Die ganze Welt	My world is all
Ist mir vergällt.	As bitter gall. (F: 3378–80)

Gretchen's happiness and even her life depend on Faust, and when he is away she is buried in bitterness. While she hopes to live without work or worry, Faust can live without her and so their courtship ends when he abandons her and she is condemned to death for the crime of infanticide. Her song of lament represents the body-machine (spinning wheel) relationship in the way she is left at the mercy of forces beyond her, while Faust's callousness embodies the fusion of human-and-animal in the freedom he enjoys to leave her behind without remorse. In this regard, he resembles not just the vampire-capitalist feeding off living labour but also the werewolf-capitalist hunting for human quarry: 'But in its blind and measureless drive, its voracious werewolf-hunger [*Werwolfsheißhunger*] for surplus labour, capital oversteps not only the moral but even the merely physical limits of the working day' (C: 375; also 353). As Gretchen falls prey to Faust's insatiable craving for more experience and more life the development of her own expansive desires and capabilities is cut short by the small-town prejudices of those around her.

on the working day, the insatiable desires of capital appear in the Gothic figure of the vampire who repeatedly returns from the dead to feed off the living:

> As a capitalist, he is only capital personified. His soul is the soul of capital. But capital has one sole driving force, the drive to valorize itself, to create surplus-value, to make its constant part, the means of production, absorb the greatest possible amount of surplus labour. Capital is dead labour, which vampire-like, lives only by sucking living labour, and lives the more the more labour it sucks. (C: 342)

The capitalist strives to extend working hours beyond the light of day and into the night, but even in these nocturnal pursuits it 'only slightly quenches the vampire thirst for the living blood of labour' (C: 367). Marx thus dramatically intensifies the scene of the worker sweating through the pores of the working day with this horrific image of the bleeding labourer whose vital forces are sucked dry by a voracious monster lurking in the darkness (Carver 1998: 14–20; McNally 2012: 113–51). Living labour 'raises the means of production from the dead merely by entering into contact with them', and in turn the undead feed parasitically off the blood of the living (C: 308). As Mark Neocleous argues, this hyperbolic figure of monstrosity serves as a beacon (*monstrare*), a revelation (*monstrum*), and a sign (*monstra*) of the inhuman fears and superhuman desires that exceed all natural and moral limits: 'The vampire as monster both demonstrates the capabilities of capital and acts as a warning about it' (Neocleous 2003: 684).

To heighten the drama even further, Marx lets the victimized proletarian worker speak on her own behalf in response to the unconvincing claim by vampire-capital simply to be following the inhuman laws of commerce:

> Suddenly, however, there arises the voice of the worker, which had previously been stifled by the sound and fury of the production process: […] 'You pay me for one day's labour-power, while you use three days of it. That is against our contract and the law of commodity exchange'. (C: 342–3)

Although this speech is Marx's own invention, he goes on to provide ample evidence of its factual basis by quoting at length from the factory inspection reports, the so-called Blue Books, many of which record the voices of workers speaking about their own experiences. Among the documents he summarizes and cites are the 'depositions of exploited children' who suffer horribly in the production of matches, wall-paper, glass, steel, iron, silk, and textiles (C: 354–67). With a touch of sadness and sarcasm, he describes in gruesome detail the death from overwork of a young seamstress at the hands of her heartless employer: 'Mary Anne Walkley, 20 years old, employed in a highly respectable dressmaking establishment, exploited by a lady with the pleasant name of Elise [...] who worked uninterruptedly for 26.5 hours, with sixty other girls, 30 in each room [...], died from long hours of work in an overcrowded work-room, and a too small and badly ventilated bedroom' (C: 364–5). Marx's purpose in summarizing and quoting from these otherwise bland reports is not just to heighten the pathos of his own critique but also to provide empirical evidence for the effects of increasing the ratio of surplus to necessary labour (his theory of absolute surplus-value) with vivid examples of the human costs of extending the working day. In Marx's graphic words, laws have occasionally been enacted that acknowledge these costs and 'the state has here and there interposed as a barrier to the transformation of children's blood into capital' (C: 382). These documents thus provide both scientific evidence and moral justification for the 10 Hours Bill, among other pieces of factory legislation, which Marx calls a modest 'Magna Carta of the legally limited working day'. For once workers were able to 'put their heads together and, as a class, compel the passing of a law, an all-powerful social barrier by which they can be prevented from selling themselves and their families into slavery and death by voluntary contract with capital' (C: 416). In Durkheimian terms, the social solidarity that emerges when workers combine their hearts and minds had finally become effective in appealing to the collective consciousness of the bourgeoisie and in evoking the compassion of legislators who could make significant changes in their working lives.

* * *

Despite the critical distance that Durkheim takes from Marxist theory and socialist politics throughout his career, all his writings seek to deepen and expand his investigation into the communal, civic, social, and symbolic sources of private property regimes under conditions of market competition and capitalist industry (Bottomore 1981). Already in his youthful essays of 1887 on legal and moral theories in Germany, he concerns himself with the 'socialists of the chair' (*Kathedersozialisten*), such as Karl Menger, Adolph Wagner, and Gustav Schmoller, who had such a profound influence on Max Weber and Georg Simmel (Kemple 2014: 215; Kemple 2018a: 6; Marx himself took up a serious study of Wagner in his final years; CW 24: 531–59). In various ways, these academic socialists promote state regulation of business enterprise and social welfare on behalf of the working classes, and they take a stand against the abuses of employers and attempts by political leaders to undermine worker solidarity (Durkheim 1993: 58–77). The 'new discipline' that the times require should not be imposed by the state or 'improvised in the silence of the study', he insists, but can only emerge 'under the pressure of internal causes that render it necessary' (DL: 340). Thus, Durkheim is deeply suspicious of any socialism that is merely theoretical, such as the abstract belief among Marx's rivals in France that the universal exchangeability of commodities is somehow 'the absolute summit of human freedom and individual independence':

> This philistine utopia is depicted in the socialism of Proudhon. […] No school of thought has thrown around the world 'science' more haphazardly than that of Proudhon, for
>
> *wo Begriffe fehlen,* — just where concept's lacking,
> *da stellt zu rechten Zeit ein Wort sich ein.* — a word in time supplies the remedy.
> (C: 161; quoting F: 1995–6)

Borrowing from Mephistopheles's cynical advice to a young student of Faust to parody Proudhon's 'scientific socialism', Marx anticipates Durkheim's scepticism that mere words without ideas mean nothing, or that theories without action are enough to address injustices.

In his 1895–1896 lecture course at Bordeaux on the history of socialism, Durkheim insists that 'socialism is not a science, a sociology in miniature—it is a cry of grief, sometimes of anger, uttered by men who feel most keenly our collective *malaise*' (Durkheim 1958: 41). Echoing Marx's critique of religion, he suggests that socialism expresses the groans of a sick society rather than a diagnosis or a cure for what ails it. He praises *Capital* as 'the strongest work—the most systematic, the richest in ideas—that this school has produced' and at the same time declares that 'there cannot be a scientific socialism' (40). Though socialism is not a scientific theory of social facts, 'it is a social fact of the greatest importance', and therefore best understood as a collective representation like any other sacred symbol (Durkheim 1978: 137). For these reasons, he was closer in sympathy to the reformist socialism of his school friend Jean Jaurès (1859–1914) than to the revolutionary syndicalism of his rival Georges Sorel (1847–1922) (Lukes 1973: 320–30).

In later writings and lectures, Durkheim analyses the anomic character of modern society as a pathology that may be treated through liberal democratic state policies, moral education, and professional ethics that foster cultural regulation and social integration. In this regard, he anticipates the later writings of his nephew and collaborator Marcel Mauss whose *Essay on the Gift* from 1925 concludes with a moral lesson and a legal argument on the enduring significance of non-commodified exchanges and reciprocal obligations in modern societies:

> French legislation on social insurance, and accomplished state socialism, are inspired by the principle that the worker gives his life and labour partly to the community and partly to the bosses. If the worker has to collaborate on the business of insurance then those who benefit from his services are not square with him simply by paying him a wage. The State, representing the community, owes him and his management and fellow-workers a certain security in his life against unemployment, sickness old age and death. (Mauss 1967: 65)

Durkheim and Mauss thus reclaim the 'chair' or 'seat' (*katheder*) occupied by socialism and Catholicism in progressive social reform by reconceiving the full range of modern secular institutions, including the state and the market, as civic cathedrals in miniature with the power to regenerate sacred values and sustain social solidarity at large. For his part, Marx is more suited to the chair of his study or the Reading Room of the British Museum than to the socialist's chair in the university, and even less to any secular version of the bishop's cathedra.

Marx's concern is decidedly with social conflict, especially the struggle for a normal working day through the regulation of working conditions and the re-classification of workers in a system which requires children to work as hard and as long as adults (C: 253–67, 392); extends the workday long into the night (C: 367–74); forces free workers to be treated as slaves and freed slaves to become wage-labourers (C: 377–9, 414–5); compels women to work the same long hours as men (C: 364–5); and treats housework as an extension of factory-labour (C: 411–2). In this regard Pierre Bourdieu's influential work in the second half of the twentieth century extends Marx's insights to include cultural and other forms of capital and by expanding the notion of class conflict to include 'class(ification) struggles': 'The "real" class is [...] the mobilized class, a result of the *struggle of classifications*, [...] a properly symbolic (and political) struggle to impose a vision of the social world' (Bourdieu 1998: 11). Bourdieu thus updates Durkheim and Mauss's classic 1903 essay from on primitive classification systems where they show that categories of genus, time, space, and force derive from human collectives that encompass a range of social, cultural, and natural fields (Durkheim and Mauss 1963: 82–3). As Durkheim notes, in modern societies human-made conditions and naturally induced events that give rise to anomie upset categorical distinctions and undo established classifications: 'In the case of economic disasters, indeed, something like a declassification occurs which casts certain individuals into a lower state than their previous one' (Durkheim 1957: 252). Combining the insights of Marx and Durkheim, Bourdieu formulates his own concept of 'symbolic capital' to account for how class conflicts and classification struggles over the accumulation and conversion of various forms of capital occur in social space and take place over historical time. Like their classical predecessors, contemporary sociologists like Bourdieu are driven by the desire for knowledge to inform action and by the determination to foster individual personality through social solidarity.

N.B.: I often modify existing English translations, drawing on German or French editions readily available online or from print sources. References to *Faust* are by line number as indicated in both English and German editions.

Works Cited and Consulted

Abbreviations Used

C—Marx, Karl (1976). *Capital: A Critique of Political Economy, Volume 1.* Ben Fowkes trans. Ernest Mandel intro. London: Penguin Books.

CW—*The Collected Works of Karl Marx and Friedrich Engels 1844–1895.* 47 Volumes. New York: International Publishers. (Electronic Edition, Charlottesville, Virginia).

DL—Durkheim, Emile (2004). *The Division of Labor in Society.* W. D. Wells trans. Lewis Coser intro. New York: The Free Press.

F—Goethe, Johann Wolfgang von (1986). *Faust: Eine Tragödie.* Erster und Zweiter Teile. Stuttgart: Philipp Reclam Jun.

Goethe, Johann Wolfgang von (1976). *Faust: A Tragedy.* Walter Arndt trans., Cyrus Hamlin ed. New York: W. W. Norton & Company.

PE—Weber, Max (2009). *The Protestant Ethic and the Spirit of Capitalism, with Other Writings on the Rise of the West.* Fourth edition. Stephen Kalberg trans., intro. Oxford: Oxford University Press.

PM—Simmel, Georg (2004). *The Philosophy of Money.* Thomas Bottomore, David Frisby trans. London: Routledge.

Alexander, Jeffrey C. (1989). 'Rethinking Durkheim's Intellectual Development: On the Complex Origins of a Cultural Sociology'. In *Structure and Meaning: Rethinking Classical Sociology.* New York: Columbia University Press, pp. 123–55.

Arendt, Hannah (1958). *The Human Condition*. Chicago, IL: University of Chicago Press.

Baehr, Peter (2019). *The Unmasking Style in Social Theory*. London: Routledge.

Bottomore, Thomas (1981). 'A Marxist Consideration of Durkheim'. *Social Forces* 59(4): 902–17.

Bourdieu, Pierre (1998). *Practical Reason*. Stanford, CA : Stanford University Press.

Burkett, Paul (2014). *Marx and Nature: A Red and Green Perspective*. Chicago: Haymarket Books.

Carver, Terrell (1998). *The Postmodern Marx*. University Park, PA: Penn State University Press.

Dean, Jodi (2020). 'Neofeudalism: The End of Capitalism?'. *Los Angeles Review of Books*. https://lareviewofbooks.org/article/neofeudalism-the-end-of-capitalism/

Durkheim, Emile (1995). *The Elementary Forms of Religious Life*. Karen E. Fields trans. New York: The Free Press.

Durkheim, Emile (1993). *Ethics and the Sociology of Morals*. R. T. Hall. Prometheus Books. Amherst, NY: Prometheus Books.

Durkheim, Emile (1982). *The Rules of Sociological Method*. W. D. Halls trans. New York: The Free Press.

Durkheim, Emile (1958). *Socialism and Saint Simon*. C. Sattler trans. London: Routledge and Kegan Paul.

Durkheim, Emile (1957). *Suicide*. J. A. Spaulding, G. Simpson trans. New York: The Free Press

Durkheim, Emile (1978). On Institutional Analysis. Mark Traugott ed., trans. Chicago, IL: Univerisity of Chicago Press.

Durkheim, Emile and Marcel Mauss (1963). *Primitive Classification*. Rodney Needham trans. Chicago: The University of Chicago Press.

Elson, Diane (1979). 'The Value Theory of Labour'. In *Value: The Representation of Labour in Capitalism*. Atlantic Highlands, New Jersey: Humanities Press. Pp. 115–80.

Finn, Ed (2017). *What Algorithms Want: Imagination in the Age of Computing*. Cambridge, MA: The MIT Press.

Follert, Micheal (2019). 'Contractual Thought and Durkheim's Theory of the Social: A Reappraisal'. *Journal of Classical Sociology* 8(4): 447–66.

Goethe, Johann Wolfgand von (1983). *Selected Poems*. Christopher Middleton ed. London: John Calder.

Harvey, David (2018). *Marx,* Capital *and the Madness of Economic Reason*. Oxford, UK: Oxford University Press.

Hobbes, Thomas (1968). *Leviathan*. C. B. Macpherson ed. London: Penguin Books.

Hochschild, Arlie (2012). *The Managed Heart: The Commercialization of Human Feeling*. Berkeley, CA: The University of California Press.

Jarvikoski, Timo (1996). 'The Relation of Nature and Society in Marx and Durkheim'. *Acta Sociologica* 39(1): 73–86.

Kemple, Thomas (1995). *Reading Marx Writing: Melodrama, the Market, and the 'Grundrisse'*. Stanford: Stanford University Press.

Kemple, Thomas (2018a). *Simmel*. Cambridge, UK: Polity Press.

Kemple, Thomas (2014). *Intellectual Work and the Spirit of Capitalism: Weber's Calling*. Basingstoke, UK: Palgrave Macmillan.

Khatib, Sami (2017). '"Sensuously Supra-Sensuous": The Aesthetics of Real Abstraction'. In *Aesthetic Marx*. S. Gandesha, J. Hartle eds. London: Bloomsbury, pp. 49–72.

Lukács, Georg (1968). *Goethe and his Age*. R. Anchor trans. London: Merlin Press.

Lukes, Steven (1973). *Émile Durkheim: His Life and Work*. London: Penguin Books.

Marx, Karl (1989). *Le Capital*. M. J. Roy trans., entièrement révisée par l'auteur. *Marx Engels Gesamtausgabe* II/7 and Apparat. Berlin: Dietz Verlag.

Mauss, Marcel (1967). *The Gift*. I. Cunnison trans. NY: W.W. Norton & Co. Inc.

McNally, David (2012). Monsters of the Market: Zombies, Vampires, and Global Capitalism. Chicago: Haymarket Books.

Neocleous, Mark (2003). 'The Political Economy of the Dead: Marx's Vampires'. *History of Political Thought* 24(4): 668–84.

Roberts, William Clare (2017). *Marx's Inferno: The Political Theory of Capital*. Princeton University Press.

Said, Edward W. (1978). *Orientalism*. New York: Vintage Books.

CHAPTER 3

Capitalism as a Vocation: *Capital* and the Work Ethic

Abstract In contrast to other classical sociologists, Weber develops a more sustained reading of Marx's writings which is nevertheless at times selective, sporadic, and superficial. He deepens Marx's discussion of machinery and large-scale industry in *Capital* by showing how the ethical motivation stemming from the Protestant idea of industrious work in a 'calling' or 'vocation' (*Beruf*) provides the cultural basis for 'formally free labour'. Weber also examines how the separation of workers from the means of production sets the pattern for similar institutional arrangements in state bureaucracies and the modern professions. Adapting the emerging outlook expressed in the Faust legend, Marx and Weber each assume that action in the world is the presupposition if not the ultimate goal of modern knowledge and mature understanding.

Keywords Machinery • Protestantism • Weber • Separation • Cyclops

Capital does more than simply argue that the organization of social labour is the basis for the exchange and production of commodities, themes taken up in Parts I and II of the book. What I am calling Marx's *surplus-value theory of labour-power*, first laid out in Part III, goes further to examine how the human capacity to work is itself commodified when skills and time are exchanged for a wage or a salary, and when labour-power

T. Kemple, *Marx's Wager*, Marx, Engels, and Marxisms,
https://doi.org/10.1007/978-3-031-08065-4_3

produces more value than what is needed to reproduce and maintain it. In particular, Chapter 10 details how this process takes place in the factory system in the course of an ordinary working day for the women, children, and men of the nineteenth century. Marx focuses on the struggle among workers and factory inspectors for a 'normal working day' that does not require overwork, overtime, and overspecialization, or the constant threat of unemployment, injury, and death. In Parts IV, V, and VI of *Capital* (Chapters 12–22), he turns his attention to the role of large-scale machinery and other labour-saving techniques. These industrial innovations increase the productivity and profitability of the work process without necessarily improving working conditions or increasing wages. The hinge on which the whole of *Capital* turns (consisting of the two middle chapters out of six in the first edition) is an account of this double tactic of extending the working day while accelerating production:

> I call that surplus-value which is produced by the lengthening of the working day, *absolute surplus-value*. In contrast to this, I call that surplus-value which arises from the curtailment of the necessary labour-time, and from the corresponding alteration in the respective lengths of the two components of the working day, *relative surplus-value*. (C: 432)

Using the analogy of a line marking time, Marx describes how the rate and mass of surplus-value produced by any individual or organization encounters an *absolute limit* (*Schranke*) in the hours that make up the working day and at the point where factors such as the physical capacity of the body or access to natural resources are exhausted (C: 340). By contrast, the rate and mass of surplus-value reaches only a *relative barrier* (*Grenze*) that can be surpassed insofar as the proportion of necessary to surplus labour is altered within the fixed timeline of the working day (C: 429). This relative productivity varies according to the speed of the work process, the skill of workers, and above all the efficiency of the instruments of production. *Capital* is Marx's effort to explain the underling mechanism that drives the capitalist system in producing, trading, and profiting from more goods on an expanding scale and in more intensive ways. Surplus-value is the name he gives to this mechanism.

Living and writing in the period of rapid industrialization and urbanization in Germany after the Franco-Prussian war of 1870–1871 (the so-called *Grunderzeit*), Max Weber takes these arguments as his point of departure for examining what he and his contemporaries came to call capital*ism*. He extends Marx's singular focus on 'the capitalist mode of production'—the market exchange, industrial production, and monetary distribution of commodified goods and services that emerged in Europe and expanded through its colonial empires from the sixteenth to the nineteenth century—by considering a wide range of social practices for the creation, calculation, and acquisition of profit. What Weber loses from Marx's analytical precision he gains in the historical-comparative breadth and theoretical clarity by which he identifies the cultural specificity of *occidental capitalism*. In the magisterial 'Prefatory Remarks' to his collected essays in the sociology of religion, he calls capitalism 'the most fateful power of modern life' while insisting that the concept not be reduced to clichés about 'the pursuit of goods, gain, or profit' (PE: 208). Capitalism has existed in many political, entrepreneurial, and commercial forms in all world civilizations throughout history, but the 'rational, industrial capitalism' that emerged in the modern era in the West must be defined in more precise terms, specifically: (1) the (formally) rational calculation of earnings and losses through systematic bookkeeping; (2) the methodical organization of (formally) free labour; and (3) the (formal) separation of business from household activities (PE: 210–2). Following Marx and Engels, Weber focuses on the social significance of middle class (bourgeois) industrial (entrepreneurial) capitalism (*das bürgerliche Betriebskapitalismus*) (PE: 214).

Here I consider how this canonical founder of modern sociology offers a sustained reading of Marx's writings and ideas, a reading which is also at times selective, sporadic, and superficial. Like Durkheim, Weber places particular stress on the industrial and capitalist organization of work without which modern-day class struggles and their state socialist alternatives would be unthinkable: 'The modern opposition between large-scale industrialists, as employers, and free workers paid a wage is completely lacking outside the West' (PE: 213). From his first university lectures on 'national economics' to his last course on 'general economic history', Weber periodically yet persistently engages with the reception and elaboration of Marx's writings and with 'historical materialism' more broadly (Swedberg 1998: 46–7). Like Emile Durkheim, he tends to read Marx indirectly through the writings of the professorial 'socialists of the chair' (*Kathedersozialisten*) in Germany, especially the historical economists Karl Knies (1821–1898) and Wilhelm Georg Friedrich Roscher (1817–1894) as well as the legal scholar Rudolf Stammler (1856–1938), all of whom Weber commented on extensively. In the increasingly baroque footnotes added to the second edition of *The Protestant Ethic and the Spirit of*

Capitalism published in 1920, Weber defends himself against the critiques of other academic socialists, especially his colleagues Werner Sombart (1863–1941) on the rise of the bourgeoisie and Lujo Brentano (1944–1931) on the origins of occidental capitalism (PE: 209n9, 458–9n1). Anticipating pedantic objections to his arguments in *Capital*, Marx himself is scathing in his mocking attacks on Roscher, while Engels in his Preface to the final edition of 1890 defends Marx against Brentano's accusation of deliberately adulterating a quotation.[1] Despite their contrasting political views and scholarly styles, Marx, Engels, and Weber share an approach to 'scientific socialism' which is grounded in a rigorous critique of the political economy capitalist industry, a broadly sociological understanding of modern workaday life, and a moral-political commitment to social justice.

Weber and Marx agree on *the primacy of action* in the world as the presupposition and ultimate aim of knowledge and understanding, even when action is not the sole objective of academic work. In various ways and to different ends, they are guided by the motto of the frustrated Faust in his study as he heretically re-translates the Gospel of John:

[1] A full consideration of how Engels, Marx, and Weber engaged with the 'socialists of the chair' (*Kathedersozialisten*) or 'academic socialists' of their time would require a study in itself. Marx is especially insulting to Roscher, whom he mocks as a 'man of learning' who 'seldom loses the opportunity of rushing into print with ingenious apologetic fantasies', such as the idea that nature produces exchange-value, 'like the foolish virgin who admitted she had a child "but only a very little one"', or that 'surplus-value somehow originates in "thrift"' (C: 314n3; 326n6). Engels goes to great pains to refute Brentano's claim that Marx had forged a compromising parliamentary speech on 16 April 1863 by Prime Minister Gladstone on how the '"intoxicating accumulation of wealth and power [is] entirely confined to classes of property"', citing the stenographic account of the speech as evidence against newspaper reports on it the following day (C: 115–20, discussing 805–6). For his part, Weber more soberly establishes some critical distance from his teachers and 'great masters' Roscher and Knies, noting how their weaknesses 'lead us to reflect on those general presuppositions with which we approach our scientific work', and even to rethink the convoluted writing styles of many intellectuals (Weber 2012: 3, 29; Kemple 2014: 204). Weber is also respectful in arguing with Brentano who was co-founder of the Association for Social Policy (*Verein für Sozialpolitik*) which supported liberal trade and union policies and chair of economics at the Ludwig-Maximilian University in Munich which Weber took over in 1919 (Weber 1988: 645–6). Finally, though 'strongly opposed' to parts of Sombart's 'refutation of historical materialism', Weber concedes that he and other critics are indebted to his 'manifold investigations and their acute formulations' (PE: 468n14; Kemple 2014: 208–10). Arguably, the passionate polemics among these scholars were formative rather than merely incidental in developing their respective intellectual projects.

Geschrieben steht:'Im Anfang war das Wort!'	'In the beginning was the *Word*': thus runs the text.
Hier stock ich schon! Wer hilf mir weiter fort? [...]	Who helps me on? Already I'm perplexed! [...]
Mir hilft der Geist! Auf einmal seh ich Rat	The spirit speaks! And lo, the way is freed,
Und schreibe getrost: Im Anfang war die Tat!	I calmly write: 'In the beginning was the *Deed!*'
	(F: 1224–5, 1236–7)

In a jocular way Marx cites the last of these lines in *Capital* when describing how 'in their difficulties, our commodity-owners think like Faust' (C: 180). They exchange commodities with one another on the basis of their respective needs or desires, but without considering what makes these products of labour or use-values equivalent to one another as exchange-values: 'they have therefore already acted before thinking' (C: 180). On a more serious note, Weber remarks that the business activities of the early Calvinists were often caught in the paradox that Goethe expresses in his maxim about acting without a moral conscience, since '"only those who observe have a conscience"' (PE: 138, quoting Goethe's *Maxims*). By engaging in business activities without considering the consequences, the Calvinists also seem to act before thinking. Where Marx approaches theoretical critique as the task of moving from the page to the deed and from interpreting to changing the world, Weber considers how the words and deeds of historical actors inform speech and motivate action in the present. Like the early Christians, each adopts a version of the motto of the charismatic thinker and leader who speaks against established teachings: '"It is written, but I say unto you"' (Weber 2019: 376, quoting the Gospel of Matthew).

I

Expanding on Marx's observation that 'the determination of the value of labour-power contains a moral and historical element', Weber takes a more focused approach than Durkheim to the ethical motivations and religious sanctions that inform modern industrial work processes and which in turn make 'labour-time' a measure of economic value (C: 274). In particular, he focuses on the origins of the Protestant idea of the 'calling' or 'vocation' (*Beruf* in German) introduced during the Reformation through Martin

Luther's translation of the Bible (PE: 89–90, 473–80n1–10). The divine command to engage in this-worldly work would later take on broader practical meaning and secular significance as a bureaucratic 'profession' or capitalist 'occupation' (also *Beruf*). Weber concludes *The Protestant Ethic and the Spirit of Capitalism* (1905/1920) by noting that he wishes only to supplement rather than to substitute the guiding thread of Marx's studies of how material conditions give rise to cultural values and ideological ideas: 'It can not be [...] the intention here to set a one-sided spiritualistic analysis of the causes of culture and history in place of an equally one-sided "materialistic" analysis. *Both are equally possible*' (PE: 159). His aim rather is to trace some of the catalysing connections or 'elective affinities' (*Wahlverwandtschaften*) between two key ideas which are necessary conditions (though not adequate causes) for the rise and spread of industrial capitalism—the work ethic of Protestantism and the cultural ethos of acquisition, which together make capitalism itself the vocation of modern civilization.

Weber's argument pivots on his interpretation of the semantic overlap and cultural resonance between two specific notions, exemplified, on the one hand, in the sermons of the seventeenth-century English Puritan preacher Richard Baxter, who preached 'work hard in your calling', and, on the other hand, in the popular aphorisms of the eighteenth-century American diplomat, politician, and popular writer Benjamin Franklin, who declared that 'time is money' (PE: 143, 70). These texts place a moral premium and psychological sanction on the ascetic compulsion to work as an ethical imperative rather than out of material necessity. In Chapter 1 of *Capital*, Marx also quotes 'the famous Franklin' to praise him for recognizing labour-time as the fundamental basis of commerce. Although Franklin does not distinguish between the qualitative (use-value) and the quantitative (exchange-value) aspects of labour, he understands how commodities embody and are measured against the labour-time needed to produce them: '"Trade in general being nothing else but the exchange of labour for labour, the value of all things is justly measured by labour"' (C: 142, quoting the Sparks edition of Franklin's works which Weber also cites). Anticipating Weber's argument concerning the ascetic character of the Protestant work ethic, Marx notes that 'Protestantism, by changing almost all the traditional holidays into working days, played an important part in the genesis of capital', and that 'the "spirit" of Protestantism' informed the poor laws and their middle-class defenders (C: 387n92, 882n9). Where Marx examines the objective forces that propel labour-power to produce surplus-value, Weber studies the subjective motivations that drove the capitalist work ethic in the first place.

Weber's argument takes the form of a paradox: the consistent adherence among the early Protestant believers to the principle of hard work sanctioned by God inadvertently led to a worldly life of sin and a culture of material distractions. In the words of the eighteenth-century founder of the Methodist sect John Wesley, '*we must exhort all Christians to gain all they can, and to save all they can; that is, in effect to grow rich*' (PE: 154; Weber's emphasis). By preaching and practicing the methodical-rational organization of life, the Puritans and other ascetic Protestants condemn all 'covetousness' and 'mammonism' while at the same time 'accumulating wealth in ways that encourage greed and temptation' (PE: 151). As Weber notes with some irony, the unintended consequence of this ethic was that ascetic Protestantism became '"the power that perpetually wanted good and perpetually created evil"' (PE: 151). That is, their actions effectively reversed Mephistopheles's description of himself when first encountering Faust as:

Ein Teil von jener Kraft,	Part of that force,
Die stets das Böse will und stets das Gute schafft.	That would do ever evil, and does ever good.
	(F: 1336–7)

Despite the Protestants' belief in God's omniscience regarding who among the elect will be saved in the next world, they held fast to the divine command that everyone, without distinction, must persist in doing good in *this* world. From their perspective, Cyprian's Catholic dictum 'no salvation outside the church' (*nulla ecclesia salus*) amounts to accepting the injustices of institutional hierarchy and clerical authority, while Luther's Reformist rule of 'salvation by faith alone' (*sola fides*) applies equally to every believer. For Weber, the Reformation thereby radicalized the freedom of individual conscience while also upholding an ideal of *social equality*. The unintended effect was not just to create egalitarian cultural and economic conditions through the capitalist compulsion that everyone must work, but also to define social justice in terms of moral and political equality, which amounts to the revolutionary call to abolish inherited inequalities (Marianne Weber 1988: 476; Weber 1978: 1209–10; Kemple 2014: 102).

Weber is well known for stressing the darker side of these unexpected developments in the levelling of social distinctions and the homogenizing effects of rationalization that accompany the rise of industrial capitalism. Where the Protestant work ethic required everyone to engage freely in worldly activities through willing submission to God's command, hard work would later be enforced as a secular compulsion that no one can opt out of:

> The Puritan *wanted to* be a person with a vocational calling [*Beruf*]; we *must* be. For to the extent that asceticism moved out of the monastic cell, was transferred to the life of work in a vocational calling, and then commenced to rule over this-worldly morality, it helped to build the mighty cosmos of the modern economic order—namely, an economy bound to the technical and economic conditions at the foundation of mechanized, machine-based production. (PE: 157)

In referring to the technological conditions of industry, Weber's investigation into the religious and moral obligation to work from the seventeenth to the eighteenth century merges with Marx's examination of the mechanical and material requirement to work from the late eighteenth through the nineteenth century. Despite the austere piety of the Puritans in their disdain for accumulating riches, the worldly ethic of asceticism they lived by played a crucial role in propelling capitalist production and accumulation. In the continuation of this celebrated passage, the echo of Marx's discussion in Chapter 15 of *Capital*, 'Machinery and Large-Scale Industry', is especially palpable:

> This cosmos today determines the style of life of all individuals born into this grinding mechanism [*Triebwerk*], and *not* only those directly engaged in economically productive activity. It does so with overwhelming force—and perhaps it will continue to do so until the last ton of fossil fuel has burnt to ashes. (PE: 157)

Where Marx and Engels envision a world in which 'everything established and stable evaporates', like steam wafting off the engines of the ships, factories, and trains building the new global order, Weber prophesizes the collapse of carbon capitalism with the inevitable exhaustion of energy reserves as they literally go up in smoke (CM: 65; C: 617n29). In his devastating concluding reflections Weber invokes the epic figure of confinement and containment that has haunted sociology ever since, exceeding even Marx's dramatic image of capital as 'a colossal accumulation of commodities':

> The concern for material goods, according to Baxter, should lie upon the shoulders of his saints like "a lightweight coat that one can throw off at any time." Yet fate allowed this coat to become a steel-hard casing [*ein stahlhartes Gehäuse*]. To the extent that asceticism undertook to transform and influence the world, the world's material goods acquired an increasing and, in the end, inescapable power over people—as never before in history. (PE: 157–8; quoting Baxter's *Saints' Everlasting Rest*)

Baxter's light mantel, which was only intended to protect against the elements, here becomes a steel straightjacket that conceals and constrains anyone who wears it.[2] After demonstrating the causal influence of certain cultural ideas in the advance of modern industry, Weber concludes by emphasizing the inexorable force of material conditions on everyone and by projecting the effects of this process on present and future developments. The ascetic work ethic, at least in its Protestant form, is no longer required as a support (*Stütz*) for the capitalist spirit now that it solidly rests on mechanical-technological foundations (PE: 158).

[2] In contrast to Weber's coat-cum-straightjacket, we might imagine how the mass-produced and tattered coat that Marx examines in the opening chapter of *Capital* is manufactured, bought, and sold among workers and merchants before being pawned, discarded, and dumped for re-use among the world's poor (Stallybrass 1998). The stories of the coat that Marx and Weber tell in their own way can also be understood as an elaboration of the Faust legend. A master of disguises, Mephistopheles embodies the magical power of metamorphosis that Weber pictures so ominously in the transformation of the Puritan's 'light cloak' into the capitalist's 'steel-hard casing', and that Marx sees in the almost metaphysical capacity of the commodity-owner to exchange linen (or any comparable good) for a coat of equal or more value. In describing the capitalist's delight in having to pay the worker only a half a day's labour for a whole day's work, Marx recalls Mephistopheles's magical transfiguration when appearing to Faust for the first time: 'Our capitalist foresaw this situation, and that was the cause of his laughter [*der Kasus macht ihn lachen*]' (C: 301). Here Marx feigns a version of Faust's expression of astonishment in discovering that the poodle that followed him home is actually a 'scholar', or rather, Mephistopheles disguised in a disguise:

Das also war das Pudels Kern? *Ein fahrender Skolast! Der Casus macht mich lachen!*	So this was at the poodle's core? A traveling scholar? Most amusing case!' (F: 1323–4)

Like Mephistopheles who insists that his pact with Faust is fair and just, the capitalist senses that his 'good luck' in buying the worker's labour-power will generate a profit which is 'by no means an injustice toward the seller' (C: 301). That is, in keeping to the terms of the wage contract with the worker, the capitalist has only followed the laws of commodity exchange in which equivalent has been freely exchanged for something of equal value. At the conclusion of this scene in Faust's study, Mephistopheles spreads his 'mantel wide' and miraculously sweeps Faust away on his fabulous new career (F: 2045–71).

Part IV of *Capital*, 'Relative Surplus-Value', accounts for the displacement of early modern manufacture by large-scale industry while leaving aside the religious, cultural, and moral motivations for this historical shift that most concern Weber. Marx's analysis turns on the combination of motor-, transmission-, and working-mechanisms (*Bewegungs-, Transmissions-, Arbeitsmaschinen*) in which the manipulable implements of handicraft are replaced by the mechanical instruments of industry:

> An organized system of machines to which motion is communicated by the transmitting mechanism from an automatic centre is the most developed form of production by machinery. Here we have, in place of the isolated machine, a mechanical monster whose body fills whole factories, and whose demonic power, at first hidden by the slow and measured motions of its gigantic members, finally bursts forth in the fast and furious whirl of its countless working organs. (C: 503)

By characterizing capital as a mechanical monstrosity, Marx begins to narrate his own quasi-mythological tale by adding the ancient Cyclops to his menagerie of metaphors that includes the medieval vampire: 'But the huge masses of iron that had now to be forged, welded, and cut, bored and shaped required for their part machines of Cyclopean dimensions, which the machine-building trades of the period of manufacture were incapable of constructing' (C: 506). In three bracing pages that rival the epic high drama of Weber's apocalyptic lines on the end-times of capitalism, Marx describes the 'Cyclopean machinery' of railways, ocean-steamers, and telegraphs along with the colossal 'machines that produce machines' on a superhuman scale and that spell the doom of earlier cooperative modes of production (C: 506–8; Jameson 2011: 54–5). This new 'material mode of existence [...] necessitates the replacement of human force by natural forces, and the replacement of the rule of thumb by the conscious application of natural science' (C: 508). In contrast to the refined, malleable, and delicate steel alloy that Weber envisions, Marx traces the primitive sources of this mechanized system to the extraction and smelting of iron directly out of the earth and to its deployment in the heavy machinery of large-scale industry.

The capitalist class of Cyclops in this modern version of the mythical legend are therefore descendants not of the cave-dwelling shepherds in

Homer's *Odyssey* who try to impede the hero on his journey to glory, but rather of the iron-welding assistants of the smith-god Vulcan (Hephaestus) in Virgil's *Aeneid*. By forging the thunderbolts, chariots, and armour that the hero needs for battle, they also equip him with the material means to found a new nation, the future Roman Empire. In the climactic passage on the general law of capitalist accumulation, Marx invokes this story in describing the 'despotism' of capital over the mass of toiling labourers: 'the law which holds the relative surplus population or industrial reserve army in equilibrium with the extent and energy of accumulation rivets [*schmied*] the worker to capital more firmly than the wedges of Hephaestus held Prometheus to the rock' (C: 799). Obeying a law laid down by the blacksmith god of metalworking, the Cyclops forge the instruments that punish the sacrilege of stealing fire from heaven for human and civil use. In both their ancient and modern incarnations, these cruel, cannibalistic, and uncivilized giants serve under more powerful forces and are as ignorant of the devastation they bring to humankind as they are blind to human suffering, since they can only see through a single round eye.[3]

II

Chapter 15 of *Capital*, 'Machinery and Large-Scale Industry', is by far the longest at 150 pages (twice as long as the chapter on the working day). Combining historical narrative and empirical documentation on the

[3] Marx first introduces the Cyclops in Chapter 10 of *Capital*, 'The Working Day', in denouncing the savagery of the Messrs Cammell & Co., owners of 'Cyclops Steel and Iron Works' (C: 372; also see the 1875 painting by Adolph von Menzel 'The Forge (A Modern Cyclops)' on the cover of the most recent Penguin edition of *Capital*). These 'Cyclopean gentlemen', as he calls them, complained to the Governing Commissioner that prohibiting the night-work of children and young people would ruin their business, even though in fact only a fraction of their workforce is made up of minors. In dismissing the 'cynical naiveté' of arguments like these steel by manufacturers, Marx turns to Hegel's *Logic* to note how nowadays corruption can be justified on almost any grounds: 'In a time so rich in reflection and so devoted to *raisonnement* as our own, he must be a poor creature who cannot advance a good ground for everything, even for what is worst and most depraved' (C: 373n70, quoting Hegel 1977: 178, para. 121). By justifying even the most inhuman working conditions in the interests of turning a profit, the capitalist Cyclops seems to combine superhuman strength with convoluted powers of reasoning (C: 347, 363).

structure and organization of the nineteenth-century factory system, Marx examines the devastating impact of handicrafts, manufacture, agriculture, and domestic industry on the vitality and longevity of workers of all ages and genders:

> Insofar as machinery dispenses with muscular power, it becomes a means for employing workers of slight muscular strength, or whose bodily development is complete, but whose limbs are all the more supple. The labour of women and children was therefore the first result of the capitalist application of machinery! (C: 517)

Laws implemented to regulate unhealthy, immoral, and uncivil working conditions are at the same time the inevitable outcome of these conditions: 'Factory legislation, that first conscious and methodical reaction of society against the spontaneously developed form of its production process, is, as we have seen, just as much the necessary product of large-scale industry as cotton yarn, self-actors, and the electric telegraph' (C: 610). Marx does not advance any simple thesis that economic forces are the only causes of the breakdown of working families or that the 'anarchy of production' can simply be reined in by regulatory controls (C: 608). He is concerned rather with how the technical process of labour in particular and the organization of social life more generally have been radically changed ('revolutionized') by the capitalist mode of production. To develop this multi-faceted argument he examines a mass of empirical evidence in Part IV and then offers a sophistical theoretical analysis in Part V through a series of technical investigations ('*nouvelles recherches*' in the French edition) into how absolute and relative surplus-value operate in combination. These hypothetical models, in which the length, productivity, or intensity of labour are held constant or assumed to be variable, are designed to illuminate how older work processes are taken over by or absorbed into new production regimes. On the one hand, 'the formal subsumption' of labour under capital leaves the work process more or less as it was while exploiting it from the outside, like a predatory vampire that merely sucks living labour without transforming it into something else. On the other hand, 'the real subsumption' of labour under capital accelerates the technical conditions of the production process by reorganizing it from within, like a cannibalistic Cyclops that consumes a body whole and becomes something bigger and more powerful than it was before. With the shift from small manufacture into large-scale industry, 'the formal subsumption is then replaced by a real subsumption' (C: 645).[4]

Weber's insights into this history consist in recovering the cultural sources of technological change and the moral motivations of capital accumulation. In defining 'formally free labour' as the crucial feature of industrial capitalism, he suggests that work may be legally or technologically emancipated from earlier forms of servitude or slavery, and yet remain unfree, restrained, or controlled in other unforeseen ways. Weber's formulation draws on Marx's argument in the penultimate chapter of *Capital* that 'capitalist private property [...] rests on the exploitation of alien, but formally free labour' (C: 928). Where Marx describes how 'new forces and new passions spring up in the bosom of society', Weber emphasizes how austere attitudes and ascetic habits inform the ethical obligation to work by providing new justifications for the relationship between necessary labour for oneself and surplus labour for others. As Marx describes this transformation in Part VI of *Capital* on 'wages' (in the first edition the continuation of Chapter 5), the value-form of wage-labour makes the reality of exploitation and inequality appear to be freely chosen and the result of an equal exchange:

> The wage-form thus extinguishes every trace of the division of the working day into necessary labour and surplus labour, into paid labour and unpaid labour. [...] In wage-labour [...] even surplus labour, or unpaid labour, appears as paid [...], and the money-relation conceals the uncompensated labour of the wage-labourer. (C: 680)

[4] Marx's discussion of the conceptual distinction between the formal and real subsumption of labour under capital anticipates the arguments of later writers like Weber on the expansion of the world market and the acceleration of technological innovation. These phases are more fully examined in a section of Marx's posthumously published chapter of *Capital* drafted in 1863–1836, 'The Results of the Immediate Process of Production' (included as an appendix in C: 1019–38). Here he describes the historical difference between the seizure of traditional production processes by extending the working day and increasing the scale and size of factory operations, on the one hand, and the reorganization and intensification of working conditions through specialization and mechanization, on the other hand. Marx seems to have conceived this larger perspective on 'absolute' versus 'relative' surplus-value initially as an extension of the discussion of 'primitive accumulation' in the final two chapters of Part VIII (the concluding sections of Chapter 6 in the first edition) and thus as a kind of bridge to Volume 2 of *Capital* on the expansion of the circulation process (see Ernst Mandel's editorial notes in C: 943–7). Here and in his brief remarks on formal and real subsumption in Part V of the German editions (which he deleted in the French translation), he beings to sketch the beginnings of a more refined theory of 'accumulation by dispossession' advanced by recent theorists of colonial and imperial capitalism (Harvey 2003; Ince 2018, 2021; Pinho 2021: 13).

The wage-form wraps a harsh reality within a more palatable or alluring mystery by covering every track (*löscht jede Spur aus*) left by earlier working regimes under the fluctuations of financial transactions. To this argument Weber adds that workers do not submit to the monetary regime of wages and salaries out of mere cultural delusion or sheer force, but rather because of the different motivations they have for working. In his empirical investigations into the selection and adaptation of occupations (*Berufe*), for example, he includes a social survey of workers designed to recover the 'psychophysical' principles of pace, skill, rhythm, and stress levels as they affect industrial productivity (Weber 1971; Brain 2001). Time-wages, piece-wages, and other forms of remuneration on their own are insufficient motivations for work under capitalism, which also requires a complex system of interconnected environmental factors, affective promptings, skills training, ethical ideals, and emotional controls to keep the components of the production process in motion.

What then remains of the work ethic when the Puritan-Christian sources of its ascetic and disciplinary form are no longer needed and when industry comes to rest on a foundation of large-scale machinery? In Part VII of *Capital*, 'The Process of Accumulation of Capital', Marx indirectly takes up this question by considering how political economists promote a kind of 'abstinence theory' of acquisition and investment: 'While the capitalist of the classical type brands individual consumption as a sin against his function, as "abstinence" from accumulating, the modernized capitalist is capable of viewing accumulation as "renunciation" of pleasure' (C: 740–1). Unlike the entrepreneurs and merchants of the early modern period, the industrial capitalists supposedly must abstain from enjoying riches by reinvesting their extra earnings and consuming wealth productively. By this logic, the capitalist earns 'interest' which requires abstinence (*Enthaltung*) in being reinvested while the worker earns 'wages' which are spent on consumption for mere maintenance (*Erhaltung*). Marx finds these convoluted explanations of the profit motive and the work ethic wholly inadequate, and notes contemptuously that they are adorned with the Christian connotations of renunciation (*Entsagung*) in the writings of economic scholars like Wilhelm Roscher, who was later Weber's teacher (C: 338n12). Such a 'catechism' or 'gospel of abstinence and saving' hypocritically preaches to capitalists that they repudiate worldly pleasures while paying near starvation wages to workers, whom they exhort to restrain themselves from the supposedly 'extravagant' expense of large families (C: 298).[5]

Marx suggests that, in fact, the 'vocational asceticism' that gave birth to the idea that a worldly calling applies to everyone no longer needs a religious foundation but only the general acceptance of the need to specialize and submit to discipline. As Weber puts this point, the new work ethic requires 'renunciation of the Faustian multi-dimensionality of the human species'; that is, it entails the replacement of the cultivated human being by the specialist. To illustrate he alludes to the mature Wilhelm Meister in Goethe's novel who joins a group of fellow-travellers called 'the renunciants' and the ageing Faust who learns the discipline needed to reorganize the world according to his own methodical plans (PE: 157). Weber's later writings take up these themes by turning to the study of worldly professions, careers, and occupations (*Berufe*) in a variety of modern cultural spheres, including private enterprises and public bureaucracies, and most famously in science and politics, the two vocations that most concerned him personally. Towards the end of his lectures on 'Science as a Vocation' (1917) and 'Politics as a Vocation' (1919), he cites a speech by Mephistopheles (in Act Two of the second part of *Faust*) as a way of admonishing his audience members against falling for the fashionable pursuit of 'sensation' and 'experience' (Weber 2004: 27, 91):

[5] In Chapter 25 of *Capital*, Marx proposes his own 'general law of capitalist accumulation' as an alternative to the general 'law of population' that was popular among economists in his day and influential in the passage of the nineteenth-century poor laws. In the book's longest footnote, worthy of Weber with its intricate detail and complex reasoning, Marx declares that the 'hour of the Protestant had struck' with the publication of Thomas Malthus's well-known 'sermon' on 'the principle of population for the workers' (C: 766–8n6). He notes that most population theorists are Protestant clerics bent on preaching austerity for poor (Joseph Townsend, Thomas Chalmers, and now Malthus), while the early political economists were philosophers (Thomas Hobbes), medical men (William Petty), or businessmen and statesmen (Benjamin Franklin). Against the natural and quasi-theological laws of selection and scarcity proclaimed by 'the parsons', Marx offers a working hypothesis in the form of a law of population under the capitalist mode of production and considers its political and moral implications. By taking account of social conditions and historical contingencies, this 'law' therefore meets the modest criteria that Weber formulates for the 'ideal type': 'Anyone who has ever worked with Marxist concepts will be aware not only of the eminent, indeed unique, *heuristic* importance of those ideal types, when they are used for *comparisons* with reality, but also of how dangerous they can be whenever they are presented as empirically valid, or even as *real* (which in fact means: metaphysical) "effective *forces*", "tendencies" etc.' (Weber 2012: 132–3). In proposing a general law of capitalist accumulation, Marx offers a critique of the discourse of population among his contemporaries which sets a precedent for Weber's historical investigation of the Protestant source of the work ethic.

Ihr bleibt bei meinem Worte kalt,	I see my discourse leaves you cold,
Euch guten Kindern laß ich's gehen;	Dear kids, do not take offense;
Bedenkt: der Teufel, der ist alt,	Recall: the Devil, he is old,
So werdet alt, ihn zu verstehen!	Grow old yourselves, and he'll make sense! (F: 6815–8)

On each occasion Weber himself implicitly takes on the role of 'the old devil' by exhorting his young listeners to take a long view of the diabolical ways of the world and to stand up to the harsh realities of life with 'trained ruthlessness', patience, and maturity (Kemple 2014: 49–55). As we learn in the next scene of the play, Mephistopheles's speech takes place while Faust's assistant Wagner is working on an experiment in his laboratory to 'crystalize' a tiny human—the Homunculus—out of pure light, reason, sound, and speech. Like Weber's sombre remarks, Mephistopheles's cold words serve as a warning to today's youth about a future in which the modern sciences can engineer life in a laboratory and traditional political rule gives way to the cynical exercise of power.

Weber's later writings on the comparative sociology of the world religions, which the earlier essay on the Protestant ethic came to serve as both prelude and centrepiece, are concerned with examining both the material and ideal sides of the causal chain. His larger project expands the scope of Marx's *Capital* by considering how a variety of culturally specific 'economic ethics' may either propel or hinder the expansion of the material forces of occidental capitalism across the globe. In particular, the idea of salvation evokes different images of a world without suffering and death among Christian, Muslim, Hindu, and Jewish believers with contrasting practical, material, and economic consequences. In his general introduction to the larger series of studies, he invokes the striking figure of the railway worker to describe these divergences:

> Not ideas, but material and ideal *interests,* directly govern a person's activities. Yet very frequently the 'world images' that have been created by 'ideas' have, like switchmen determined the tracks along which action has been pushed by the dynamic of interest. (PE: 241)

The figure depicts the influence of ideas and world images on the direction that particular agents and social practices may take within historical systems. In the context of his larger comparative sociology of world religions, for example, he identifies a kind of axial turn in which the 'occidental' worldviews of Judaism, Christianity, and Islam, which stressed world-mastery, branched off from the ancient 'oriental' worldviews of Hinduism, Buddhism, and Confucianism, which emphasized world-flight. Drawing upon conventional typologies of Orientalist and theological scholarship, he argues that each of these 'cultural mentalities' or 'economic ethics' in turn broke off into orthodox and heterodox strains through the instigation of particular 'culture carriers' (*Kulturträger*), such as the sixteenth- and seventeenth-century reformers who split Christianity into Protestant and Catholic branches (Said 1978: 259). Invoking the railway metaphor in another context to formulate the larger implications of this process, Weber asks what factors distinguish the western trajectory towards particular strains of methodical action and rational ideas across a wide range of institutional domains: 'How did it happen that scientific, artistic, [legal], and economic development, as well as state-building, were directed into those tracks [*Bahne*] of *rationalization* specific to the West?' (PE: 215).[6] His 'switchman theory of world history' is an attempt to answer this question by accounting for the emergence of pivotal historical individuals, such

[6] As products of nineteenth-century Europe, Marx and Weber have characteristically close personal and intellectual ties to railways. Among Weber's formative early memories was the shattering spectacle of a catastrophic train wreck, which he later recalled as his 'first experience of the transitoriness of the great and beautiful on this earth' (Marianne Weber 1988: 32; Kemple 2014: 155). Perhaps as a symptom of this recollection, one of his favourite metaphors when describing the direction of historical development is that of a vehicle that cannot reverse course at will or a locomotive that has gone 'off track' (*aus der Bahne*) (Weber 2004: 81–2; Kemple 2014: 216–23). During one of the most desperate periods for Marx and his family, having lost the income from his editorial work for the *New York Daily Tribune* due to the outbreak of the Civil War, he applied for a job as a clerk in a railway station but was rejected for his bad handwriting (CW 41: 436). In *Capital*, he describes a railway accident that has 'dispatched hundreds of passengers into the next world' and denounces the routine overwork imposed on 'ordinary men, who are not Cyclops'. He also remarks with considerable scorn on the disruption of mealtimes by factory clocks, which were themselves set to railway clocks (C: 363, 608). In an often-quoted sentence from his articles on 'The Class Struggles in France' (1848–1850), Marx writes that not the ballot box but rather 'revolutions are the locomotives of history' (CW 10: 122). The age of railways, which extends into our own day, is therefore both a material foundation for the dangerous acceleration of capitalist accumulation and a metaphorical site for critically imagining a world beyond it (Traverso 2021: 32–77).

as Buddha, Confucius, Moses, Jesus, Mohammad, Luther, and Franklin over the course of millennia and their influence on the formation of general categories of important culture-carriers, such as monks, priests, peasants, and city-dwellers.

Weber's argument regarding the cultural-carriers of history can also be interpreted broadly to include economic class and social status positions, such as those Marx and Engels group under the headings 'bourgeoisie' and 'proletariat' or 'wage-labour' and 'capital'. The figure of the 'switchmen' alludes to the now-automated function of the class of railroad worker charged with manually switching tracks to allow trains to shift directions towards different destinations. Today we might think of air traffic

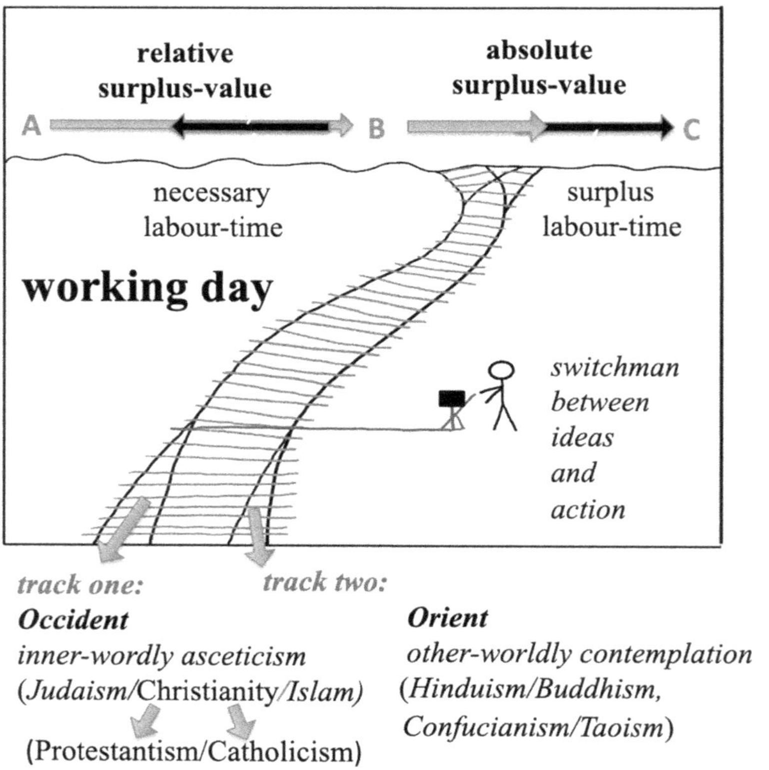

Fig. 3.1 The railroad of capitalism (Marx and Weber on work-time and world-views)

controllers and other technically trained experts who monitor transportation networks as well as civil engineers who design traffic lights and plan road signs. Figure 3.1 presents Weber's metaphor of the 'switchman between ideas and action' as a literal illustration of Marx's discussion of the collective labourer under capital, here exemplified by the railway worker. As Marx reminds us, 'the collective worker, who constitutes the living mechanism of manufacture, is made up of one-sidedly specialized workers' (C: 458). The emergence and divergence of world civilizations over the past three millennia that Weber envisions is shown here alongside Marx's line-metaphor depicting the proportion of surplus to necessary labour in the working day. On the one hand, this ratio depends on whether surplus labour-time is extended by lengthening the hours worked, such as when a railway worker is required to put in overtime (the production of absolute surplus-value). On the other hand, necessary labour-time may be shortened relative to surplus labour by being employed more efficiently, such as when automated devices or rapid transportation systems are introduced (the production of relative surplus-value). In *The Communist Manifesto* Marx and Engels consider these developments on a large scale, noting that bourgeois society is sustained by the 'subjection of Nature's forces to man, machinery, application of chemistry to industry and agriculture, steam-navigation, railways, electric telegraphs, clearing of whole continents for cultivation, canalization of rivers, whole populations conjured out of the ground' (CM: 66). They marvel over how the centuries-long struggle to form unions of craftsmen in the Middle Ages can now be accomplished in just a few years, thanks to railway connections between modern workers (CM: 70–1). The nineteenth-century railroad served as a kind of information highway and internet of trade facilitating local commodity chains and cultural exchanges on a continental and global scale.

Marx and Weber differ from Durkheim in how they define modern industrial capitalism not just in terms of the specialized division (*Teilung*) of labour but also the spatial separation (*Scheidung*) of city and country and the socio-economic separation of workers from the means of production: 'Capitalist production therefore reproduces in the course of its own process the separation between labour-power and the conditions of labour' (C: 723). The appropriation of land, by which landowners displace peasants from their means of subsistence and colonial settlers remove indigenous people from their way of life—'so-called primitive accumulation'—is reproduced constantly and intensified daily in the factory and private enterprise where workers neither own nor control the instruments of production. Weber's later sociological and political writings, such as

'Parliament and Government in Germany' (1918), repeatedly point out that Marx's insight can be extended to include a wide range of leading institutions in capitalist society, including the bureaucratic state and the organizations it administers:

> Whether the organization is a modern state apparatus engaging in power politics or cultural politics or pursing military aims, or a private capitalist business, the same, decisive economic basis is *common* to both, namely the 'separation' of the worker from the material means of conducting the activity of the organization—the means of production in the economy, the means of war in the army, or the means of research in a university institution or laboratory, and the financial means in all of them. (Weber 1994: 147)

As the means of operation become concentrated in the hands of judges, officials, officers, foremen, clerks, soldiers, and technicians who control the bureaucratic apparatus, the socialization of professional organizations increasingly entails bureaucratization. Rather than merely an effect or epiphenomenon of capitalist forces of production, bureaucracy is a strategy for remotely reproducing and managing social relations apart from the ownership of private enterprise. In 'Politics as a Vocation', Weber notes the nearly complete 'expropriation' of civil servants from the means of administration employed by the modern state and of soldiers from the weapons of war: 'In the modern "state" [...] the "separation" of the administrative staff [...] of officials and employees from the material resources of administration has been completed' (Weber 2004: 38). In 'Science as a Vocation' he points out that 'the major institutes of science and medicine are "state capitalist" enterprises [characterized by] "the separation of the worker from the means of production", while this process has only partially been accomplished in the arts and social sciences where cultural and intellectual workers typically own many of the tools of their trade' (Weber 2004: 3).

In early writings Weber traces the origins of state capitalist enterprise to precedents in the agrarian empires of antiquity and commercial partnerships in the Middle Ages and considers how each type of regime is characterized by distinctive class struggles. In the version of *Economy and Society* he was working on when he died, he further generalizes these ideas by formulating a sociological ideal type of 'class' in terms of a group or a person's life-chances and skill-levels are tied to market position, not just ownership of the means of production, access to income, or control over resources:

> The 'class position' of an individual is the typical opportunity or possibility [*Chance*]: 1. of provision with goods, 2. of outer position in life, 3. of inner life-fate, that follows from the extent and nature of a power of disposition (or the absence of such power) over goods and educational or technical qualifications [*Leistungsqualifikationen*], and from the given form in which they might be valorised in seeking access to income or revenues within a given economic order. (Weber 2019: 450)

Weber goes on to note that the unfinished problem Marx addresses in *Capital* is concerned with how the working classes may be unified politically despite their different qualifications, their location in various labour markets, or their classification by age and sex, particularly as semi-skilled labour workers replace skilled workers with the introduction of machinery (Weber 2019: 454; C: 788). With this broader sociology of class (*Klasse*) in mind, he then considers the distinctive impact of rank or status (*Stand*) on social inequality with respect to the cultural estimation of certain life-styles, the prestige of different kinds of life-conduct, and the significance of birth, occupation, cultivation, or education with respect to a person's social standing (Weber 2019: 455). Adding a sociological dimension to the categories of political economy he inherited from Marx's era, Weber argues that status distinctions and social hierarchies that inform struggles over political power and social recognition often follow a cultural logic that diverges from the economic logic of class position based on the production or distribution of wealth and the acquisition of property.

* * *

Weber calls Marxism a prominent example of 'the purely *logically* compelling power of ideas' on empirical-historical events in view of its widespread diffusion and influence on people's minds even when its original sources of inspiration are not acknowledged (Weber 2012:129). His challenge to Marxian theory and to socialist thought more broadly lies in his insistence that bureaucratization is the 'inevitable' condition for modern industrial production, whether managed by state institutions or private enterprise. As he argues in his 1918 lecture 'Socialism', 'Everywhere we find the same thing: the means of operation within the factory, the state administration, the army and university department are concentrated by means of a bureaucratically structured human apparatus in the hands of the person who has command over [*beherrscht*] this human apparatus'

(Weber 1994: 281). Although he calls Marx's statement regarding the 'separation of workers from the means of production' a 'socialist slogan', he adopts it as the guiding thesis for his own study of modern organizations: 'as discipline was required for capitalist industry so "factory *discipline* [...] gave birth to modern socialism"' (Weber 1994: 283). In both capitalist and socialist societies the army operates through the apparatus of the officer corps; mines are managed by engineers; factories are ruled by specialist personnel; university departments are governed by senior administrators, and yet in none of these contexts can bureaucrats call the institution their 'property'. In *Economy and Society* Weber echoes some of Marx's critical views on the brutal conditions of struggle and domination that the capitalist economy presupposes and exacerbates: 'A further specifically material irrationality of the economic order is that the greatest extent of formal rationality in capitalist calculation is possible only where the worker is completely subject to the rule of entrepreneurs' (Weber 2019: 245). He credits Marx with distinguishing 'between an evolutionary socialism oriented to production linked especially with Marxism and a form of distributional socialism organized around a rational planned economy (which is today once more called "communism")' (Weber 2019: 207). Weber was not surprised to witness the breakout of revolution in his home city of Munich a year after the revolution in Russia, which in 'Science as a Vocation' he describes in Marxian terms as an 'attempt to bring about the expropriation of this expropriator of the resources of politics and hence of political power' (Weber 2004: 38).

Writing in the early decades of the twentieth century, Weber occasionally paused to look back on the intellectual world of the early nineteenth century in ways that speak uncannily to our own dilemmas in the early decades of the twenty-first century. In the concluding remarks of his 1904 essay on 'objectivity' in the social and economic sciences, for instance, he muses about how literary scholars and social scientists often seem to waver between tirelessly gathering facts, statistics, and documents, on the one hand, and impatiently collecting worldviews, essences, and profound ideas, on the other. He then trails off with a poetic flourish that contrasts starkly with his more sombre scholarly prose. In an age where every cultural scientist must specialize, he suggests, only rarely do we reflect on how the facts are anchored in ultimate 'value ideas' or consider how viewpoints that once seemed to illuminate a whole field of research are now eclipsed as new problems emerge and 'the way forward fades away in the twilight':

Doch scheint die Göttin endlich wegzusinken;	At last, it seems, the god is downward sinking;
Allein der neue Trieb erwacht,	Yet a new urge awakens the mind,
Ich eile fort, ihr ew'ges Licht zu trinken	I hasten on, his ceaseless radiance drinking,
Vor mir den Tag und hinter mir die Nacht,	The day ahead of me, night left behind,
Den Himmel über mir und unter mir die Wellen.	The waves below, overhead the sky. (Weber 2012: 138, quoting F: 1084–8)

The irony in using a quotation from Faust's speech to his young assistant Wagner in the context of a theoretical discussion would not have been lost on Weber. In this early scene (later parodied in the speech by Mephistopheles that Weber quotes from in his lectures on science and politics), Faust himself seems to succumb for a moment to the romance of science as he takes a stroll with his naïve protégé outside the city gates. Weber's striking figural turn here can be read as an invitation for us to reflect on both his legacy and that of Marx, if not from the 'summits of thought' then from the vantage point of historical hindsight over a hundred years after their deaths.

Notwithstanding his commitment to the scholarly calling, Weber was also profoundly engaged with political affairs throughout his career. He did not argue for a separation of political action from scientific understanding, except as a logical necessity and as a principled matter of professional integrity or a pragmatic question of personal humility. In the second half of the twentieth century, sociologist Immanuel Wallerstein emerged as one of the most influential heirs to the legacies of both Marx and Weber in arguing that critique and analysis must inform one another and be taken up together. Rather than ascend to abstract theories and local disciplinary disputes, he argues, the critical sociological analyst must descend into the messy complexities of global political controversies. With Marx and Weber as his guide, Wallerstein investigates the dynamics of the capitalist world system since its emergence in the sixteenth-century Europe with the establishment manufactories and the expansion of world markets. Since world-economies like the capitalist world system 'lack the unifying cement of an overall political structure or a homogeneous culture, what holds them together is the efficacy of the division of labour' (Wallerstein 2004: 24).

State power and legal institutions do not guarantee stability in the capitalist world system, while class positions and status identities are largely reproduced in markets, firms, states, and households that serve as socializing agents for the global circulation of surplus-value (Wallerstein 2004: 35–6). The capitalist world economy today is characterized much as it was in Weber and Marx's time, namely by the uneven accumulation of wealth among nation-states, the global division of labour between rich and poor countries, and the unequal distribution of surplus-value in 'core', 'semi-peripheral', and 'peripheral' areas. Then as now it is an open question whether riots, revolts, reforms, or revolutions can leverage credible anti-systemic alternatives, whether socialist or otherwise.

N.B.: I often modify existing English translations, drawing on German or French editions readily available online or from print sources. References to *Faust* are by line number as indicated in both English and German editions.

Works Cited and Consulted

Abbreviations Used

C—Marx, Karl (1976). *Capital: A Critique of Political Economy, Volume 1.* Ben Fowkes trans. Ernest Mandel intro. London: Penguin Books.

CW—*The Collected Works of Karl Marx and Friedrich Engels 1844–1895.* 47 Volumes. New York: International Publishers. (Electronic Edition, Charlottesville, Virginia).

DL—Durkheim, Emile (2004). *The Division of Labor in Society.* W. D. Wells trans. Lewis Coser intro. New York: The Free Press.

F—Goethe, Johann Wolfgang von (1986). *Faust: Eine Tragödie.* Erster und Zweiter Teile. Stuttgart: Philipp Reclam Jun.

Goethe, Johann Wolfgang von (1976). *Faust: A Tragedy.* Walter Arndt trans., Cyrus Hamlin ed. New York: W. W. Norton & Company.

PE—Weber, Max (2009). *The Protestant Ethic and the Spirit of Capitalism, with Other Writings on the Rise of the West.* Fourth edition. Stephen Kalberg trans., intro. Oxford: Oxford University Press.

PM—Simmel, Georg (2004). *The Philosophy of Money.* Thomas Bottomore, David Frisby trans. London: Routledge.

Brain, Robert M. (2001). 'The Ontology of the Questionnaire: Max Weber on Measurement and Mass Investigation'. *Studies in History and Philosophy* 32(4): 647–84.

Harvey, David (2003). *The New Imperialism*. Oxford, UK: Oxford University Press.

Hegel, G. W. F. (1977). *Phenomenology of Spirit*. A. V. Miller trans. Oxford, UK: Oxford University Press.

Ince, Onur Ulas (2021). 'Deprovincializing Racial Capitalism: John Crawfurd and Settler Colonialism in India'. *American Political Science Review* (September 2017): 1–17.

Ince, Onur Ulas (2018). *Colonial Capitalism and the Dilemmas of Liberalism*. Oxford, UK: Oxford University Press.

Jameson, Fredric (2011). *Representing 'Capital'*. London: Verso Books.

Kemple, Thomas (2014). *Intellectual Work and the Spirit of Capitalism: Weber's Calling*. Basingstoke, UK: Palgrave Macmillan.

Kemple, Thomas (2011). 'The Spatial Sense of Empire: Encountering Strangers with Simmel, Tocqueville and Martineau'. *Journal of Classical Sociology* 11(4): 340–355.

Pinho, Rodrigo Maiolini Bebello (2021). 'The Originality of Marx's French Edition of *Capital*: An Historical Analysis'. *International Marxist Humanist*. 3 September: 1–45. https://imhojournal.org/articles/the-originality-of-marxs-french-edition-of-capital-an-historical-analysis/

Said, Edward W. (1978). *Orientalism*. New York: Vintage Books.

Stallybrass, Peter (1998). 'Marx's Coat'. In *Border Fetishisms: Material Objects in Unstable Spaces*. P. Spyer ed. London: Routledge, pp. 183–207.

Swedberg, Richard (1998). *Max Weber and the Idea of Economic Sociology*. Princeton, NJ: Princeton University Press.

Traverso, Enzo (2021). *Revolution: An Intellectual History*. London: Verso.

Wallerstein, Immanuel (2004). *World-Systems Analysis: An Introduction*. Durham, NC: Duke University Press.

Weber, Marianne (1988). *Max Weber: A Biography*. H. Zohn trans. New Brunswick, NJ: Transaction Books.

Weber, Max (2019) *Economy and Society: A New Translation*. Keith Tribe trans. Cambridge, UK: Harvard University Press.

Weber, Max (2012). *Collected Methodological Writings*. H. H. Bruun trans. H. H. Bruun, S. Whimster eds. London: Routledge.

Weber, Max (2004). *The Vocation Lectures*. R. Livinstone trans. D. Owen, T. B. Strong eds. Indianapolis, IN: Hackett.

Weber, Max (1994). *Political Writings*. P. Lassman, R. Speirs trans, eds. Cambridge, UK: Cambridge University Press.

Weber, Max (1978). *Economy and Society, Volumes 1 and 2*. G. Roth, C. Wittich eds. Berkeley, CA: University of California Press.

Weber, Max (1971). *Max Weber: The Interpretation of Social Reality*. D. Hytch trans. New York: Charles Scribner's Sons.

CHAPTER 4

The Capitalist's Two Souls: *Capital* and the Money Economy

Abstract Simmel's philosophical sociology of the modern money economy deepens Marx's analysis of the ruthless dynamic of capitalist accumulation in *Capital*. Leaving aside a closer examination of the mechanisms of exploitation and expropriation, Simmel's cultural theory of modernity explores the underlying dynamics of modern social life and the inner experience of urban individuality. Marx's general formula for capital (buying cheap to sell dear) is thus expanded into a social psychology of endless consumption and a relativist metaphysics of infinite accumulation. Simmel's sees the tragedy of modern culture in the alienation, mechanization, and reification of life, and advocates for social assistance to the poor rather than for socialism as a solution to the problems of modern existence. Simmel and Marx envision the modern soul as divided between the passion for accumulation or enjoyment and the austere requirement to save or invest, like Faust who is torn between ever wanting more and needing to restrain his desires.

Keywords Value • Simmel • Accumulation • Reification • Juggernaut

In the final Parts VII and VIII of *Capital, Volume 1* (Chapters 23–33, which together made up the concluding Chapter 6 of the first edition), Marx considers 'capitalist accumulation' from the point of view of the

T. Kemple, *Marx's Wager*, Marx, Engels, and Marxisms,
https://doi.org/10.1007/978-3-031-08065-4_4

immediate process of production. Rather than examining accumulation from the perspective of trade in commodities or the investment of money on the market, his focus here is on the transformation of surplus-value into capital. Anticipating the subsequent volumes, he takes a couple of pages to sketch a general overview of the work as a whole: after examining the exchange of money for labour-power, raw materials, instruments, and machines employed in the production of surplus-value in Volume 1, the following two volumes would consider the circulation of surplus-value and its distribution as profit, interest, and rent (C: 709–10). In contrast to the volume's opening lines, where he describes a colossal collection (*Sammlung*) of things, that is, a miscellany of goods for purchase and sale, here he examines the cyclical accumulation (*Akkumulation*) of people, places, and processes and the systematic organization of labour, land, and life itself in the pursuit of surplus-value. From the worker's standpoint, the accumulation process entails the productive consumption of the means of production as well as the individual consumption of means of subsistence. The latter includes reproduction through the sale (C—M), purchase (M—C′), and consumption of basic commodities necessary for the perpetuation of the working class (C: 717–8). From the capitalist's standpoint, the accumulation process appears as the acquisition of commodities (M—C), including labour, materials, and machines, and their employment for a surplus-value realized through profitable sale and reinvestment (C—M′). The cycle of simple reproduction is thus transformed into a spiral of expanding and accelerating accumulation (M—M′) where capital appears to create more capital (C: 727). As Marx irreverently puts it, the capitalist's cardinal commandment—'Accumulate, accumulate! That is Moses and the prophets!'—is echoed in the 'shibboleth' of the classical economists, who call for the acceleration of accumulation and more rapid 'production on a constantly increasing scale' (C: 742–3). Marx's last word on the production process of capital takes the form of a 'general law' of capitalist accumulation (Chapter 25, at 110 pages the second longest chapter), itself premised on the 'historical tendency' of ongoing expropriation and colonization (Chapters 32 and 33, together just 13 pages, which I discuss in the Conclusion).

Georg Simmel's *Philosophy of Money* (*Philosophie des Geldes*, published in 1900, a revised edition in 1907) broadens the scope of Marx's concern with the accumulation process in *Capital* by thinking beyond the confines of political economy and in some sense 'beneath' its materialist critique:

> The attempt is made to construct a storey beneath [*ein Stockwerk unterzubauen*] historical materialism such that the explanatory value of the incorporation of economic life into the causes of intellectual culture is preserved, while these economic forms themselves are recognized as the result of more profound valuations and currents of psychological or even metaphysical preconditions. (PM: 54)

Without disputing that material conditions give rise to intellectual culture, Simmel argues that these conditions are also shaped by even more fundamental psychic and metaphysical processes. In the opening chapters, for example, he implicitly takes Marx's discussion of use-value and exchange-value in Chapter 1 of *Capital* as the point of departure for his own elaboration of the theory of value, which he reformulates in terms of the deeper dialectic of subjective desire and objective privation. In pursuing a 'philosophy of money' rather than an economics of industrial capitalism, Simmel shows how economic life is incorporated into even the most refined and remote areas of culture. In any case, he shares Marx's main concern in discussing the money economy partly in terms of the distinctively modern problem of accumulation. Side-stepping Marx's analysis of the commodification and exploitation of labour-power (the problematic of surplus-value), however, he expands the general formula for capital—buying cheap order to sell dear—into a social psychology of endless consumption and a sociology infinite accumulation. Simmel's celebrated sociology of spiritual, cultural, and mental life (*Geistesleben*) in modern metropolises (*Großstädte*), especially in 'The Metropolis and Mental Life' (1903), begins from these insights into the intellectual and psychological impact of 'money economy' (*Geldwirtschaft*) on the inner experience and psychic life (*Seelenleben*) of the modern individual. His broader philosophical aim is to elaborate on the relativist metaphysics or 'relational' worldview inaugurated by the capitalist money economy and established in the modern metropolis, and to consider whether this emerging world picture may be itself grounded in ultimate ideals or absolute principles (PM: 54; Kemple 2018a: 24–5).

In what follows I examine the convergence and divergence between Marx's analysis of the ruthless dynamic of capitalist accumulation and Georg Simmel's philosophical sociology of the tragedy of modernity epitomized in the rise of the modern money economy. As if to anticipate Simmel's insights into the psychic contradictions of capitalist life, Marx cites the famous words of Faust early on in Goethe's play in characterizing the division within the capitalist mind between new and old ways of viewing wealth. Like Faust who is torn between ever wanting more and yet needing to restrain his desires, the capitalist soul is split between the passion for accumulation and the austere requirement to save money rather than enjoy life:

> While the capitalist of the classic type brands individual consumption as a sin against his function, as 'abstinence' from accumulating, the modernized capitalist is capable of viewing accumulation as 'renunciation' of pleasure:

Zwei Seelen wohnen, ach! In meiner Brust,	Two souls, alas, are dwelling within my breast;
Die eine will sich von der andern trennen	And either would be severed from its other.
	(C: 740–1, quoting F: 1112–3)

Marx's parody of the old-school capitalist who 'abstains' (*enthalt*) from accumulation, in contrast to the new-fangled capitalist who 'renounces' (*entsagt*) pleasure, recalls the moral maxims of Protestant asceticism discussed by Weber. It also evokes the deeper tension between Faust's eternal striving and his determination to 'do without' (*entbehrt*), such as when the world spirit calls out to him in the moments leading up to his pact with Mephistopheles:

Entbehren sollst du! Sollst du entbehren.	Abstain, it calls, You must abstain!'
	(F: 1549)

Simmel takes these reflections a step further than Marx and Weber by characterizing mental life in the modern metropolis as inherently and irreparably torn between the desire for distinction and the passion for equality, and as a conflict between intense involvement and blasé detachment. In an excursus on the expansion of groups and the development of modern individuality in the final chapter of his monumental *Sociology* (1908), he describes the psychological and sociological aspects of selfhood in terms of the duelling commitments of the spectator who studies the world and the participant who strives to change it. Alluding to Faust's famous speech, Simmel describes the relationship between self and others as a field of conflicting interests and contradictory imaginings: 'then will "two souls in one breast" sympathize and imitate the relationships of conflict and reconciliation, separation and unity, domination and subservience that occur between the targets of interest' (Simmel 2009: 667). Leaving aside a closer examination of the mechanisms of exploitation and expropriation in the capitalist economy, Simmel's philosophy of money and cultural theory of modernity excavate the underlying metaphysical dynamics of modern social life and the inner experience of (in)dividuality.

I

Where Durkheim and Weber start out from Marx's analysis of the relations between capital and labour, their contemporary (and occasional interlocutor) Simmel focuses on Marx's theory of commodity exchanges, money transactions, and capital accumulation. Throughout his career Simmel develops a broad philosophical conception of the reciprocal causes and effects between all things, and of the interactions and relations between human and more-than-human beings.[1] Within this

[1] Simmel's master concept of the interaction (*Wechselwirkung*) among humans and between human and natural beings, where each acts on the other, can be understood to complement Marx's notion of the metabolism (*Stoffwechsel*) between humans and nature, the process by which humans exchange properties with the natural environment and are themselves transformed (C: 283–4). Each idea is drawn from the biological and physical sciences of the day, the objective of which was to articulate the dynamics of ecological and cultural change (*Wechsel*), and more broadly to express the essentially relational character of all existence (Kemple 2018a: 10–11; Saito 2017: 199–137; Marx 1989: 146). Both Marx and Simmel express the problem of the modern world order in terms of a fundamental break, rift, or alienation within human-natural processes (as I discuss below). But where Simmel imagines the fateful working out of the virtually inevitable consequences and fateful effects (*Wirkungen*) of this process, Marx insists that the human capacity to transform the world of matter (*Stoff*) through the labour-process has the potential for creating alternatives. In the *Grundrisse* Marx himself employs the language of interaction (*Wechselwirkung*) in a somewhat looser sense than Simmel. There he describes how interactions between conquering and conquered people may lead to a new cultural formation (as with the Germanic conquests), and more broadly he describes the reciprocal cause and effect within an economic totality between the different moments of production, consumption, distribution, exchange, and circulation (CW 28: 35, 37).

framework, exchanges of every kind appear to make up the very texture of social life: 'every interaction [*Wechselwirkung*] has to be regarded as an exchange [*Tausch*]—every conversation, every affection (even if it is rejected), every game, every glance at another person' (PM: 79). Exchange is the process by which the grammar of interindividual interactions become manifest and through which the syntax of social relationships become orderly: 'The same synthesizing mental process that turns the mere co-existence of things into a systematic relationship [...] has seized upon the natural rhythm of our existence, and through exchange has organized its elements in a meaningful interconnection' (PM: 80). Where Marx examines exchange primarily in terms of the exchange-value materialized in commodity and money transactions, Simmel probes deeper into the underlying material and even metaphysical processes that give rise to such exchanges and that imbue meaning and value into these interactions in the first place. (My remarks here selectively revise and expand on some points made in Kemple 2018a: 23–74, b).

Simmel thus reformulates the general problem of value in terms of the metaphysics of desiring subjects and the recalcitrant objects that resist the desire to acquire them. Philosophically speaking, value emerges 'from the separation between the subject and the content of enjoyment as an object that stands opposed to the subject as something desired and only to be attained by the conquest of distance, obstacles, and difficulties' (PM: 63–4). Any gain or profit acquired through exchange entails some kind of sacrifice or privation, though not necessarily in equal measure or as a zero-sum transaction. In a rare reference to Marx in the *Philosophy of Money*, Simmel notes that with the growth of a capitalist economy in a society based on commodity production, use-values are set aside, eliminated, or 'switched off' (*ausgeschaltet*) in favour of exchange-value, and that 'the pure form of exchangeability' is only ideally attained in a money economy (PM: 128). Implicitly extending Marx's notion of 'the formal and real subsumption of labour under capital', Simmel argues that relationships mediated by money potentially absorb the whole of social life, not just economic activities. Not only are the rhythms of meal-time and play-time regulated by the rhythms of work-time and capital-time, for example, but as a common saying puts it, 'money is a claim upon society' (PM: 176; Dodd 2014: 386). Simmel develops this essential point by observing that money is a kind of claim, command, or instruction (*Anweisung*) which directs how social exchanges may unfold anonymously, without notice, or despite resistance though a multitude of people, networks of trust, and institutional settings: 'Money appears, so to speak, as a bill of exchange from which the name of the drawee is lacking, or alternatively, which is guaranteed rather than accepted' (PM: 176). Without elaborating on the inner logic and historical source of the capitalist valuation of labour, land, and life, Simmel turns to the larger philosophical implications of this transformation of qualitative differences into quantitative equivalences. In Marx's terms, the reduction of experiential use-values into the numerical measure of abstract cash-value or market price entails reformulating the question 'how' and 'what' as a matter of 'how much' and 'how many' (C: 136). In particular, the social custom of using a precious metal like gold (*Gold*) to calculate money (*Geld*) emerges historically from its function as the equivalent form (measure and medium) of value (C: 149). Simmel takes these insights a step further by examining the effects of the process by which social relations and cultural values more broadly are 'monetized', 'quantified', and 'calculated'. For example, social standardization in the form of weights and measures, or in the valuation of things by their price, is the ultimate foundation for the calculation and enumeration of all human and more-than-human life. Simmel calls this tendency towards quantification 'the first step towards that objectivity in the free exchange of property between individuals which is the essence of exchange' (PM: 97).

In the first 'analytical' part of the *Philosophy of Money*, Simmel's discussion of how values emerge through exchange, along with his reflections on the material worth or intrinsic value (*Substanzwert*) of money, largely complement and deepen Marx's analysis of commodities and exchange in the first part of *Capital*.[2] However, their perspectives diverge in the emphasis Marx places on the buying and selling of *labour-power* as the driving force of value-formation under capital in the second part of *Capital*. Here he examines the historical process by

[2] Marx's primary interest is to develop a critique of political economy rather than a philosophy of money or a cultural theory of modern social relations, as is already evident in the *Grundrisse*, the seven preparatory notebooks for *Capital* that he filled in 1857–1858. In the 'Chapter on Money', he takes the global financial crisis of the time as the impetus to engage in a polemic with French socialists who assume that money and metal reserves are the source of the world's troubles and the cause of the unjust suffering of workers. Like the scheming Mephistopheles in the second part of Goethe's *Faust*, they assume that paper money can create wealth or guarantee credit, and that social and economic problems can be solved through the financial magic of merely printing more paper currency:

Man wird sich nicht mit Börs und Beutel tragen, *Ein Blättchen ist im Busen leicht zu tragen.*	One is no longer plagued by purse or package, A note borne next the heart is easy baggage. (F: 6103–4; Binswanger 2017)

Marx's critique goes on to develop a conceptual analysis of the functions of money as measure, medium, and store of value in different historical epochs. Metal coins, paper bills, credit notes, and time chits in Marx's day (like the crypto-currencies in our own) cannot solve the contradictions between use-value and exchange-value, he argues, nor can they harmonize the social conflicts on which they are based:

> The various forms of money may correspond better to social production at various stages of its development; one form may remove certain shortcomings with which the other cannot cope; but none of them, so long as they remain forms of money, and so long as money remains an essential relation of production, can resolve the contradictions inherent in the money relationship; they can all only express these contradictions in one form or another. (CW 28: 61)

Like Marx, Simmel assumes that value relations expressed through money are founded on irresolvable contradictions and that social strife is the consequence of such contradictions, including class conflicts stirring within the social relations of capitalist production (Kemple 2018a: 71–4; Varoufakis and Morozov 2022).

which labour-power is assigned a price through the wage contract and then circulated and consumed as a commodity among other commodities. In other words, the commodification and employment of labour-power for a specified period of time (as in the exemplary case of 'the working day') is the primary motor of capital, not just the monetization of forces of production and relations of consumption through exchange.

While Simmel acknowledges the increasing precariousness and impoverishment of workers, he is even more concerned with the expansion of individual freedoms established through the wage relationship: 'Certainly the worker is tied to his job almost as the peasant to his lot, but the frequency with which employers change in a money economy and the frequent possibility of choosing and changing them that is made possible by the form of money wages provide an altogether new freedom within the framework of his dependency' (PM: 300). These new-found 'freedoms' include the capacity or compulsion to exchange an ever-expanding range of human abilities for money, not just the skills of manual labour but of emotional and mental labour as well. In Simmel's view, Marx treats the work of the hand as the value-standard for the work of the heart and the head: 'The labour theory of value searches for [...] a concept of labour that is equally valid for manual and mental labour and, in so doing, actually appeals to manual labour as the primary value or value-producing entity that is valid as the measure of work as a whole' (PM: 414). In eliding Marx's distinction between *labour* and *labour-power*, Simmel treats all mental, affective, and physical capacities as potentially utilizable within the money economy, and conceives the metabolism between natural and human beings as equally malleable and valuable. And by ignoring Marx's analysis of exploitation and appropriation, he avoids a closer consideration of how these interactions and relationships are unevenly employed for profit and how these capacities and powers are unequally extracted for surplus-value (the increment or excess created beyond the original value).

Despite these glosses and gaps, Simmel's excavation of the underlying layers of the money economy offers sharp insights into the reification of human life and the reduction of persons to mere things. Marx views this process as inherent in the dynamics of general commodification, where anything and anyone can be evaluated and assigned a price in principle if not always in practice: 'there is an antithesis, immanent in the commodity, between the conversion of things into persons and the conversion of persons into things [*Personifizierung der Sachen und Versachlichung der Personen*]' (C: 209). Like the Faustian dilemma of the capitalist's two souls, this antithesis expresses different sides of the same process of commodification. Likewise, Simmel suggests that the tendency to reduce human beings, or at least parts of their personal life and embodied existence, to the measure of money 'not only makes money the measure of man, but it also makes man the measure of money' (PM: 357–8). Even abstract and exalted human capacities such as intellectual work can be subjected to quantitative calculation and monetary valuation. The most private and intimate of human interactions, such as sexual relations, can also be valorized as transactional tokens through monetary exchange: 'The indifference as to its use, the lack of attachment to any individual because it is unrelated to any of them, the objectivity inherent in money as a mere means which excludes any emotional relationship—all this produces an ominous analogy between money and prostitution' (PM: 379). As Marx and Engels famously proclaim in the *Manifesto*, the lack of warm emotional bonds is characteristic of both the proletarian family and public prostitution, since for each the common denominator of relations between individuals is the cold cash nexus (CM: 78). That is, sex work combines the cultivated skills and techniques of manual, intellectual, and emotional labour in ways that challenge the practical and conceptual distinction between labour-power in the abstract and the labouring body of the worker.[3]

[3]The figure of the prostitute seems to pose a perennial problem for classical social theories of money, especially in the capitalist context of generalized commodification (Kemple 1995: 228–9; 2018a: 52–3). In the *Grundrisse*, Marx describes the relations of utility and instrumentality exemplified in the so-called oldest profession as the epitome of capitalist corruption: 'The exchangeability of all products, activities, relationships for a third, *objective* entity, which in turn can be exchanged for everything *without distinction*—in other words, the development of exchange values (and of monetary relationships) is identical with general venality, with corruption. General prostitution appears as a necessary phase in the development of the social character of personal inclinations, capacities, abilities, activities' (CW 28: 99–100). In *Capital* he is especially scandalized by the living and working conditions of actual prostitutes, who along with vagabonds and criminals make up the most degraded layers of the relative surplus population, the lumpenproletariat (C: 797). Simmel too writes passionately about the miserable conditions of poverty, illiteracy, poor health, and isolation of street prostitutes in his native city of Berlin (Simmel 1997: 262–70; cf. PM: 378–82). Where Simmel metaphorically diagnoses the 'moral syphilis' infecting clients and sex workers, Marx musters a poetic figure of venal corruption to denounce the ruling classes after the revolutions of 1848 in their efforts to salvage the principles of property, family, and religion through a coalition of 'landowners and capitalists, stock-exchange sharks and small-time shopkeepers, Protectionists and Freetraders, government and opposition, priests and freethinkers, young whores and old nuns' (C: 397). This last phrase comes from a popular poem 'v. Krüdener' (1818) where Goethe condemns the chorus of reactionary forces calling for the formation of the Holy Alliance in the final years of Napoleon's reign:

Junge Huren, alte Nonnen	Young whores and old nuns
Hatten sonst schon viel gewonnen	Would do us all a few good turns
Wenn, von Pfaffen wohlberaten,	If, by priests put through their paces,
Sie im Kloster Wunder taten.	They'd work miracles in monastic places.
	(Goethe 1983: 234–5)

For both Marx and Simmel, prostitution in a modern context is a topic of intense fascination and personal disgust, a provocation for ethical compassion as well as political outrage, an exemplary resource for empirical demonstration and an occasion for polemical performance.

Value emerges through the exchange process just as money mediates the 'sequence of purposes' and connects the series of instrumental relationships by which the means become the ends because, as Simmel puts it, 'in the last analysis, the ends are only the means' (PM: 236). To illustrate this key point, Simmel devotes an extended discussion to the contrast between the figure of the miser, who takes money not as a means but as the absolute end in itself, and that of the spendthrift, who treats money as a mere means and pursues infinite acquisition of goods as an ever-elusive end (PM: 228–52). Although these character-types appear to be diametrically opposed, both see the material substance of money as having been dissolved in the pure desire of things or in self-subsisting values: 'spendthrifts are concerned only with the value of the *thing*, whereas misers are concerned only with the *value* of the thing' (Simmel 1997: 236). The extravagant spender or consumer craves the sheer bliss of squandering money and shopping for goods, regardless of their price or intrinsic worth. By contrast, the stingy money-hoarder or greedy banker relishes in acquiring the mere symbol of value without really enjoying the material things money can buy. To be sure, the life of the dissolute spendthrift is hardly sustainable for long, and the fevered mind of the mad miser is ultimately tempered and tamed when inserted into the rational circuit of savings and investments, as Marx points out:

> This boundless drive for enrichment, this passionate chase after value, is common to the capitalist and the miser; but while the miser is merely a capitalist gone mad, the capitalist is a rational miser. The ceaseless augmentation of value, which the miser seeks to attain by saving his money from circulation, is achieved by the more acute capitalist by means of throwing his money again and again into circulation. (C: 254–5)

The capitalist's motivating drive does not lie in endlessly stockpiling merchandize or perpetually enjoying goods, but rather in the severe and systematic acquisition of exchange-values and the methodical augmentation of profits (surplus-value). In contrast to the mania of the miser ruled by an insane psychology of avarice and a personal pathology of greed, the capitalist is 'capital personified' and thus a mere cog in a larger social mechanism (C: 739). Propelled by the double demands of inciting desire and deferring its consummation, the modern capitalist embodies the soul of the miser and the soul of the spendthrift within the machinery of investment and accumulation.

II

The capitalist money economy runs on a system of social and natural interdependencies that also foster the expansion of new freedoms and new obligations: 'the money economy makes possible ... a specific kind of mutual dependence which, at the same time, affords room for a maximum of liberty' (PM: 295). Simmel characterizes the tension between liberty and domination as inherently *tragic* insofar as cultural progress lays down the conditions for its own destruction and anticipates its potential transformation into something else. In his programmatic essay, 'The Concept and the Tragedy of Culture' included in the collection *Philosophical Culture* (1911), he describes the inner tendency of culture to succumb to annihilating forces that lie in the deepest layers of human interactions with natural forces. In the modern age, the specifically capitalistic manifestation of this inexorable dynamic is just one instance of a pervasive logic in which the products of culture are destined to become estranged from their sources and ends:

> The 'fetishistic character' which Marx attributed to economic objects in the epoch of commodity production is only a particularly modified instance of this general fate of the contents of our culture. These contents are subject to the paradox—and increasingly so as 'culture' develops—that they are indeed created by human subjects and are meant for human subjects, but follow an immanent developmental logic in the intermediate form of objectivity which they take on at either side of these instances and thereby become alienated from both their origin and their purpose. (Simmel 1997: 70)

Simmel's allusion here to the notorious fourth section of Chapter 1 of *Capital*, which Marx expanded on in later editions, illustrates his general thesis that products of culture outstrip their intended ends and become estranged from their origins as they take on an almost transcendent life their own. In Marx's words, the commodity-form is 'nothing but the definite social relation between men which assumes here, for them, the fantastic form of a relation between things' (C: 165). Simmel interprets this argument broadly to include the stockpiling of technical inventions, communicative media, and built environments that constitute the modern metropolis and propel capitalist accumulation. As he writes in the final pages of 'The Metropolis and Mental Life', 'the individual has become a mere cog in an enormous organization of things and powers which tear from his hands all progress, spirituality, and value in order to transform them from their subjective form into the forms of a purely objective life' (Simmel 1997: 184). Where Marx and Engels in *The Communist Manifesto* characterize the living worker as a 'mere appendage of the machine', Simmel describes the relentless and reckless tendency of the products of objective culture to outstrip and overwhelm any subjective attempts to control or comprehend the conditions of life itself (CM: 68; also C: 614, 719, 798).[4]

In *Capital* Marx likewise describes the process of capital accumulation as 'the diminution of the subjective factor of the labour process as compared with the objective factor' (C: 773). When beasts of burden and hand-held instruments become redundant, machines driven by steam-engines increase in scale while means of transport expand across space and accelerate in time. Simmel considers this modern problematic within the small scale of everyday life by examining, for instance, how the pocket watch regulates the rhythms of ordinary existence (PM: 450). He also characterizes the vending machine (*Warenautomat*), a new invention at the end of the nineteenth century, as the epitome of modern efficiency: 'By mechanical means, human relationships are completely eliminated, even in the retail trade where the exchange of commodities was long carried out between one person and another, and the money equivalent is

[4] Marx is more cautious than Simmel in insisting that the capacity to shape the course of history and the conditions of existence does not ultimately derive from a divine or a natural power, but expresses rather a limited human potential for directing fate. In the course of discussing the specialization of tools and instruments in early modern manufacture, Marx approvingly quotes from Charles Darwin's *Origin of Species* (1859) on the differentiation of the natural organs of plants and animals through the 'laws of variation'. He then draws an analogy between the evolution of organic forms through 'natural selection' and the cultivation of human implements designed for various purposes through a kind of historical selection (C: 461n6). Later in discussing the development of machinery in large-scale industry, Marx makes a comparison between Darwin's natural history of species and Giambattista Vico's critical history of technology, praising Vico's materialist method for examining worlds made and unmade by humans for themselves: 'Technology reveals the active relation of man to nature, the direct process of the production of his life, and thereby it also lays bare the process of the production of his life, and of the mental conceptions that flow from those relations' (C: 493n4). Marx extends this argument to account for how even the fantastic forms of religion emerge from 'the actual, given relations of life' and are not more mystifications that contain a kernel of human truth or earthly reality. Marx and Vico therefore complement Darwin and Simmel in grounding the social and natural sciences in a humanist method for understanding the ecology of physical and cultural worlds (O'Neill 2020: 73–4).

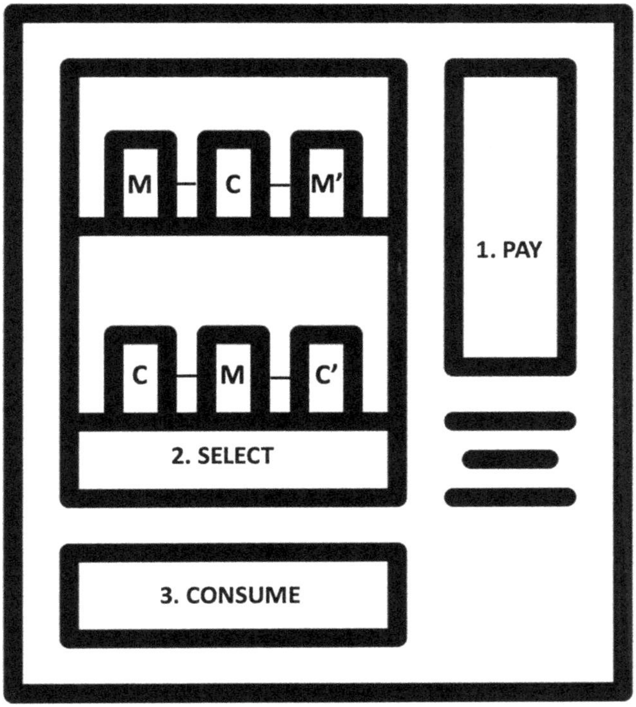

Fig. 4.1 The capitalist's vending machine. (Marx and Simmel on money economy and commodity culture)

now mechanically exchanged against the commodity' (PM: 460–1). As displayed in Fig. 4.1, his point complements and completes Marx's insight into the mechanization of work and the production process by accounting for the mechanical mediation of commerce and consumption as well. That is, money is a 'claim on society' in prescribing a set of orders, instructions, or commands (*Anweisungen*) which are programmed into everyday social interactions and mediated by commodity exchanges: (1) insert coin; (2) select from an assortment of goods; (3) consume right away or set aside for later use. Marx's general formulas for capital and consumption—buying in order to sell for a profit (M—C—M') and selling one thing in order to buy something else (C—M—C')—are accomplished here without face-to-face negotiations between persons but rather at the sheer interface of the individual and the machine. Simmel therefore anticipates the rise of a *self-service culture* where the consumer works on behalf of the producer, as we now experience in supermarket check-out lines, internet retailers, and automated tellers. He also envisions the *mechanization of social life*, where use-values may be elided or cancelled out by exchange-values and human relationships themselves are eliminated or switched off (*ausgeschaltet*) as bodies are replaced by machines and technologies are incorporated into social life.

Marx calls this process of mechanization through incorporation the 'general law of capitalist accumulation', which accounts for the influence of the growth of capital on the fate (*Geschick*) of the working class (C: 762). In more technical terms, the organic composition (*organische Zusammensetzung*) of capital consists of the proportion of the value of labour-power ('variable capital') relative to the value of the means and materials of production ('constant capital'). When more hands, hearts, and heads are employed (thereby increasing the rate of absolute surplus-value) or more efficient technology is introduced (increasing the rate of relative surplus-value), the movement of capital accumulation drives the movement of exploitable labour-power. As Marx expresses this relationship mathematically, 'the rate of accumulation is the independent [...] variable, the rate of wages the dependent [...] variable' (C: 771). He is careful in this context to refute the adherents of the 'currency principle' who conclude that price fluctuations are an effect of whether too much or too little money is in circulation rather than a reflection of more profound changes in the ratio of human labour and economic capital. He also describes at some length the contradictory tendencies of centralization and concentration, which would hypothetically reach their absolute limit 'only when the entire social capital was in the hands of either a single capitalist or a single capitalist company' (C: 779). Finally, he turns to the underside of this dynamic in the production of a relative surplus population of workers. Here Marx introduces a third figure of capitalist monstrosity, after the blood-sucking vampire and the mechanical Cyclops of earlier chapters, namely the unstoppable juggernaut that mercilessly mangles everything and relentlessly crushes anyone in its path:

> [A]ll means for the development of production undergo a dialectical inversion so that they become means of domination and exploitation of the producers; they distort the worker into a fragment of a man, they degrade him

> to the level of an appendage of a machine, they destroy the actual content of his labour by turning it into a torment; they alienate from him the intellectual potentialities of the labour-process in the same proportion as science is incorporated in it as an independent power; [...] they transform his life-time into working-time, and drag his wife and child beneath the juggernaut of capital. (C: 799)

Despotic capital appears here in an unyielding chariot bearing the icon of money and trampling down the worker's family under its wheels. In Marx's dramatic vision, the fetish-cult of capital exerts an almost supernatural force by devouring all living beings in its path in order to keep its dead objectivity operating.[5]

[5] Marx's metaphor of the 'juggernaut of capital' (C: 799) obviously draws upon an orientalist fantasy in projecting a coded image of Asiatic despotism onto the inner logic of capital accumulation personified as 'lord of the world' (the literal meaning of juggernaut in ancient Sanskrit). In the first of two articles on the British rule in India for the *New York Daily Tribune* (1853), Marx indulges in this mid-nineteenth-century trope by characterizing 'the religion of Hindoostan' in terms of the generic tension between sensual exuberance and self-torturing asceticism, and more precisely as the contradiction between egalitarian communalism symbolized by the Lingam and self-annihilating fanaticism symbolized by the juggernaut (CW 12: 125–6). In the second article, this exoticizing imagery is redeployed in an explicitly critical way to denounce the cruelties of British imperialism rather than to criticize the stagnant backwardness of Indian traditionalism. He alludes to how the colonial agents of the East India Company protected the priests of the juggernaut temple in Orissa and Bengal who staged sumptuous festivals leading to the death and self-torture of believers, and then confiscated vast sums of money from pilgrims and prostitutes. Marx sums up these grim events in a passage that has often been quoted out of the cultural context he provides for them: 'The profound hypocrisy and inherent barbarism of bourgeois civilization lies unveiled before our eyes, turning from its home, where it assumes respectable forms, to the colonies, where it goes naked' (CW 12: 221–2, 662n179). The historical and cultural specificity of Marx's allusion along with its political charge are lost in Anthony Giddens's use of this figure to describe the unintended and uncontrollable effects of globalization more broadly: 'The high consequence global risks which we all now run are key elements of the runaway, juggernaut character of modernity, [...] a runaway engine of enormous power which, collectively as human beings, we can drive to some extent but which also threatens to rush out of our control and which could render itself asunder' (Giddens 1990: 137, 139). While retaining a trace of its humanist inspiration, this use of the metaphor to describe modernity-at-large loses the reference to capitalist imperialism.

From Simmel's perspective a generation later, the juggernaut of capital loses none of its mobility and monstrosity even as it shrinks in scale to the more congenial proportions of a simple cash transaction between a consumer and a stationary vending machine. 'Money is the purest example of the tool', he argues, in its capacity to mediate the transformation material means into ideal functionality and cultural values into material goods (PM 210). As money becomes more pervasive and circulates more quickly, exchange-value predominates over use-values and the functional-value (*Funktionswert*) of money prevails over a thing's intrinsic worth or substance-value (*Substanzwert*): 'The value-as-function of money exceeds its value-as-substance the more extensive and diversified are the services it performs and the more rapidly it circulates' (PM: 142). Simmel emphasizes the widespread monetization and instrumentalization of social relationships even beyond commodity exchanges: 'money is the embodied function of being exchanged; [...] the materialization of the pure relationship between things as expressed in their economic motion' (PM: 175). In an argument that made a profound impression on later critical theorists like Georg Lukács, Simmel redescribes what Marx calls the 'fetishism' of commodities as the 'becoming substance' (*zur Substanz gewordene*) of social relationships and highlights the alienating character of this 'reification' on both collective and personal experience: 'These counter-tendencies, once started, may press forward to an ideal of completely pure separation in which all the material contents of life become increasingly objective and impersonal, so that the remainder that cannot be reified becomes all the more personal, all the more the indisputable property of the self' (PM: 474; quoted in Lukács 1971: 156–7). The virtual erasure of personal qualities as they become ever more objectified (*immer sachlicher*), he suggests, is all the more remarkable when even an individual's most intimate, private, or unique properties—as expressed though sexuality, vocal mannerisms, or writing style, for instance—retreat into the residual part of oneself that are not standardized or reified (*der nicht zu verdinglichende Rest*). In Simmel's view, the organic composition of capital does not just grow as an inexorable technological force of accumulation imposed from the outside; it also shrinks insofar as it is internalized as a dimension of one's own innermost self.

Foundational to Simmel's conception of modern experience is the tendency towards a completely pure separation (*absolut reinliche Scheidung*) between the subjective, personal and the objective, material sides of culture. As he notes in the opening sentence of 'The Concept and the Tragedy of Culture', the human being is not integrated unthinkingly into the world of nature, but rather 'confronts it' as a subject in opposition to an object, 'demanding, struggling, violating and being violated by it' (Simmel 1997: 55). In the world of culture this violent struggle may be pacified through the constant measuring and weighing that takes place in commercial transactions and also though 'the democratic levelling where everyone counts as one and no one counts as more than one' (PM: 444). As people from far away are brought into closer proximity through rapid transportation networks and communication systems, they become paradoxically more estranged from one another and more remote from themselves: 'Man has thereby become distanced from himself; an insuperable barrier of media, technical inventions, abilities and enjoyments has been erected between him and his most distinctive and essential being' (PM: 489). Marx traces this cultural dynamic of separation (*Scheidung*) to the historical process of original or primitive accumulation with reference to land enclosures and colonial dispossessions that cut people off from the material and ecological resources that had sustained their communal livelihood and cultural vitality for centuries: 'A separation between the product of labour and labour itself, between the objective conditions of labour and subjective labour-power, was therefore the real foundation and starting points of the process of capitalist production' (C: 716). This separation becomes the alienation (*Enfremdung*) of human beings from the natural world and from one another as the process and products of labour are appropriated by the owners of the means of production and incorporated into capital.[6] For Marx, the tragedy of culture is not just an historical fate that may be

[6] Throughout his career Marx developed a conception of nature that includes land (air, water, earth) and labour (mental, manual, emotional), what in *Capital* he calls 'the original sources of all wealth' embodied in 'the soil and the worker [*die Erde und den Arbeiter;* in French: *la terre et le travailleur*]' (C: 638; Marx 1989: 439). All natural things can be commodified and capitalized in principle if not in practice; or as Simmel would add, even life itself (animal, vegetable, mineral) is potentially monetizable. Marx's *Economic and Philosophical Manuscripts* elaborates on the overlap, interchange, and folding together of organic, inorganic, and human processes in almost poetic terms:

> The human being *lives* from nature—means that nature is his *body*, with which he must remain in a continuous interchange [*in beständigen Prozeß*] if he is not to die. That the human being's physical and spiritual life is linked to nature means simply that nature is linked to itself, for the human being is a part of nature. (CW 3: 276; O'Neill 2020: 74–5)

After studying more deeply the soil science of the day, especially the work of Justus von Liebig (1803–1873), Marx later refines this broad philosophical view of human-natural processes to adopt an explicitly ecological perspective on the metabolism (*Stoffwechsel*) among all things, including the exchange of material properties between humans and other living beings (Foster 2000: 147–54; Saito 141–75). In the third volume of *Capital* drafted in the early 1860s, he examines the breakdown and break up of this ecological balance with the emergence of large landed property which drove the agricultural population from the countryside into industrial urban centres. This shift 'creates conditions which induce an irreparable break [*einen unheilbaren Riß*] in the continuity and balance of the social metabolism prescribed by the natural laws of life [*des gesellschaftlichen und durch die Naturgesetze des Lebens vorgeschriebene Stoffwechsels*]' (CW 37: 799). In the final pages of the chapter on 'Machinery and Large-Scale Industry' in volume 1 of *Capital*, he attributes the separation of agriculture and manufacture and the push towards urban concentration to capitalist production as a whole, which 'disturbs the metabolic interaction [*stört den Stoffwechsel;* in French: *trouble encore la circulation matérielle*] between humans and the earth' (C: 637; Marx 1989: 438). Marx's wording in German to describe this 'process of destruction' (*Zerstörungsprozeß*) and in French (*procès de destruction*) does not amount to a complete account of ecological disturbances and environmental imbalances emerging from the intervention of capitalist processes into natural cycles. Nevertheless, as John Bellamy Foster has argued, 'contrary to those who believe that he wore an ecological blinder that prevented him from perceiving natural limits to production, Marx employed the concept of *metabolic rift* to capture the material estrangement of human beings in capitalist society from the natural conditions of their existence' (Foster 1999: 383; my emphasis). Writing in the middle and late nineteenth century, Marx struggled to keep up with the latest discoveries of the soil and climate sciences that contributed to the second agricultural revolution (1815–1880). He was aware that technological 'improvements', such as the replacement of pasturing cattle with oil-fuelled tractors, require advanced scientific knowledge of the dynamic interactions between complex sociological, cultural, meteorological, and biochemical processes (Foster 1999: 390).

regrettable or even redemptive but also a historically contingent process of estrangement that humans might eventually learn from and potentially transform.

Simmel is neither ignorant of nor insensitive to the miseries wrought by the capitalist money economy, especially in industrialized urban centres like London, Paris, and Berlin. In a chapter of *Sociology*, 'The Poor Person', he considers the problem of pauperism not in terms class struggle or social domination but rather as an issue concerning the liberty of individuals who are members of unequal social groups and who share bonds of solidarity with one another. He contrasts the provision of welfare, where the state intervenes to alleviate poverty in the name of humanity in general, and private charity or philanthropy, which forges a moral connection between persons from different social worlds (Simmel 2009: 431). In either case, 'the right to support belongs to the same category as the right to work and the right to one's existence', and such support may be provided by state and municipal officials, by community and parish members, or within familial and friendship circles (Simmel 2009: 411). Care for the poor person is in the interests of the propertied and prosperous classes, whose humanity is reflected in the social whole to which everyone belongs and mirrored in the public good where each person is included (Simmel 2009: 417). *Capital* likewise treats the problems of poverty with considerable moral compassion and personal empathy, but also in excruciating empirical detail and with a clear political commitment to poor relief and proletarian revolution. 'Pauperism is the hospital of the active labour-army and the dead weight of the industrial reserve army', Marx writes, and 'along with the surplus population, pauperism forms a condition of capitalist production, and of the capitalist production of wealth' (C: 797). His notorious 'general law of accumulation' outlined at length in Chapter 25 is not a thesis about the inevitable immiseration of the working classes or a theory of the absolute impoverishment of the unemployed, as is sometimes assumed. Marx offers instead an account of the socio-economic conditions in which 'accumulation at one pole is [...] at the same time accumulation of misery, the torment of labour, slavery, ignorance, brutalization, and moral degradation at the opposite pole' (C: 799). In the long final section of the chapter, Marx again draws on the factory inspection reports and Engels's research to provide details on the working and living conditions of the 'worst paid part of the industrial proletariat and the agricultural labourers, who together form the majority of the working class' (C: 802–70). This series of 'illustrations' depict the most brutal experiences of poverty—from the slavery of the workhouse to the nomadic population in England and Ireland, and from the best-paid workers to the most oppressed, malnourished, disease-prone, and brutally treated—while making a moral and political case for change.

* * *

Simmel insists that neither private philanthropy nor public welfare can advance a socialist policy of social equality. While charity and social support take from the prosperous and give to the poor, they cannot result in 'an equalization of these individual positions and [...] will not at all overcome the tendency for the differentiation of society into rich and poor' (Simmel 2009: 413). In a reference to the third volume of *Capital* in the *Philosophy of Money*, he argues further that the measure of value in a socialist state cannot be grounded in use-value, social need, or labour-time as a universal standard apart from the circulation and exchange of money (PM: 430). He thereby assumes that Marx's 'labour theory of value' treats all kinds of labour and various needs analytically as 'of equal value' and ignores Marx's surplus-value theory of labour-power, which explains how some classes are structurally positioned to exploit and profit from the working capacity of others. Conflating Marx's ideas with 'historical materialism' understood as both a social theory and a political project, Simmel arrives at what he calls the 'diametrically opposed psychic roots' of socialism in the isolation of the individual, at one extreme, and in the collectivization of group enthusiasms and sympathies, at the other extreme:

> Undoubtedly, socialism is directed towards a rationalization of life, towards control of life's chance and unique elements by the law-like regularities and calculations of reason. [...]. On the one hand, socialism is the final developmental product of the rationalistic money economy, and on the other, it is the embodiment of the most basic instincts and emotions. (PM: 347–8)

In Simmel's view, socialism is not just the rational supersession of capitalist standards of value along with the modern forms of individuation and association they give rise to; socialism is above all the supreme expression of the duelling tendencies within the modern soul itself.

These critical remarks articulate Simmel's scepticism regarding Marx's theoretical innovations and his pessimism over whether the contradictions of the capitalist money economy can ever be practically overcome. Money serves as a kind of absolute value or god-term of contemporary life, a metaphysical principle that accounts for the relativistic character of the modern worldview. The tendency of the money economy is to eliminate use-value in the pursuit of 'the ultimate means' and in an effort 'to realize the possibility of all values as the value of all possibilities' (PM: 221). As Simmel writes in the notebook of aphorisms he kept in his later years,

> Money is the only cultural formation that is pure power, that has fully eliminated material supports from itself, in that it is absolutely pure symbol. To this degree, it is the most characteristic among all the phenomena of our time, when dynamism has gained command of all theory and practice. The fact that it is *pure relationship* (and thus likewise characteristic of our time) without including any of the content of the relationship does not contradict this. For in reality, power is nothing but relationship. (Simmel 2010: 186)

The myriad techniques of soft surveillance and social control that characterize our world today can be traced to the subtle forms of commodification and financialization implied in Simmel's account of money as 'pure power', 'absolutely pure symbol', and 'pure relationship', where anything is potentially exchangeable and everything may be treated as fungible. With considerable irony, in the *Philosophy of Money* he alludes to Marx's concluding call to revolution in *Capital* as the epitome of the perpetual changes that would dominate a world beyond the money economy: 'The all-embracing substance, the only absolute that remains, can now be disregarded without thereby affecting the content of reality—the expropriator will be expropriated, as Marx says of a process that is similar in form—and nothing remains but the relativistic dissolution of things into relations and processes' (PM: 116–7, paraphrasing C: 929). As a modernist intellectual who is nevertheless committed to exploring the eternal verities of antiquity and the enduring ideals of tradition, Simmel resists this descent into a world where everything established and stable evaporates, and in the words of the *Manifesto*, in which 'all that is solid melts into air' (CM: 65).

Reflecting on the philosophical and historical 'turn toward ideas' in his last book, *View of Life*, Simmel describes the shift of human culture away from immediate empirical reality towards a metaphysics of transcendent values. In our experiences of longing and of resignation, he muses, time seems to stand still and the mind or spirit (*Geist*) appears to look at the flux and flow of life from the aspect of eternity (*sub specie aeternitatis*, as he occasionally writes with reference to Spinoza's *Ethics*). Leaving aside his own philosophical prose at this point, he cites the lyrical lines of Goethe's 'Dedication' to *Faust* to express the contradictory sentiments of his own personal view of life:

Was ich besitze, seh ich wie im Weiten,	What I possess I see as though from a distance,
Und was verschwand, wird mir zu Wirklichkeiten.	And what has passed, to me becomes existence.
	(Simmel 2010: 51, quoting F: 31–2)

Hope and loss finally become expressible when we assume the standpoint of artistic detachment and intellectual distantiation, impassivity, and objectification with respect to the intense immediacy of life. Yearning and forbearance for the creative writer as for the intellectual thereby anticipate a 'relation to time as displacement from the genuinely full life', as these unique affects and individual desires are shaped into the sociable cultural forms of art and science.

In contrast to Simmel's concern with 'the law of the individual' in the last chapter of *View of Life* and his search for the principle of the uniqueness of 'life', Marx never wavers in his concern to address the problem of collective agency as the lever of social reproduction and historical transformation. At the same time, he is attentive to how flexible, short-term, interventions at the level of everyday practices may have long-term effects on maintaining or changing large-scale cultural patterns and institutional orders (Giddens 1984: 186–9; Jungmann 2020: 52). Writing in the wake of developments in post-war American sociology and European critical theory, Anthony Giddens has attempted to replace the philosophical dualism of objectivism and subjectivism, already a prominent organizing principle in Simmel's philosophical sociology, with the duality of agency and the 'structuration' of institutions (Giddens 1984: xx–xxi). In part, his aim is to locate Marx's method of treating 'individuals as bearers of economic categories' within time-space relationships of situated actors on multiple scales, from local workplaces and urban centres to global markets and long-range historical epochs. Capitalist accumulation can therefore be treated as an instance of this larger process of structuration, where relations of private property and general commodification are understood to contribute to the reproduction and transformation of rules and resources, including those that constitute class exploitation and surplus-value extraction (Giddens 1984: 185–93). Giddens's deconstruction of the progressivist timeline of 'historical materialism' and the structuring principles of 'Marxism' is in some ways an elaboration on Marx's polemical comment in *The 18th Brumaire of Louis Bonaparte* (1851–1852): 'human beings make their own history [...], but not of their own free will' (CW 11: 103, in Giddens 1984: xxi). Following Marx's sarcastic remark in *Capital*, Giddens might have added that human beings do not enjoy unlimited agency any more than a commodity can 'begin to dance of its own free will' (C: 164). The German idiom Marx uses on each occasion—*aus freien Stücken*; literally, 'out of free pieces'—suggests people are not at liberty to assemble things in any way they wish just as an artisan cannot craft something without taking into account the properties of the materials available, the parts they are made up of, the instruments at hand, and the demands and desires of others. Just as we cannot create a world from nothing or construct an artefact out of free-floating pieces from nowhere, so history is made from circumstances inherited from past and materials which are themselves made and remade through the innumerable interactions among human and more-than-human beings.

N.B.: I often modify existing English translations, drawing on German or French editions readily available online or from print sources. References to *Faust* are by line number as indicated in both English and German editions.

Works Cited and Consulted

Abbreviations Used

C—Marx, Karl (1976). *Capital: A Critique of Political Economy, Volume 1*. Ben Fowkes trans. Ernest Mandel intro. London: Penguin Books.

CW—*The Collected Works of Karl Marx and Friedrich Engels 1844–1895*. 47 Volumes. New York: International Publishers. (Electronic Edition, Charlottesville, Virginia).

DL—Durkheim, Emile (2004). *The Division of Labor in Society*. W. D. Wells trans. Lewis Coser intro. New York: The Free Press.

F—Goethe, Johann Wolfgang von (1986). *Faust: Eine Tragödie*. Erster und Zweiter Teile. Stuttgart: Philipp Reclam Jun.

Goethe, Johann Wolfgang von (1976). *Faust: A Tragedy*. Walter Arndt trans., Cyrus Hamlin ed. New York: W. W. Norton & Company.

PE—Weber, Max (2009). *The Protestant Ethic and the Spirit of Capitalism, with Other Writings on the Rise of the West.* Fourth edition. Stephen Kalberg trans., intro. Oxford: Oxford University Press.

PM—Simmel, Georg (2004). *The Philosophy of Money.* Thomas Bottomore, David Frisby trans. London: Routledge.

Binswanger, Hans Christoph (2017). 'Nutzen und Nachteil der Alchemie für die Wirtschaft: Eine geldtheoretische Faust-Deutung'. In *Wie man ein Arschloch wird: Kapitalismus und Kolonisierung.* Carl Hegemann ed. Berlin: Alexanderverlag, pp. 88–108.

Dodd, Nigel (2014). *The Social Life of Money.* Princeton, NJ: Princeton University Press.

Foster, John Bellamy (2000). *Marx's Ecology.* New York: Monthly Review Press.

Foster, John Bellamy (1999). 'Marx's Theory of Metabolic Rift: Classical Foundations for Environmental Sociology'. *American Journal of Sociology* 105(2): 366–405.

Giddens, Anthony (1990). *The Consequences of Modernity.* Stanford, CA: Stanford University Press.

Giddens, Anthony (1984). *The Constitution of Society: Outline of the Theory of Structuration.* Cambridge, UK: Polity Press.

Goethe, Johann Wolfgand von (1983). *Selected Poems.* Christopher Middleton ed. London: John Calder.

Jungmann, Robert (2020). 'Kollektives Handeln und die neue Kollektive: eine praxistheoretische Heuristik'. *Zeitschrift für Soziologie* 49(1): 49–65.

Kemple, Thomas (2018a). *Simmel.* Cambridge, UK: Polity Press.

Kemple, Thomas (2018b). 'Infinite Ends and the Tempo of Life: Notes on the Marx/Simmel Convergence/Divergence'. *Dissonância* (2)2: 137–66.

Kemple, Thomas (1995). *Reading Marx Writing: Melodrama, the Market, and the 'Grundrisse'.* Stanford: Stanford University Press.

Lukács, Georg (1971). *History and Class Consciousness.* R. Livingstone trans. London: Merlin Press.

Marx, Karl (1989). *Le Capital.* M. J. Roy trans., entièrement révisée par l'auteur. *Marx Engels Gesamtausgabe* II/7 and Apparat. Berlin: Dietz Verlag.

O'Neill, John (2020). *Writing the Body Politic: A John O'Neill Reader.* M. Featherstone, T. Kemple eds. London: Routledge.

Saito, Kohei (2017). *Karl Marx's Ecosocialism: Capital, Nature, and the Unfinished Critique of Political Economy.* New York: Monthly Review Press.

Simmel, Georg (2010). *The View of Life: Four Metaphysical Essays, with Journal Aphorisms.* J. A. Y. Andrews, D. Frisby trans. Chicago: Chicago University Press.

Simmel, Georg (1997). *Simmel on Culture.* D. Frisby, M. Featherstone eds. London: SAGE Publications.

Simmel, Georg (2009). *Sociology: Inquries into the Construction of Social Forms.* 2 vols. A. Blasi, A. K. Jacops, and M. Kanjirathinkal. Leiden: Brill.

Varoufakis, Yanis, and Evgeny Morozov (2022). 'Yanis Varoufakis on Crypto & the Left, and Technofeudalism'. *The crypto syllabus.* https://the-crypto-syllabus.com/yanis-varoufakis-on-techno-feudalism/

CHAPTER 5

Conclusion: Capital as Animated Monster: Sociology *Contra* Marxism?

Abstract The expansion of colonial capitalism and the vicissitudes of international socialism provoked a variety of responses from classical sociologists in Europe and North America. These concluding remarks take the final two chapters of *Capital* on 'the historical tendency of capitalist accumulation' and 'the modern theory of colonialism' as a frame for considering how classical sociologists in America engage with Marx's radical vision, including W. E. B. Du Bois on the racialization of capital-labour relations; Charlotte Perkins Gilman on the world-building force of 'mother-power'; and Thorstein Veblen on the value-creating work of leisure and business enterprise. Finally, Marx's comment on the 'dream-world' of settler colonialism is examined through Sigmund Freud's discussion of 'dream-work' in terms of an analogy with capitalist enterprise. Marx's sociology of revolution does not project a heavenly utopia, as in Goethe's vision of Faust's redemption, but focuses instead on the conditions of the past that produce present realities and project future possibilities.

Keywords Colonialism • Du Bois • Gilman • Veblen • Psychoanalysis

Can a volume that promises two sequels have an ending? And can a body of work that both interprets the world and insists on changing it be considered complete? *Capital, Volume 1* presents a conundrum for anyone trying to answer either question, since it is decidedly unfinished as a text and

T. Kemple, *Marx's Wager*, Marx, Engels, and Marxisms,
https://doi.org/10.1007/978-3-031-08065-4_5

lacking in a satisfactory plan for action. In fact, the final Part VIII offers no clear call for revolution or explicit ending, only an historical digression into the origins of the modern capitalist mode of production and a brief review of its global expansion. In the first edition, these remarks are appended to the long Chapter 6, 'Capitalist Accumulation', and take the form of a critical commentary on Adam Smith's notion of 'previous accumulation' by way of a history of the enclosure movement in England, and on E. G. Wakefield's 'theory of colonialism' as applied to the British Empire. Marx's uneasiness in closing the work this way is apparent in the second German edition, where he restructures the text so that these discussions become the final Chapters 24 and 25, respectively. In the French version—the last edition he brought to publication—and in later English translations they appear as a separate part divided up into eight short chapters (one of which—Chapter 30, 'The Genesis of the Capitalist Farmer'—is only three pages long). Marx's general argument in Part VIII is that the secret of 'so-called primitive accumulation [...] is nothing else than the historical process of separating [*Scheidungsprozeß*] the producer from the means of production'—specifically the peasants from the soil and more broadly the workers from the conditions of production—and that this history 'is written in the annals a humankind in letters of blood and fire' (C: 874–5).

The penultimate Chapter 32 dramatically describes this historical tendency of capitalist accumulation as ultimately bursting asunder the capitalist shell (*Hülle*) of socialized production as if through an abrupt explosion: 'the expropriators are expropriated' (C: 929). On the one hand, Marx's classic account of original accumulation thus seems to end with the tragedy of the closure of the commons where producers are stripped of their means of subsistence and compelled to submit to the command of capitalist industry before rising up and seizing the means of production. On the other hand, however, the final Chapter 33 argues that while all countries of Western Europe are going through this same development, 'the secret both of the prosperity of the colonies and of their cancerous affliction [is] their resistance to capitalist settlement [*ihres Widerstands wider die Ansiedlung des Kapitals*]' (C: 934). His critique of the modern theory of colonization then appears to conclude as a farce rather than with a bang (perhaps as a way of eluding the censors), where settlers casually shake off the shackles of capital and venture into the new world on their own: 'Horror of horrors! [...] The end of the world has come!' (C: 936).

As I have tried to show, the whole of *Capital, Volume 1* is designed as a kind of horror story in which the opening image of an immense collection of commodities (in Chapter 1) metamorphosizes into the terrifying figures of capital as blood-sucking vampire (Chapter 10), mechanical Cyclops

(Chapter 15), and life-destroying juggernaut (Chapter 25). Echoing the notorious invocation of 'the spectre of communism' in the opening line of *The Communist Manifesto*, Marx jokingly alludes to his critical aim in deploying these metaphors of monstrosity in the Preface to the first edition of *Capital*: 'Perseus wore a magic cap so that the monsters he hunted down might not see him. We draw the magic cap down over our own eyes and ears so as to deny that there are monsters' (C: 91). Marx rejects disguises and disappearing acts in taking on his role as a courageous mortal facing off against the colossus of capital, and he asks his readers to follow his lead in witnessing and listening compassionately to the cries of its victims. In the pivotal Chapter 7 on the production of use-value and surplus-value, he presents his most extreme depiction of capital as an animated monster (*beseeltes Ungeheuer*) absorbing all life into itself and setting to work on its own:

> By turning his money into commodities which serve as the building materials for a new product, and as factors in the labour process, by incorporating living labour-power into their dead objectivity, the capitalist simultaneously transforms value, i.e. past labour in its objectified and lifeless form, into capital, value self-valorizing on its own, an animated monster which begins to 'work', as if its body were by love possessed. (C:302; Marx 1989: 160)

As with so many crucial turning points in *Capital*, at the climactic moment of this passage Marx casually adapts a line from Goethe's *Faust*. In this instance, he invokes the scene of 'Auerbach's Wine-Cellar in Leipzig' which immediately follows Faust's pact with Mephistopheles. Here a group of 'jolly follows' are invited to join in the chorus of a drinking song:

Geb acht! Ein Lied zum neusten Schnitt!	Attend! A song in latest vein!
Und singt den Rundreim kräfitg mit!	Chime in with vigorous refrain!
	(F: 2214–5)

In an almost unconscious and automatic way, Marx himself chimes in on the refrain—'as if it had love in its body [*als hätt' es Lieb' im Leibe*]'—at the very moment he is describing the subsumption of living labour into the dead body of capital. The crudeness of this raunchy chorus-line ironically reverses the scenario described at the beginning of the passage, suggesting that capital does not just possess labour but is itself possessed by the soul of living labour-power, like a devil in the flesh (*comme s'il avait le diable au corps* in the French version) which somehow controls the lifeless objectivity of capital from within (Marx 1989: 160). This *total subsumption of labour by capital* is thus at the same time the tragic end and the comic undoing of protagonist in the story Marx is telling about the historical tendency of capitalist accumulation to absorb the whole of life under its command and control.[1]

[1]The refrain from the drinking song in the scene of 'Auerbach's Wine-Cellar in Leipzig' is evidently among Marx's favourite lines from Goethe's *Faust* as he quotes or paraphrases it on a number of occasions. The first is at the climax of what has come to be known as 'The Fragment on Machines' in the *Grundrisse*, where Marx is describing how the activities of workers are transformed into mechanical operations: 'Thus the appropriation [*Aneignung*] of labour by capital confronts the worker in a gross-sensuous way; capital as absorbing living labour into itself as though it had love in its bosom [*als hätt' es Lieb' im Leibe*]' (CW 29: 90; I discuss this passage in detail in Kemple 1995: 30–43). In a second instance, Marx discusses the formal and real subsumption of labour under capital in a draft chapter of *Capital* that examines how the instrument of labour itself becomes 'a conductor, an agency, for this *process of absorption*': 'By incorporating living labour-power into the material constituents of capital, the latter becomes an animated monster and starts to act as if consumed by love [*als hätt' es Lieb' im Leibe*]' (C: 1007). The refrain appears yet again in volume 3 of *Capital* in the discussion of how interest-bearing capital continues to increase whether 'asleep or awake, at home or abroad, by day or by night':

> In this way, a capital = 1000 is fixed as a thing [...] which is transformed after a certain period into 1100 just as wine stored in a cellar improves its use-value after a certain period. Capital is now a thing, but as a thing it is capital. Money now has love in its body [*hat jetzt Lieb' im Leibe*]. (CW 37: 391; also CW 32: 526)

This last allusion indirectly conjures up the scene in Goethe's *Faust* where drunken revellers in a wine-cellar sing a song about a cellar-rat writhing in agony after being poisoned by the cook upstairs:

Sie tät gar manchen Ängstesprung,	Tried many a leap in fear and pain,
Bald hatte das arme Tier genung,	But all it tried was tried in vain,
Als hätt' es Lieb' im Leibe!	As if the love bug bit it!
	(F: 2138–40)

In its incarnation as machinery or as money, capital is represented in these references as a monster living off the love-energy of labour-power, the body of the worker in turn living off it as a kind of parasite, like the jolly reveller who sees in the dying rat an image of his own 'natural kin and counterpart [*sein ganz natürlich Ebenbild*]' (F: 2157; Pyyhtinen 2014: 67–94). Elsewhere in *Capital, Volume 1* Marx ironically suggests that the remedy for the rapacious pestilence of worker demands—for food, health, hygiene, rest, and so on—lies in the passage of new laws that facilitate capitalist expansion rather than eliminate the problems such expansion creates: 'No poison kills vermin with more certainty than the Factory Act removes such "natural barriers"' (C: 605). These moments in Marx's writings are not simply interruptions, digressions, or pauses in the dialectical movement of his argument; they are the mark of its inner incommensurability and a symptom of its outer limits (Lukàcs 1968: 237).

The following concluding remarks take up this apocalyptic limit-case of Marx's argument in *Capital* with a focus on the book's final two chapters. First, I consider how a generation of American classical sociologists engage with and then deepen Marx's radical vision of the end of capitalism, but also side-step or gloss over some of the critical insights of 'Marxism' and 'socialism' in the process. W. E. B. Du Bois (1868–1963) moves beyond Marx's comments on commodified chattel slavery to consider the racialization of capital-labour relations in post-Civil War America, while Charlotte Perkins Gilman (1860–1835) provides a crucial supplement to Marx's ideas about social reproduction (drawing on Engels's thesis concerning women's subordination) by examining the world-building force of 'mother-power'. Thorstein Veblen (1957–1929) likewise extends Marx's emphasis on production and labour by considering the value-creating work of consumption and leisure, on the one hand, and of business and enterprise, on the other, while George Herbert Mead (1863–1931) investigates the body-mind relationship as foundational to all social life, including the free association of individuals in any socialist alternative to capitalism. Following the First International (1865–1875) in which Marx and Engels were active participants, these classical sociologists share the sceptical views of their European counterparts—including Emile Durkheim, Max Weber, and Georg Simmel—concerning the theoretical narrowness of the Second International (1889–1916) and the political inflexibility of the Third International (1919–1943). Finally, I consider one of the most formidable challenges to Marxist theory and socialist practice in the twentieth century, namely the psychoanalytic insights of Sigmund Freud (1956–1939). In the last chapter of *Capital*, Marx rejects the dream-world (*Traumreich*) of colonial expansion in a way that anticipates Freud's curious elaboration of the dream-work (*Traumarbeit*) through an analogy with capitalist enterprise. Marx's vision of revolution does not project a utopia of heavenly salvation, as in Goethe's depiction of Faust's redemption, but instead focuses as Freud does on conditions of the past that produce present realities and project future possibilities. With these arguments in mind, I suggest that the question 'sociology *contra* Marxism?', which still remains unanswered today, implies the question 'Marxism *cum* psychoanalysis?' and may therefore entail a detour into the workings of the modern mind.

I

The penultimate Chapter 32 of *Capital*, 'The Historical Tendency of Capitalist Accumulation', imagines the inversion of the law of capitalist appropriation in decisive and dramatic terms. The capitalist mode of production elicits new forces and new passions, Marx declares, which are struggling to break free from the fetters imposed on them by limitations of private property. Capital thereby creates the material means for its own destruction: 'It has to be annihilated; it is annihilated' (C: 928). Toying with Hegelian terminology, he suggests that capitalist private property constitutes 'the first negation' of traditional regimes of property founded on the cooperative and individual labour of the owners of wealth. This movement of expropriation potentially brings about 'the negation of the negation' through the dynamic realization of autonomous labour-creating value (Roberts 2017: 240). Marx's revolutionary rhetoric reaches a high pitch with this striking proclamation of the hour of death of this mode of production as 'the knell of capitalist property sounds [*die Stunde des kapitalisten Privateigentum schlägt*]' (C: 929). The chapter ends not with a loud explosion but with the quiet scene of proletarian workers digging the graves of their bourgeois rulers, as depicted in a memorable passage of *The Communist Manifesto* that Marx quotes here in a footnote:

> The advance of industry, whose unwilling and unstoppable instrument is the bourgeoisie, replaces the isolation of the workers due to competition by their revolutionary combination due to association. The development of big industry, therefore, cuts from under its feet the very foundation on which the bourgeoisie produces and appropriates products. It produces, above all, its own grave-diggers. Its fall and the victory of the proletariat are alike inevitable. [...] Of all the classes that stand face to face with the bourgeoisie today, the proletariat alone is a really revolutionary class. The other classes decay and go under in the presence of big industry, the proletariat is its very own product. (C: 930n2, quoting CM: 72, 73–4)

Just as the *Manifesto* does not paint a precise picture of a future socialist or communist society, apart from a vague reference to 'a free association in which the free development of each is the condition for the free development of all', so *Capital* projects only the faintest outlines of a world based on 'co-operation and the possession in common of the land and the means of production produced by labour itself' (CM: 82; C: 929). Far from predicting the demise of the 'bourgeois sorcerer' and the triumph of his proletarian gravediggers, Marx can only proclaim the apocalyptic end of capitalist society and hint in general terms at how its overthrow may regenerate some new mode of production.[2]

This broad sketch of the revolutionary energy building up within capitalist society is only specified in a smattering of places in *Capital.* Among them is the reference in the Preface of the first edition to the explosive potential of the American Civil War to signal transoceanic change: 'Just as the in the eighteenth century the American War of Independence sounded the tocsin for the American middle class, so in the nineteenth century the American Civil War did the same for the European working classes' (C: 91). Building on editorials he wrote for the *New York Daily Tribune* from 1852 to 1862, he treats the defeat of this 'pro-slavery rebellion' as the alarm bell announcing the emergence of an international movement of

[2] The irony of Marx's historical narrative, in which the bourgeoisie creates the conditions for its own destruction, evokes the tragic scene of Faust's downfall. In the final act of the play, Faust in his final incarnation as colonizer ruthlessly clears the land that he claims for his own domain. His ambition costs the lives of the generous Philomon and Baucis, since their modest home impedes his plan to build canals and dikes and obstructs his view of the empire:

Die Alten, droben sollten weichen,	That aged couple must surrender,
Die Linden wünscht ich mir zum Sitz,	I want their linden for my throne,
Die wenig Bäume, nicht mein eigen,	The unowned timber-margin slender
Verderben mir den Weltbesitz	Despoils for me the world I own.
	(F:11239–43)

The bells that remind Faust of his guilt over the death of the kindly old couple only propel him even more relentlessly to pursue his plans to develop his domain at the same time as they sound his own death-knell. Faust's victory is followed by his defeat at the hands of the workers he has exploited to build his kingdom—figured as ghostly spirits (*lemures*) of the restless dead from Greek mythology—who are already digging his grave and stand ready to lower him down as he utters his final words:

Im Vorgefühl von solchem hohen Glück	Foretasting such high happiness to come,
Genieß ich jetzt den höchsten Augenblick.	I savor now my striving's crown and sum.
	(F: 11585–6)

As Marshall Berman notes, these passages anticipate the climactic scene of *The Manifesto* where the bourgeoisie ruthlessly destroys the achievements of the past while creating the conditions for its own downfall at the hands of the proletariat (Berman 1988: 60–71).

workers beyond the borders of race and ethnicity (Anderson 2019: 201–2, 2010: 79–114). As he writes in the chapter on the working day, 'labour in a white skin cannot emancipate itself where it is branded in a black skin' (C: 414).

W. E. B. Du Bois develops this argument further in the second chapter of *The Souls of Black Folk* (1903), where 'the problem of the color-line' is framed in terms of the inequalities of wealth, education, and political power that the Freedman's Bureau had tried to address on behalf of the newly emancipated slaves. The influence of Marx on Du Bois's reading of post-Civil War class and race relations is especially palpable in *Black Reconstruction in America* (1935) which considers the rise in tensions between Black and White workers. Du Bois expresses his disappointment that Marx's friends and allies who had migrated to the United States supported abolition while tacitly condoning the exclusion of Blacks from the labour movement. He then examines the threat to worker solidarity in the debilitating competition between White and Black labourers, each exploited by an alliance between plantation owners in the South and entrepreneurs in the North. With the transformation of commodified chattel slavery into capitalist wage-labour, the Black worker has been left abandoned and 'bent at the bottom of a growing pyramid of commerce and industry':

> Out of the exploitation of the dark proletariat comes the Surplus Value filched from human beasts which, in cultured lands, the Machine and harnessed Power veil and conceal. The emancipation of man is the emancipation of labor and the emancipation of labor is the freeing of that basic majority of workers who are yellow, brown and black. (Du Bois 1995: 606)

Du Bois and Marx argue that racial classifications are both established and challenged through class struggles within capitalist social relations, and so the colour-line can only be erased by establishing bonds of solidarity among all exploited workers. What Du Bois refers to as his 'double-consciousness'—as both an African and an American—is expressed in these later writings as the duelling subjectivities of race and class (Kemple 2018a: 126–31).

Marx's empirical focus in *Capital* on broadly European and specifically English industrial conditions tends to restrict his view of the racial conflicts that prop up capitalist imperialism in both Britain and America. Likewise, his emphasis on the conditions of the poorest strata of the working classes tends to skew his perspective on the gendered and intergenerational dynamics of capitalist social relations. For instance, in Chapter 23 of Part V, 'Simple Reproduction', which follows Part VI, 'Wages', and anticipates Part VII, 'The Process of Accumulation of Capital', he only alludes in general terms to how workers consume both means of production and means of subsistence. Elsewhere he notes that the relationship between unpaid and paid labour is a 'popular expression' for the formula for the rate of surplus-value, that is, the ratio of surplus labour over necessary labour (C: 71). He therefore glosses over the many kinds of unpaid activities that reproduce wage-labour itself, including care-work, child-raising, and household labour (Fraser 2014: 61). As Silvia Federici has argued, not only were land and other natural resources expropriated as private property through the process of original accumulation in the early modern period of 'primitive accumulation', but so too were women's work and reproductive capacity (Federici 2004: 97).

Drawing on Marx's ethnological notebooks on non-capitalist social formations, Engels formulates this argument in *The Origin of the Family, Private Property, and the State* (1884) as the historical 'overthrow of mother-right' in which the man took command of the private sphere of the home, and concludes that 'the first precondition for the emancipation of woman is the introduction of the entire female sex into public industry' (CW 26: 165, 182; Anderson 2010: 196–236). Elaborating on Engels's influential study a decade later, feminist sociologist Charlotte Perkins Gilman refines this thesis in her classic *Women and Economics* (1898) which traces the evolutionary process by which work relations become sexualized and sexual relations commercialized (Gilman 1989: 165–6). In subsequent writings, especially her masterpiece, *The Man-Made World: Our Androcentric Culture* (1911), Gilman extends the Marxian theory of commodified surplus-labour to include what she calls 'mother-power':

> Industry, at its base, is a feminine function. The surplus energy of the mother does not manifest itself in noise, or combat, or display, but in productive industry. Because of her mother-power she became the first inventor and laborer, being in truth the mother of all industry as well as all people. (Gilman 1989: 212)

The expropriation of all activities as 'man's work' lays the foundation of 'androcentric culture', Gilman's term for the wide range of male-dominated domains that reach beyond the domesticated pillar of 'patriarchal society'. She argues that industry, politics, science, and art—indeed all the achievements of Western civilization—are born in the cradle of the home, but the 'proprietary family' becomes their tomb if they remain there. Outlining a reformist programme of evolutionary change rather than a revolutionary project of socialist overthrow, Gilman draws on her own divided experience as both an activist and an intellectual, and her dual subjectivity as both a public figure and a private citizen.[3]

Capital is consistently concerned with the problem of how work is valued and which activities are to be counted as 'non-work' or 'unproductive labour'. Marx's historical remarks on primitive accumulation trace the origins of these classifications to the period when the early industrial capitalists and their counterparts in the countryside, the capitalist farmers, replaced the guild masters in the towns and the feudal lords on the estates. This massive shift was carried out by others who literally cleared the ground and soil (*Grund und Boden*) for expropriation, especially bailiffs,

[3] Gilman's maternal-feminist critique of androcentric culture can be characterized as *gynocentric* in method and *humanist* in its objectives. That is, she writes from the standpoint of her own experience as a woman in an androcentric culture while appealing to the general human sensibilities of her readers. By contrast, Georg Simmel assumes the existence of a separate domain of 'female culture', made up of the independent energies, emotions, and sensibilities of women that cannot be fully incorporated into a public sphere traditionally claimed by men. In this regard, his sociology of gender and his metaphysics of sex extend Goethe's sublime trope of the 'eternal feminine' (Kemple 2018a: 91–5, 176–8). Faust's salvation as he is ushered into heaven by the spirit of Gretchen suggests for him a model of exodus from this world via an other-worldly miracle of redemption, transfiguration, and regeneration:

Das Unbeschreibliche,	Human discernment
Hier ist's getan;	Here is passed by;
Das Ewig-Weibliche	Woman-Eternal
Zieht uns hinan	Draw us on high.
	(F: 12110–1)

For Goethe as for Simmel, the inner tension that tears at the human soul can attain only a figural resolution in the other-worldly realm of the imagination and language rather than in any material realm through worldly struggles. In this regard, Gilman's effort to develop a gynocentric worldview within androcentric culture through an enlarged conception of human civility resonates with W. E. B. Du Bois's attempt to unify his 'double-consciousness' as 'an American, a Negro' by striving to become 'a co-worker in the kingdom of culture' (Du Bois 1995: 29). Despite the impasses and blindnesses that each encounters in the course of their careers—including Du Bois's sexism and Gilman's racism—they find common ground in striving to find a way beyond Faust's wrenching dilemma in having to live between mind and body, and his frustration in failing to combine thought and action—'two souls, alas! are dwelling in my breast [*Zwei Seelen, ach! in meiner Brust*]' (F: 1112).

sharecroppers, and yeomanry: 'The knights of industry [...] only succeeded in supplanting the knights of the sword by making use of events in which they had played no part whatsoever' (C: 875; Roberts 2017: 237). Classical sociologists writing a generation after Marx and Engels would focus on the remnants and survivals of these older systems with the rise of large-scale industry and global finance, especially in the United States.

In *The Theory of the Leisure Class* (1899) Thorstein Veblen famously examines how old-order status hierarchies place the norms of reputability, displayed through conspicuous consumption, over traditional codes of workmanship, associated with industrial production (Veblen 1948: 125). Despite his damning characterization of Marx's 'socialist economics' as a crude 'doctrine of increasing misery' and of Marx's account of production costs as a 'doctrine of labor-value', Veblen effectively updates and expands on his analysis of capitalist industry in *Capital* (Veblen 1948: 288). In Veblen's most important later work, *The Engineers and the Price System* (1921), he distinguishes what he calls the Captains of Finance, who promote salesmanship, earnings, and profits, from the Captains of Industry, whose interests lie in performance, expertise, and productivity. The fateful combination of these facets of capital, he argues, gives rise to the volatility, precariousness, and unpredictability of the industrial system with its tendency towards parochialism and short-sightedness: 'Having begun as an industrial community which centered about an open market, [business enterprise] has matured into a community of Vested Interests whose vested right it is to keep up prices by a short supply in a closed market' (Veblen 1948: 438). In Veblen's view, the long-term future of capitalism will depend on whether the discretion and responsibility for the management of industry will pass from financiers, shareholders, and other 'absentee owners' to the more intelligent rule of technicians, engineers, and experts. Such a transition would not take place not through sabotage but only as another industrial revolution (Veblen 1948: 431–7; Wilson 2004: 195, 215). Echoing Marx on the intensification of industrial discipline, Veblen details how these structural transformations are bringing about the standardization and mechanization of 'the human material' itself while inducing a profound change in the habits of mind and bodily conduct of modern individuals (Veblen 1948: 335).

In their own way, these American classical sociologists take up Marx's sarcastic characterization of commodity exchanges at the end of Part II of *Capital* as 'a very Eden of the innate rights of man' and 'the exclusive realm of Freedom!, Equality! [and] Property!' (C: 280). They share much of Marx's cynicism over how basic human rights are distorted and inverted under the regime of capital: the formal 'freedom' of Black and White labourers amounts to the right be exploited through the wage contract (Du Bois); the supposedly 'equal' exchange of goods and services in the household results in the exclusion of women from public industry (Gilman); and the assumption that everyone disposes of 'property' means that a few absentee owners can in fact control and accumulate the wealth of the majority (Veblen). Marx's joking addition to this list—'Bentham!', as a name for the right to self-interest—also comes under the critical scrutiny of the classical sociologists. The work of George Herbert Mead, for instance, develops an extended argument against the liberal postulate of a contained, indivisible, and irreducibly private 'self'. Distinguishing among a variety of human and other-than-human agents—such as 'me', 'you', and 'I'—Mead conceives social life less as a collection of isolated individuals than as a web of interconnected institutions and personal interactions in which divided selves take others into account. In his posthumously published lectures *Mind, Self, and Society* (1934) and *The Philosophy of the Present* (1932), he envisions the ideal of human society as 'a single human community of a democratic type' which can only emerge from 'a development of communication so that individuals can put themselves into the attitudes of those whom they affect' (Mead 1956: 282). Like Marx, Mead and the early sociologists dare to picture another world in which fundamental human values are not hypocritically proclaimed and then violated, but are rather made comprehensible and realizable for all: 'Let us imagine, for a change, an association of free people working with the means of production held in common, and expending the different forms of labour-power according to a concerted plan as one single social labour force' (C: 171; Marx 1989: 59). These passing remarks, included in later editions of *Capital* and probably inspired by the cooperative spirit of the Paris Commune (1871), express something of the revolutionary vision of social change that Marx shares with later thinkers who partially and selectively take up his legacy (Anderson 2019: 204–5).

II

Where Chapter 32 of *Capital* ends in the tragic mode with the scene of capital's self-annihilation, the final Chapter 33, 'The Modern Theory of Colonization', ends in the comic mode with labour's astonishing escape from capital. Here Marx sketches out what he calls the 'melodrama' where capitalist settlers in the colonies try to create both scarcity of land and a market for labour in their desperate attempt to gain a competitive advantage at home and abroad (C: 938). These anti-climactic remarks allude to how the ferocious expansion and furious intensification of capital ultimately stumble in the wide-open space and slower pace of the colonies. The target of Marx's ridicule is the plan by Edward Gibbon Wakefield (1796–1862) for the 'systematic colonization' of Australia, New Zealand, and British North America. In contrast to the anarchic, coercive, and 'spontaneous colonization' of regions such as Africa, India, and South America, this supposedly more methodical approach to capitalist settlement requires 'a social contract of a quite original kind' in which 'the mass of mankind expropriate[s] itself in honour of the "accumulation of capital"' (C: 933–4).

Although slavery and freeholding remain foundations of colonial wealth in this scheme, some degree of privatization and expropriation of the land is necessary to compel labourers to work for a wage rather than '"making a clean breast of it"' (C: 932, quoting Wakefield). As Ulas Ince has shown in his more patient and comprehensive reading of Wakefield, the dilemma of liberal colonialism in the nineteenth century consisted in channelling capital and labour from the metropole to the colonies but without creating the conditions for revolt or revolution in either: 'Sparse population and inadequate communication vitiated the material conditions of civilization (social complexity, productivity, surplus), undermined its cultural corollaries (leisure, arts, sciences, manners), and subverted social hierarchies (status, deference, order)' (Ince 2018: 132). The challenge for the early entrepreneurial settlers was thus how to combat indolence, reduce subsistence farming, and restrict petty commodity production by absorbing such non-capitalist economic activities into the wage form and other profitable contracts. Wakefield therefore 'discovered' that colonial primitive accumulation is not just an event in the past that laid the groundwork for later developments; it also establishes a durable structure of exploitation and a sustainable strategy of accumulation through dispossession in the present (Coulthard 2014; Foster et al. 2020; Harvey 2003). As Marx is quick to point out, Wakefield's practical discovery in the colonies was already expressed theoretically with reference to the industrial metropole in *Wage-Labour and Capital* (1849): 'capital is not a thing' such as a reified stock of money, infrastructure, and technology, 'but a social relation between persons which is mediated through things' (C: 932, paraphrasing CW 9: 211–2).

Here Marx is not advancing a 'modern theory of colonization' of his own but only lampooning Wakefield's, and nor is he offering an adequate account of how capital is established beyond the borders of Europe (Bhambra and Holmwood 2021). As the final lines of *Capital* remind us, the 'punchline' of this joke has already been delivered in the previous chapter: capitalist production and accumulation are founded on 'the annihilation of that private property which rests on the labour of the individual himself; in other words, the expropriation of the worker' (C: 940). The notion that colonization offers an easy escape for labour or even a promised land for capital turns out to be a mere phantasm: 'Now one would think that this instinct of self-denying fanaticism would especially run riot in the colonies, the only places where the people and the conditions exist to translate a *contrat social* from the dream-realm into reality' (C: 934). Marx does not elaborate further on how a social contract (*contrat social*) can be translated from the realm of dreams (*Traumreich*) into reality. Nevertheless, his wording points us towards one of the more troublesome paths that Marxist theory has crossed in the twentieth century, namely the challenge posed by psychoanalysis as a method of interpreting dreams.

In the final Chapter VII of *The Interpretation of Dreams* (1900), Sigmund Freud invokes a surprising analogy which is worthy of Marx in describing how the motive force (*Triebkraft*) in the formation of dreams operates as a kind of capitalist industrial process:

> A daytime thought may very well play the part of *entrepreneur* for a dream; but the *entrepreneur*, who, as people say, has the idea and the initiative to carry it out, can do nothing without capital; he needs a *capitalist* who can afford the outlay, and the capitalist who provides the psychical outlay for the dream is invariably and indisputably, whatever may be the thoughts of the previous day, *a wish from the unconscious*. (Freud 1976: 714)

Freud describes the activity of the conscious or semi-conscious mind as a kind of productive collaboration between a resourceful entrepreneur drawing on memories of waking life, on the one hand, and a capitalist who invests resources in the form of unconscious wishes for employment by nighttime thoughts, on the other hand.

Freud's simile here is not arbitrary but rather the culmination of an extended series of economic metaphors he employs to account for the dynamics of the mind (Ricoeur 1970: 87–114). He concludes that the 'cathexis' (or occupation: *Besetzung*) of the conscious mind by unconscious thoughts or perceptions takes place in the dream by reducing psychic resistances and laying down 'facilitating paths' (*Bahnungen*) between memory traces (Freud 1976: 688). In the previous chapter (by far the longest in the book), Freud elaborates on what he calls the dream-work

(*Traumarbeit*), the mechanisms and agents employed by daytime and nighttime thoughts in forming the dream. The work of condensation (*Verdichtungsarbeit*) in dreams, for example, operates like a worker in a thought factory (*Gedankenfabrik*) weaving multiple threads of images, words, and ideas together (Freud 1976: 388). By contrast, the work of displacement (*Verschiebungsarbeit*) decentres, circulates, and redistributes psychical energies along a train of associations that shift along paths in various directions (Freud 1976: 415). Both governing factors work together as 'foremen' (*die beiden Werkmeister*) whose combined activity produces the form assumed by dreams (Freud 1976: 417). In an uncanny echo of Marx's topology of economic agencies, Freud describes how these agents of the dream-work facilitate the translation of the latent contents of dream-thoughts (the infrastructure of the dream) into the manifest content (or superstructure) of the visual and verbal dream-text, 'like two versions of the same subject matter in two different languages' (Freud 1976: 381). It is as if Freud's own language for analysing the domestic economy of the mind (*psychische Haushalt*) provides a kind of translation that accounts for how the categories of capitalism are internalized.[4]

[4]Along with condensation and displacement, Freud describes two other kinds of dream-work. Dreams must also take into consideration the means of representation (*Darstellungmittel*), such as the selective use of symbols, and they often undergo the work of secondary revision or elaboration (*sekundäre Barbeitung*), including the additions, evasions, and omissions that give final form to the dream. In a remarkable moment of self-reflection, Freud acknowledges that the intellectual process employed in writing his own 'dream-book' can be described in precisely these terms. He confesses that exposing his most private, intimate, and often embarrassing thoughts to the public by reporting his own dreams in his book has come at the cost of tremendous self-discipline, and perhaps even of the distortion and deletion of the truth. To illustrate the point, he quotes a favourite line from Goethe's *Faust* where Mephistopheles tempts Faust with the knowledge and power that will come from signing a pact with the devil:

Das beste, was du wissen kannst,	The best you can expect to learn
Darfst du den Buben doch nicht sagen.	You cannot tell the youngsters anyhow.
	(Freud 1976: 223, 587; quoting F: 1840–1)

After noting that parents and teachers must often withhold embarrassing realities or refrain from conveying challenging facts to children, Freud adds that his dilemma in disclosing the sexual and aggressive wishes behind his own dreams is not unlike a writer who faces censorship: 'A similar difficulty confronts the political writer who has disagreeable truths to tell those in authority' (Freud 1976: 223). Like Marx, who after being exiled for his radical journalism felt compelled to seek out new audiences by writing *Capital* and political editorials, the psychoanalytic writer often has to resort to vague allusions, selective disclosures, evasive jokes, or outright concealment in presenting his ideas, whether deliberately or unconsciously.

Marx speculates that the language of dreams and the language of reality offer alternative translations for the social contract between capital and labour, not just in the colonies but in the metropole as well. A similar argument might be made regarding the dream-language of colonialism and the language of capitalist reality. In the last of his *New Introductory Lectures on Psychoanalysis* (1933), 'The Question of a Weltanschauung', Freud argues that the best hope for the future of humanity lies not in religion, faith, and spirituality but in science, intellect, and reason. Marxism can contribute to this modern worldview not as a source of utopian revelation but only by advancing the ethos of science: 'The strength of Marxism clearly lies, not in its view of history or the prophecies of the future that are based on it, but in the sagacious indication of the decisive influence which the economic circumstances of people have upon their intellectual, ethical and artistic attitudes' (Freud 1965: 157). Nevertheless, he adds, such a theory lacks a developed psychology of race and rank, not to mention a psychoanalysis of sexuality and gender. These perspectives provide a necessary supplement to its insights into modern social and economic conditions, 'for sociology too, dealing as it does with the behaviour of people in society, cannot be anything but applied psychology' (Freud 1965: 158). Whether or not we accept this argument, we may at least entertain the prospect of combining a Marxist sociology of capitalist industrial work with a Freudian psychoanalysis of the dream-work of colonialism.

Figure 5.1 is my attempt to provide a 'secondary revision' of Freudo-Marxism by reformulating some of the foundational questions of Marx and Freud (O'Neill 2020: 159–67; Althusser 1971: 168–9). By raising these questions I do not mean to force a synthesis between incompatible perspectives, but only to acknowledge the credit due to both Marx and Freud in helping us to imagine a psychoanalytically informed Marxist sociology.

First, how is the metabolic interaction of natural and human worlds, including the drives and instincts, commodified and monetized (valorized) within capitalist social relations of production and exchange? In his discussion of primitive accumulation, Marx graphically depicts the primordial violence of colonial capitalism in subsuming human and natural words: 'The discovery of gold and silver in America, the extirpation, enslavement and entombment in mines of the indigenous population of that continent, the beginnings of the conquest and plunder of India, and the conversion of Africa into a preserve for the commercial hunting of black skins, are all

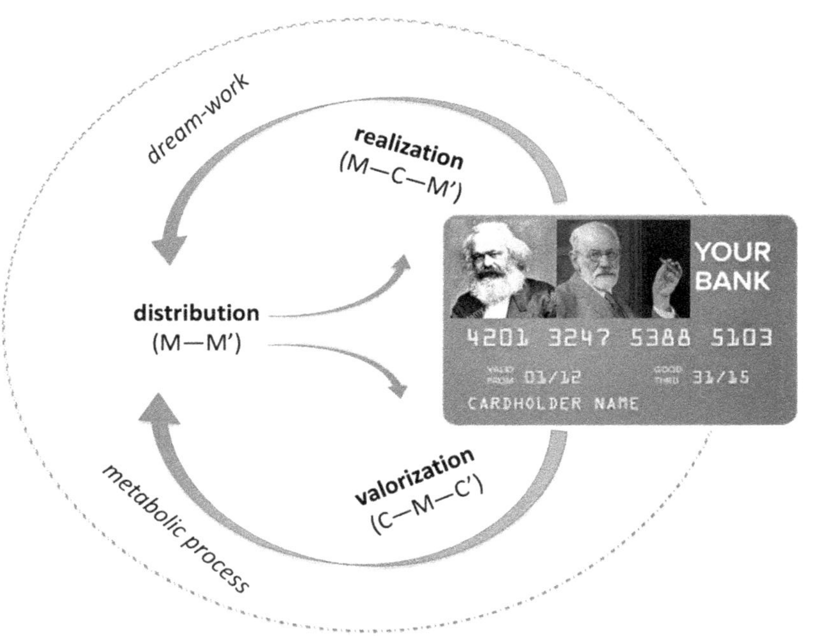

Fig. 5.1 The Marx-Freud credit card. (the dream-work of capital accumulation)

things which characterize the dawn of the era capitalist production' (C: 915). These horrors are not simply forgotten and left behind in the shadows of the rising sun of capitalism, but intensify by day and continue by night before the cycle begins again. Violence in the colonies is the foundation of the formal freedoms enjoyed in the metropole, where other forms of domination are perpetuated: 'In fact, the veiled slavery of the wage-labourers in Europe needed the unqualified slavery of the New World as its pedestal' (C: 925). As Marx reiterates in Part V of *Capital*, not just the labour-power of paid and unpaid workers but also the nature-power of lands and oceans are subjected to colonial dispossession and expropriated by capital as exploitable resources: 'The capitalist mode of production [...] presupposes the domination of man over nature' (C: 649). Natural forces are commodified as means of subsistence—'waters teaming with fish and fruitful soil'—and ecological riches are monetized as instruments of labour—'waterfalls, navigable rivers, wood, coal, etc.' (C: 648).[5] Likewise, the metabolic processes of body and mind, including natural instincts, sexual drives, and emotional sensibilities, are also seized upon and harnessed as productive forces of capital: 'The existing productivity of labour, from which [the capital relation] proceeds as its basis, is a gift, not of nature but of a history embracing thousands of centuries' (C: 647). The natural capacities that make up human work and social intelligence and that shape the eco-gifts of air, water, and land are produced by capital through a long process of cultivation and struggle and valorized through global trade networks and mass migration before being internalized through institutions of acculturation and education.

[5] Among Marx's primary empirical examples of the extraction of land and labour for surplus-value is the colonization of Ireland by England in the early decades of the nineteenth century. He details this case in two newspaper editorials for the *New York Daily Tribune*, in a confidential memorandum to the International Working Men's Association, and in the concluding section of Chapter 25 on capitalist accumulation (Anderson 2010: 115–53; C: 854–70). The agricultural revolution that transformed the Irish countryside from arable land into pasture kept pace with emigration to England, North America, and Australia. That is, with the rapid depopulation of Ireland in the 20 years after the 1844 famine and the subsequent wave of emigration, Ireland was finally able to 'fulfil her true destiny, to be an English sheepwalk and cattle pasture' (C: 869). Among the landlords and land magnates who would 'condescend to live in Ireland on their demesnes', Marx singles out Lord Dufferin for special derision. Dufferin's solution to the misery of Ireland—a slightly lower rate of migration to address depopulation and soil depletion at the same time—earns Marx's bitter sarcasm: 'what humanity from such a great Lord!' (C: 868). Here he adapts Mephistopheles's smug remark after striking his own bargain over Faust's fate with The Lord in the 'Prologue in Heaven' that opens Goethe's play:

Es ist gar hübsch von einem grossen Herrn,	Say what you like, it's quite a compliment:
So menschlich mit dem Teufel selbst zu sprechen!	A great Lord so man-to-man with the Devil! (F: 352–3)

The famine of 1846 killed a million people and led to a 20-year exodus, an 'emigration [that now] forms one of the most lucrative branches of its export trade' as well as a profitable and pleasant repose for members of the landed gentry like Lord Dufferin. Marx notes that these events sowed the seeds of revolution when Fenian nationalists in Ireland and America formed multi-ethnic alliances with impoverished peasants and industrial workers exerting their power of resistance (*Widerstandskraft*) against both capital and landed property (Anderson 2019: 201; Smith 2021: 174–83; C: 637).

Second, in what sense can the realization process expressed in the general formula for capital—buying cheap in order to sell dear (M—C—M′)—be considered a variation on the dream-work by which money somehow begets more money (M—M′) through the investment and distribution of surplus-value? In a book that focuses on the production process of capital, Marx can only offer a brief preview of the arguments he had already drafted for the following two volumes on the circulation and distribution of profit, interest, and rent (Harvey 2018: 151). Like the industrial production of commodities by wage-labour, these processes are to be considered within the global context of capitalist accumulation, colonial world markets, and the international division of labour:

> The colonial system, with its maritime trade and its commercial wars, served as a greenhouse for the credit system. [...] The only part of the so-called national wealth that actually enters into the collective possession of a modern nation is—the national debt. (C: 919)

With only a hint of hyperbole, Marx argues that public credit has become the *credo* of capital to such an extent that lack of faith in the national debt is viewed as a cardinal sin 'for which there is no forgiveness' (C: 919). Global trade and international finance serve as a kind of greenhouse (*Treibhaus*) for the cultivation of crops, raw materials, and people for colonial settlement, and as a hothouse for 'speculation via the international credit system, stock-exchange gambling, and the modern bankocracy' (C: 919; Kemple 1995: 228–9). In a passage added to the French edition of *Capital*, Marx describes the role of joint-stock companies, cartels, and financial trusts in 'welding' together the levers of centralization, thereby transforming the overall direction of capital accumulation 'from the circular to the spiral form' (C: 777–80; Marx 1989: 547–9).

Finance capital thereby emerges though a process which seems to be analogous to the dream-work of condensation (monopolization) and displacement (colonization). In Part V of volume 3 of *Capital*, Marx expands on these points in describing what he calls 'fictitious capital', a legal way of capitalizing on assets which have no material basis in productive activities or commodities. More broadly, he examines 'interest-bearing capital' (captured in the formula M—M′) as the fullest expression of the contradictions of capital, giving rise to the fantasies of an emerging financial aristocracy, 'a new variety of parasites in the shape of promoters, speculators and simply nominal directors; a whole system of swindling and cheating by means of corporation promotion, stock issuance, and stock speculation' (CW 37: 436). As we have learned again and again from the global economic crises of the twenty-first century, the financial aristocracy continues to 'govern by debt' by controlling both private and state-managed institutions (Lazzarato 2015: 136–40). At the same time, the logic of credit and debit is internalized in the ecologies of domestic life and translated into the language of everyday dreams (Featherstone 2019: 240–1; Gane 2019: 189–90).

* * *

Writing across a wide range of disciplines from the late eighteenth to the mid-twentieth century, the classical sociologists were all concerned to some degree with the problem of socialism or communism. Insofar as they read Marx and Engels, they focused either on the call to revolutionary action in *The Communist Manifesto* or on the more sober arguments of Engels's *Socialism, Utopian and Scientific*. Occasionally they also took their cue from Marx's polemical digression in Chapter 1 of *Capital* with its imaginative projection of 'an association of free producers':

> We shall assume, but only for the sake of a parallel with the production of commodities, that the share of each individual producer in the means of subsistence is determined by his or her labour-time [...]. The social relations of the individual producers, both toward their labour and products of their labour, are here transparent in their simplicity, in production as well as distribution. (C: 172)

Writing in response to the socialist theoreticians and workers' movements of the Second International (1889–1916) and the Third International (1919–1943), the classical sociologists of the early decades of the twentieth century were often critical of the scientistic dogmas and nationalist orthodoxies that would eventually divide the globe into warring camps after World War II. When they read *Capital* or other available writings by Marx and Engels, however selectively or superficially, they would offer an expanded conception of capitalism and its alternatives, whether socialist or otherwise. In particular, they broaden Marx's focus on class exploitation at the point of production by considering the representation of differently situated groups and individuals with respect to civic participation or exclusion (Emile Durkheim); the recognition of cultural statuses and individual identities within multiple institutions (Max Weber); and the redistribution of wealth between rich and poor in private and public life (Georg Simmel). Adapting the slogan of the American Revolution, in recent years Nancy Fraser has argued that there can be 'no redistribution or recognition without representation' (Fraser 2005: 79).

In fact, the classical sociologists of the United States had already elaborated on the implications of this sentiment even as they moved further away from the founding insights of *Capital*. Du Bois demonstrates how the expropriation of racialized groups is not just a presupposition of capital accumulation when exported to colonial settlements but also built into the competition between the owners of the means of production and rivalries among workers within nation-states. Likewise, Gilman shows that the unpaid work of social reproduction by women in the household and the underpaid work of care-giving more broadly are gendered in ways that are obscured by a narrow focus on the extraction of surplus-value in conventional workplaces. Veblen points to how in later phases of the industrial revolution leisure and consumption have been refashioned as value-creating work, and business management and entrepreneurial initiative have been merged into tools of the 'vested interests' while imposing the 'discipline of the machine' on the masses. These arguments anticipate Fraser's insistence that 'any politics that seeks to reform, reject or surpass capitalism must place the boundary question front and centre', especially with respect to struggles over natural and social sustainability, the borders separating affluent and impoverished states, and the lines dividing productive from unproductive work (Fraser and Jaeggi 2018: 176; Fraser 2020).

The classical sociologists do not just broaden Marx's vision to include a wider range of social relationships and institutionalized orders that reproduce state-managed capitalism; they also deepen and intensify his insights into the capitalist system by descending further into the hidden abodes of the modern mind. This social psychological dimension of contemporary life is explored in Mead's reflections on the divided identities and multiple agencies of selfhood over the life-course, and especially in

Freud's investigations into the conscious and unconscious workings of the human psyche. Freud surmises that the perception-consciousness system can be likened to a collaboration between an entrepreneur drawing on the day's residues and a capitalist providing the nighttime investment of unconscious wishes. As Michel Foucault would later argue, Freud's model of repression and sublimation can be reframed in terms of the deployment of power and knowledge in the capitalist economy: 'sexuality is originally, historically bourgeois, and [...] in its successive shifts and transpositions, it induces specific class effects' (Foucault 1978: 127). The bourgeoisie of early capitalism first turned its anxious concerns over sexuality on themselves in the name of their health, hygiene, descent, and longevity, and only later shifted their gaze to the regulation of proletarian sexuality in response to the danger of urban overcrowding, the need to maintain a vital workforce, and the surveillance of disease and immorality (Foucault 1978: 122–7). With the metamorphoses of 'human capital' in the post-liberal capitalist societies of today, we may even imagine how the government of populations, including their well-being, welfare, and productivity, may eventually be decoupled from the democratic defence and political security of sovereign territories and either 'downloaded' to populist movements or 'outsourced' to financial elites (Davies 2021: 97).

In responding to the challenge posed by *Capital*, classical sociology enlarges the Faustian pact between capital and labour by rethinking the relationship between business enterprise and nation-states along with the compact between labour organizations and private households across the divides of race and gender. Insofar as actually existing or hypothetical socialisms are found wanting in democratic freedoms, these early social scientists turn their attention to the possibility of making the capitalist world more humane and accountable. They envision how new forms of social solidarity may emerge from the industrial division of labour and the cooperation between professional groups, rather than being imposed by state power. They imagine how a renewed work ethic need not be coerced through material deprivation or the promise of profit, but freely embraced as a civic right and a social duty. And they picture an exchange economy that is not driven by market competition or class conflict but by an ethic of care and a culture of reciprocity.[6] Even before the new enclosures of the capitalist world system in the late twentieth and early twenty-first centuries had been set in place, the classical sociologists anticipate a post-liberal

[6]An ethic of entrepreneurial selfhood and a morality of self-interested exchange are the cardinal virtues of both classical liberalism and Faustian individualism, each of which *Capital* honours and denounces in equal measure. In one of the most heavily revised passages in the French edition, which Marx again annotated and revised in his own copy, he savagely criticizes John Stuart Mill for failing to find the source of surplus-value in exploitation simply by reasserting 'the productivity of labour' (C: 650–4; see the frontispiece of the present book for the facsimile in the Apparat of Marx 1989: 746. Pages 1181–3 of the Apparat summarize these revisions along with related letters by Engels to Marx and by Marx to N. D. Danielson, the Russian translator of *Capital*, as well as Marx's underlinings in the works quoted). Where David Ricardo never concerns himself with the origin of surplus-value, Marx notes, Mill only repeats the same old song (*la vieille chanson*) that evades the question of its cause and origin and ignores the buying and selling of labour-power. Mill assumes that under conditions where workers and capitalists confront each other as separate classes, '"the capitalist advances the whole expenses, including the entire remuneration of the labourer"', who in turn advances to himself not just the means of subsistence but also the means of production (labour)!' (C: 653, quoting Mill's *Principles of Political Economy*, 1868). In an absurd twist of reasoning, Mill thus presents the worker as his own wage-labourer or even his own capitalist, '"since, contributing his labour at less than the market price (!), he may be regarded as lending the difference (?) to his employer and receiving it back with interest, etc."' (C: 653, quoting Mill; Marx's parenthetical punctuation marks). Mill's conflation of labour with capital can be compared to the hubris of Faust in imagining that he alone is responsible for creating his empire, without the help of supernatural powers or the exploitation of real workers. He embraces his newfound knowledge of worldly concerns and defies the pleadings of the Spirit of Care (*Sorge*), who haunts him in the guise of an old hag like the ghost of a fairy-tale or a god resurrected from the distant past:

Der Erdenkreis ist mir genug bekannt,	I know full well the earthly sphere of men;
Nach drüben ist die Aussicht uns verrant,	The yonder view is blocked to mortal ken;
Tor, wer dorthin die Augen blinzelnd richtet,	A fool who squints beyond with blinking eyes,
Sich über Wolken seinesgleichen dichtet!	Imagining his like above the skies!
Er stehe fest und sehe hier sich um;	Let him stand firm and gaze about alert;
Dem Tüchtigen ist dies Welt nicht stumm.	To able man this world is not inert.
	(F: 11441–7)

Faust's arrogance in replacing the spiritual world with the evidence of science is punished when Care strikes him blind, rendering him even more determined to command the 'thousand hands' working under him to comply with his singular will. Faust therefore represents an important turning point in the abandonment of spiritual faith in other-worldly salvation for empirical knowledge in the service of this-worldly transformation (Foucault 2005: 310–1 and Simmel 1997: 294 each makes this point with reference to *Faust*). In this regard, Marx inherits Faust's earthly ambition while tempering the individualism of political economy with a socialist ethic of collective care.

transition to a more civil form of capitalism that embraces a covenant between generations rather than settling for a compromise between classes. As John O'Neill formulates this alternative, 'the argument for civic capitalism rests on the provision of a *civic commons* that removes the imbalance, the immodesty, and the ugliness that prevails whenever the rich are so rich that the poor are far too poor' (O'Neill 2004: 95). The overinvestment in corporate capital and the disinvestment in community and civic capital that we witness today reduce social support to private charity, refashion public welfare into entrepreneurial workfare, and transform the presumption of equality into the expectation of exploitation. To resist this dystopian dream we may find a critical resource in the work of an engaged intellectual from a century and a half ago tirelessly reading and writing in the hopes of locating the levers of change. *Capital* is more than the name for the wager that Marx wishes later scholars and activists will take up in their own way; it is also the receipt for a debt we have yet to redeem but must continue to reckon with.

N.B.: I often modify existing English translations, drawing on German or French editions readily available online or from print sources. References to *Faust* are by line number as indicated in both English and German editions.

Works Cited and Consulted

Abbreviations Used

C—Marx, Karl (1976). *Capital: A Critique of Political Economy, Volume 1.* Ben Fowkes trans. Ernest Mandel intro. London: Penguin Books.

CW—*The Collected Works of Karl Marx and Friedrich Engels 1844–1895.* 47 Volumes. New York: International Publishers. (Electronic Edition, Charlottesville, Virginia).

DL—Durkheim, Emile (2004). *The Division of Labor in Society.* W. D. Wells trans. Lewis Coser intro. New York: The Free Press.

F—Goethe, Johann Wolfgang von (1986). *Faust: Eine Tragödie.* Erster und Zweiter Teile. Stuttgart: Philipp Reclam Jun.

Goethe, Johann Wolfgang von (1976). *Faust: A Tragedy.* Walter Arndt trans., Cyrus Hamlin ed. New York: W. W. Norton & Company.

PE—Weber, Max (2009). *The Protestant Ethic and the Spirit of Capitalism, with Other Writings on the Rise of the West.* Fourth edition. Stephen Kalberg trans., intro. Oxford: Oxford University Press.

PM—Simmel, Georg (2004). *The Philosophy of Money.* Thomas Bottomore, David Frisby trans. London: Routledge.

Althusser, Louis (1971). *Lenin and Philosophy and Other Essays.* Ben Brewster, trans. New York: Monthly Review Press.

Anderson, Kevin B. (2019). 'Five explicit and implicit notions of revolution in *Capital, Volume I,* as seen from a multilinear, peripheral angle'. In *Marx's Capital after 150 Years: Critique and Alternative to Capitalism.* Marcello Musto ed. London: Routledge, Pp. 197–207.

Anderson, Kevin B. (2010). *Marx at the Margins: On Nationalism, Ethnicity, and Non-Western Societies.* Chicago & London: The University of Chicago Press.

Berman, Marshall (1988) *All that is Solid Melts into Air: The Experience of Modernity.* New York: Penguin Books.

Bhambra, Gurminder K. and John Holmwood (2021). *Colonialism and Modern Social Theory.* Cambridge, UK: Polity Press.

Coulthard, Glenn Sean (2014). *Red Skin, White Masks: Rejecting the Colonial Politics of Recognition.* Minneapolis: University of Minnesota Press.

Davies, William (2021). 'The Revenge of Sovereignty on Government? The Release of Neoliberal Politics on Economics Post-2008'. *Theory, Culture & Society* 38(6): 95–118.

Du Bois, W. E. B. (1995). *W. E. B. Du Bois: A Reader.* David Levering Lewis ed. New York: Henry Hold and Company.

Featherstone, Mark (2019). 'Ecologies of Indebtedness'. In *The Sociology of Debt.* M. Featherstone ed. Bristol, UK: Policy Press. Pp. 231–49.

Federici, Silvia (2004). *Caliban and the Witch: Women, the Body, and Primitive Accumulation.* New York, NY: Autonomedia.

Foster, John Bellamy, Brett Clark, Hannah Holleman (2020). 'Marx and the Indigenous'. *Monthly Review* February: 1–19.

Foucault, Michel (2005). *The Hermeneutics of the Subject: Lectures at the Collège de France 1981–1982.* G. Burchell trans. New York: Picador.

Foucault, Michel (1978). *The History of Sexuality, Volume 1.* R. Hurley trans. New York: Vintage Books.

Fraser, Nancy (2020). 'What Should Socialism Mean in the 21st Century?' *Socialist Register* 56: 282–294.

Fraser, Nancy (2014). 'Behind Marx's Hidden Abode: For an Expanded Conception of Capitalism'. *New Left Review* 86: 55–72.

Fraser, Nancy (2005). 'Reframing Justice in a Globalizing World'. *New Left Review* 32: 69–88.

Fraser, Nancy, Rahel Jaeggi (2018). *Capitalism: A Conversation in Critical Theory.* Brian Milstein ed. Cambridge, UK: Polity Press.

Freud, Sigmund (1976). *The Interpretation of Dreams.* J. Strachey trans., ed. London: Penguin Books.

Freud, Sigmund (1965). *New Introductory Lectures on Psychoanalysis.* J. Strachey trans., ed. New York: W. W. Norton & Co.
Gane, Nicholas (2019). 'Debt, Usury, and the Ongoing Crises of Capitalism'. In *The Sociology of Debt.* M. Featherstone ed. Bristol, UK: Policy Press. Pp. 175–95.
Gilman, Charlotte Perkins (1989). *The Yellow Wallpaper and Other Writings.* Lynne Sharon Schwartz ed. New York: Bantam Books.
Harvey, David (2018). *Marx,* Capital *and the Madness of Economic Reason.* Oxford, UK: Oxford University Press.
Harvey, David (2003). *The New Imperialism.* Oxford, UK: Oxford University Press.
Ince, Onur Ulas (2018). *Colonial Capitalism and the Dilemmas of Liberalism.* Oxford, UK: Oxford University Press.
Kemple, Thomas (1995). *Reading Marx Writing: Melodrama, the Market, and the 'Grundrisse'.* Stanford: Stanford University Press.
Kemple, Thomas (2018a). *Simmel.* Cambridge, UK: Polity Press.
Lazzarato, Maurizio (2015). *Governing by Debt.* J. D. Jordan trans. Semiotext(e). South Pasadena, CA.
Lukács, Georg (1968). *Goethe and his Age.* R. Anchor trans. London: Merlin Press.
Marx, Karl (1989). *Le Capital.* M. J. Roy trans., entièrement révisée par l'auteur. *Marx Engels Gesamtausgabe* II/7 and Apparat. Berlin: Dietz Verlag.
Mead, George Herbert (1956). *On Social Psychology.* A. Strauss ed. Chicago: The University of Chicago Press.
O'Neill, John (2020). *Writing the Body Politic: A John O'Neill Reader.* M. Featherstone, T. Kemple eds. London: Routledge.
O'Neill, John (2004). *Civic Capitalism: The State of Childhood.* Toronto, ON: University of Toronto Press.
Pyyhtinen, Olli (2014). *The Gift and its Paradoxes: Beyond Mauss.* Surrey, UK: Ashgate.
Ricoeur, Paul (1970). *Freud and Philosophy: An Essay on Interpretation.* D. Savage trans. New Haven: Yale University Press.
Roberts, William Clare (2017). *Marx's Inferno: The Political Theory of Capital.* Princeton University Press.
Simmel, Georg (1997). *Simmel on Culture.* D. Frisby, M. Featherstone eds. London: SAGE Publications.
Veblen, Thorstein (1948). *The Portable Veblen.* M. Lernier ed. New York, NY: Viking Press. Smith 2021.
Wilson, H. T. (2004). *The Vocation of Reason: Studies in Critical Theory and Social Science in the Age of Max Weber.* T. Kemple ed. Leiden: Brill.

Appendixes

Appendix A: The 'Known Marx', 1841–1941

Fig. A1 The 'Known Marx'. (Marx's published works and drafts)

For most of his life Karl Marx (1818–1883) worked in relative obscurity and solitude, and only a few of his published writings were known among his contemporaries or the next generation of scholars and activists. Much of the effort of publicizing or branding Marx's ideas was undertaken by

T. Kemple, *Marx's Wager*, Marx, Engels, and Marxisms,
https://doi.org/10.1007/978-3-031-08065-4

Marx himself in 1859 in the bio-bibliographical self-portrait he provided in the Preface to *A Contribution to the Critique of Political Economy* (Carver 2018: 16–30), and later by his friend, collaborator, and co-author Friedrich Engels. He also references his own published writings in *Capital, Volume 1,* where he highlights the *Contribution, The Poverty of Philosophy* (in French), and *The Communist Manifesto* (co-authored with Engels but originally published anonymously), as well his journal articles and even some of his unpublished writings. This 'known Marx' may be contrasted with what has been called the works of the 'unknown Marx', including the republication in the twentieth century of his early writings dating back to his 1841 dissertation, and especially manuscripts and drafts published posthumously between 1927 and 1941 in the first *Marx-Engels Gesamtausgabe* (MEGA), such as the *Economic and Philosophical Manuscripts* (1844), *The German Ideology* (1845–1847), and the *Grundrisse* (1857–1858), Ironically, today Marx is often better known for these works than he is for those published when he was alive (Kemple 1995: 199–201; Nicolaus 1968).

Marx's masterpiece, *Capital*, presents us with a complex case of this 'known Marx'. Three significantly different editions of Volume 1 appeared in his lifetime: the German editions of 1867 and 1873, and the French translation of 1872–1875 which he collaborated on and which was published in instalments. Under Engels's editorship two revised editions appeared posthumously in 1883 and 1890, along with Volumes 2 (1885) and 3 (1894). Together these works and the drafts of *Capital*, beginning with the 1857–1858 *Grundrisse,* make up 15 volumes of Section II of the second version of MEGA, the only section completed to date. (The others are Section I: published works, articles, and drafts of other works; Section III: correspondence; and Section IV: excerpts, notes, and marginalia, for a total of 114 planned volumes). As Marx notes in the Postface to the second edition of *Capital*, his mode of inquiry (*Forschungsweise*) must be formally distinguished from his mode of presentation (*Vorstellungsweise*; C: 102; Heinrich 2016; Musto 2019).

Following Engels in his Preface to the English edition and many recent scholars, I consider *Capital, Volume 1* to be an independent work and a 'dialectically articulated artistic whole', as Marx himself asserts in a letter to Engels (C: 112; CW 42: 168; Jameson 2011; Roberts 2017). The first edition of 1867 is organized into six chapters which appear loosely to follow—or 'coquette with', as Marx says in the Postface—Hegel's general mode of expression (*Ausdrücksweise*). In particular, he seems to be thinking of the three parts of the *Logic*: Chapters 1 and 2 on the circulation of commodities and money consider the being (*Sein*) of capital (quality, quantity, and measure); Chapters 3 and 4 on the production of relative and absolute surplus-value correspond to the essence (*Wesen)* of capital (existence, appearance, and reality); and Chapters 5 and 6 on the distribution and accumulation of surplus-value express the concept (*Begriff*) of capital (subjective, objective, and total aspects) (C: 103; Hegel 1975; Sekine 1984/1986; Kemple 1995: 87–92). In the second German edition Marx further divides these 6 chapters into 25, and in the 1872–1875 French translation he thoroughly revises the whole work in order to make it 'more intelligible to the reader', as he notes in the Postface (C: 105). The French translation may be considered the last definitive and authorized version that Marx approved for publication in his lifetime, and yet up to his final years he continued to make notes and revisions in anticipation of a third edition (Anderson 1983; Haug 2017; Musto 2020; Pinho 2021).

In the French and later English translations, Volume 1 is re-organized into 8 parts and 33 chapters (which roughly reflect the 8 figures and 33 footnotes of the present book) distributed into 3 groups of 11, each centred on a long historical discussion: Parts I–III (Chapters 1–11) include the extended Chapter 10 'The Working Day'; Parts IV–VI (Chapters 12–22) feature the detailed Chapter 15 'Machinery and Large-Scale Industry'; and Parts VII–VIII (Chapters 23–33) centre on the long Chapter 25 'The Law of Capitalist Accumulation'. The three historical chapters cover more than 335 pages in the English translation (almost 40% of the book) while Parts II, V, and VI comprise 10 chapters totalling just under 100 pages (about 10% of the book). Despite the 'lack of harmony in style [*des décordances de style*]' that Marx acknowledges in the Postface to the French translation, these revisions show that he was constantly refining his sense of the work's literary form (C: 105; see Appendix B).

Unless otherwise indicated, all works in the list below originally appeared in German; dates in **bold** indicate those published or written within Marx's lifetime; dates underlined indicate works co-authored, edited, or with a preface by Engels.

1842–1843 Articles in the *Rheinische Zeitung* [Rhenish Newspaper], including 'On Freedom of the Press' and 'Debates on the Law on Thefts of Wood'

1844 Articles in the *Deutsch-Französische Jahrbucher* [German-French Yearbooks], including 'Toward a Critique of Hegel's *Philosophy of Right*: Introduction' and 'On the Jewish Question' (1902)

1845	with Engels, *The Holy Family, or Critique of Critical Criticism. Against Bruno Bauer and Company* (1932).
1846	'Peuchet: On Suicide'
1847	*The Poverty of Philosophy, Answer to* The Philosophy of Poverty *by M. Proudhon* (in French; German 1884, 1892; Russian 1886)
1848	'Discourse on Free Trade' (in French; German **1848**, 1884; English 1888)
1848	with Engels, *Manifesto of the Communist Party* (as *The Communist Manifesto* in **1872**, 1883, 1890; Russian **1882**; English 1888; Polish 1892; Italian 1893)
1848–1850	Articles in the *Neue Rheinische Zeitung* [New Rhenish Newspaper], including 'Wage-Labour and Capital' (1891; English 1933) and 'The Class Struggle in France, 1848–1850' (1895; English 1924)
1852	*The Eighteenth Brumaire of Louis Bonaparte* (**1869**, 1885; English 1937)
1851–1862	Articles in the *New York Daily Tribune*, including 'History of the Opium Trade', 'The English Middle Classes', 'The Future of the British Rule in India', 'The British Cotton Trade', and 'The North American Civil War' (in English)
1859	*A Contribution to the Critique of Political Economy*
1864	*Inaugural Address of the International Working Men's Association* (in English)
1867	*Capital: A Critique of Political Economy, Volume 1: The Production Process of Capital* (**1872**,1883, 1890; Russian **1872**; French **1872–1875**, 1924; English 1887)
1871	*The Civil War in France* (in English; 1891)
1878	'Part II: Political Economy, Chapter 10: From *Kritische Geschichte*', in Engels, *Herr Eugen Dühring's Revolution in Science* (1885, 1894, 1935; English 1907)
1880	'Introduction' to Engels, *Socialism: Utopian and Scientific* (in French; revised and translated chapters from *Anti-Dühring* 1978; German 1882; English 1891)
1885	*Capital, Volume 2* (written in **1862–1865**, **1868–1870**, **1876–1881**; English 1907)
1886	'Theses on Feuerbach', in Engels, *Ludwig Feuerbach and the End of Classical German Philosophy* (written in **1847**)

1891	*Critique of the Gotha Programme* (written in **1875**; English 1918)
1894	*Capital, Volume 3* (written in **1864–1865**; English 1909)
1898	*Value, Price, and Profit* (in English, written in **1865**)
1902	*The Difference between the Democritean and Epicurean Philosophies of Nature* (doctoral dissertation; written in **1841**)
1903	'Introduction' (written in **1857** for the *Grundrisse*)
1904–1910	*Theories of Surplus Value, Capital Volume 4* (written in **1862–1863**; French 1924–1925)
1924	'Letter to Vera Zasulich' (in Russian, written in **1881**)
1926	'Conspectus on Bakunin's *Statism and Anarchy*' (in Russian, written in **1874–1875**)
1932	with Engels, *The German Ideology* (written **1845–1846**)
1932	*Economic and Philosophical Manuscripts* (written **1844**)
1939–1941	*Grundrisse* (written **1857–1858**)

Appendix B: *Capital* as Epic Drama, 1775–1875

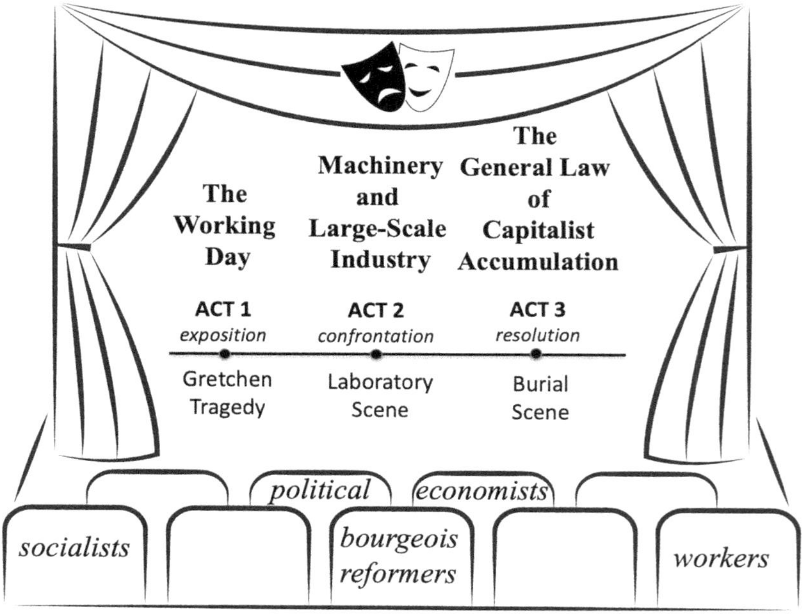

Fig. A2 *Capital* as epic drama. (Historical chapters from *Capital*, scenes from *Faust*, Marx's intended audiences)

In the process of writing *Capital* Marx looked for inspiring models from among his favourite works of literature, among them the epic drama *Faust: A Tragedy* by Johann Wolfgang von Goethe (1749–1832). Each writer began his masterpiece in his youth (Goethe completing his early draft, the *Urfaust* in 1775) and worked steadily on them into their mature age (Marx publishing his last version of *Capital* in 1875). In contrast to the artistry of other great poets whom Marx could often recite by heart, such as Aeschylus, Dante, and Shakespeare, or the novelists he often returned to, including Rabelais, Cervantes, and Balzac, Goethe stood out for him in addressing the spirit of the age by reworking older literary forms (verse, drama, and epic narrative) rather than by inventing new ones (Lukács 1968: 158). Likewise, Marx's critique of classical political economy contributes to and reconceives this specialist field but without creating a new science. He also draws on the full range of literary and scholarly resources available to him in an effort to address a variety of audiences, especially the political economists he comments on and criticizes along with bourgeois reformers, socialist writers and agitators, and educated workers, such as those in the International Working Men's Association that Marx and Engels collaborated in establishing in 1864. (Commentaries on Marx's use of literary models include Berman 1982: 37–129 on *Faust* as inspiration for *The Communist Manifesto*; Kemple 1995: 108–14 on Balzac's *Human Comedy* as a model for the *Grundrisse*; and Roberts 2017: 23–28 on Dante's *Divine Comedy* as a model for *Capital*).

The complex plot and allegorical narrative of *Faust* seem to have captured Marx's imagination as a compelling way of presenting his own critique of political economy. Where the crucial turning point early on in Goethe's play is the fateful pact between Mephistopheles and Faust (F: 1530–2072), Marx's argument hinges on a dramatic depiction of the wage contract between capitalist and worker (C: 270–80). Here Marx signals a decisive 'change in the physiognomy of our *dramatis personae*' from the scene of buyers and sellers on the market to that of capitalists and wage labourers in the factory (C: 280; Roberts 2017; Wolff 1988: 15, 39–60). This 'stage direction' concludes the examination of value in Parts I and II of *Capital* and sets up the classic three-act narrative that structures the book as a whole. Each 'act' comprises 11 chapters centred on a long historical discussion that may be read as having been inspired by a key scene in Goethe's *Faust*. The set-piece for the first act, the magisterial Chapter 10 'The Working Day', details the factory inspection reports on the exploitation of workers, with particular concern for the suffering of women and children. These descriptions mirror the tragedy of Gretchen, the spinner who is seduced and abandoned by Faust in the first part of Goethe's play. The set-piece for the 11 central chapters of *Capital* (Parts IV–VI), the elaborate Chapter 15 'Machinery and Large-Scale Industry', examines the complex division of labour and application of science and technology to industrial and agricultural production processes. These issues are prefigured in the laboratory scene where Faust's protegé Wagner fabricates a new life form, the Homunculus. The set-piece for the final 11 chapters of *Capital* (Parts VII–VIII) brings the confrontation between capitalist and worker to a climax in the long Chapter 25 'The General Law of Capitalist Accumulation'. This conflict is resolved when the death knell of capitalist property relations is sounded by the proletarian 'gravediggers' (C: 929–30), whose role is analogous to the labouring lemures who build Faust's empire in the final scenes and then bury him when he dies. In each of these three 'acts', the front-stage dramas of exploitation, domination, and expropriation are obscured by the so-called mysteries of 'the fetish-character of the commodity' (Chapter 1), 'the wage-form' (Chapter 19), and 'systemic colonisation' (Chapter 33).

The parallel literary form and narrative structure of the two works can be seen by placing their main divisions side by side:

Goethe's *Faust* (1775–1831)	**Marx's *Capital, Volume 1*(1857–1875)**
Dedication, Prelude, and Prologue	Prefaces and Postfaces
Part One: study and town scenes	Part I: Chapters 1–3: commodities/money
pact scene	Part II: Chapters 4–6: buying/selling labour-power
wine-cellar scene	Part III: Chapter 7: labour/valorization process
witches' kitchen scene/ Walpurgis night	Chapters 8 and 9, 11: absolute surplus-value
Gretchen tragedy	*Chapter 10: the working day*
	<Durkheim>
Part Two, Act 1: masque, paper money	Part IV: Chapters 12–14: relative surplus-value, scheme, classical drama cooperation, manufacturing
Act 2: Laboratory scene	*Chapter 15: Machinery and large-scale industry*
classical Walpurgis night	Part V: Chapters 16–18: magnitude/rate of exploitation
Act 3: Helena and Euphorion interlude	Part VI: Chapters 19–22: wages
	<Weber>
Act 4: Imperial war and occupation scenes	Part VII: Chapters 23–24: reproduction/transformation
Act 5: Colonization	*Chapter 25: Capitalist accumulation*
burial and salvation scenes	*Part VIII: Chapters 26–33: Primitive accumulation*
	<Simmel>

As I indicate here, this comparison between the two works may be extended to consider how the plot of the Faust story is repurposed in the work of the three canonical classical sociologists, Emile Durkheim, Max Weber, and Georg Simmel, through their reception of *Capital* and in their efforts to examine later stages of industrial capitalism. For example, Marx's detailed discussion of the industrial division of social labour in Chapters 1–11 of *Capital* (Parts I–III), which Durkheim reworks in examining the moral foundations of social solidarity, is dramatized in Goethe in his depiction of Faust's ambition to establish himself in the imperial court (Part One, and Part Two, Act 1). In a similar way, Weber's examination of the origins of the capitalist work ethic and the rise of the modern vocations, which builds on Marx's analysis of the contradictions of the wage-form and the mechanization of the labour process, are illustrated in Goethe's characters of the scientist Wagner, the dreamer Faust, and the power-hungry Emperor (Part Two, Acts 2–4). Finally, Simmel's work on the capitalist money economy, which connects Marx's broad theoretical concerns with the dynamism of commodity exchange and capital accumulation, is anticipated in Goethe's depiction of the ageing Faust building his commercial and colonial empire (Part Two, Act 5). In effect, the classical sociologists extend Marx's Faustian epic of the diabolical pact between capital and labour by considering the historical, economic, political, and social consequences of this fateful relationship for the modern age.

APPENDIX C: A FLOOR PLAN FOR CLASSICAL SOCIOLOGY, 1789–1939

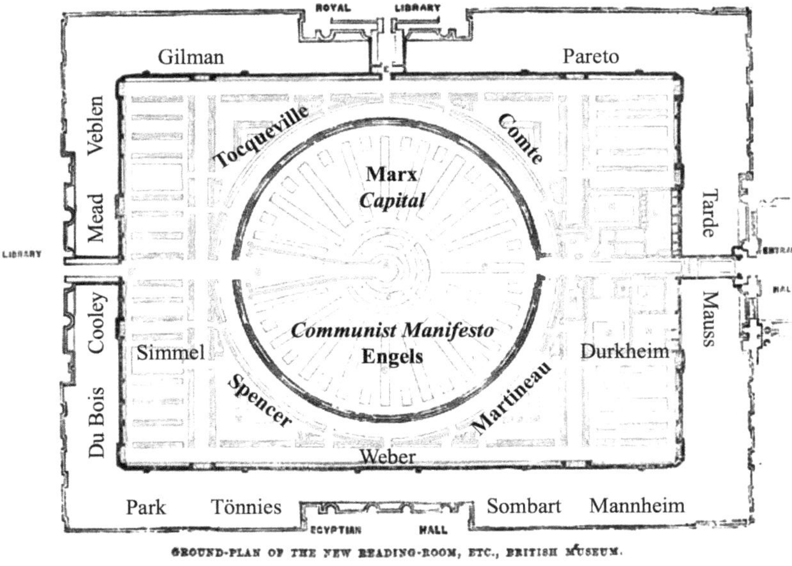

Fig. A3 A floor plan for classical sociology. (First- and second-generation classical sociologists)

Marx began his research for *Capital* in London at the British Museum in 1857, the same year its newly designed Reading Room—an impressive domed structure modelled on the Pantheon—had just re-opened to commemorate the Museum's 100th anniversary. Surrounded by the Museum's large collection of objects from all over the world and by thousands of books, he focused on the writings of political economists from William Petty to Adam Smith, Jeremy Bentham, David Ricardo, and John Stuart Mill, and of socialist writers from Charles Fourier to Ferdinand Lassalle, Jérôme-Alolphe Blanqui, and Robert Owen. In addition to having ready access to works not already in his personal library (for a list see MEGA IV/32), he could also consult parliamentary publications such as the so-called Blue Books (factory inspections, poor law reports, and public health inquiries), newspapers from Europe and North America, and the works of his favourite philosophers, poets, and fiction writers from antiquity to the present. Marx also became familiar with the fledgling field of sociology, including the writings of Harriet Martineau (such as her *Illustrations of Political Economy*), Auguste Comte (and his followers in the journal *Philosophie Positiviste*), Alexis de Tocqueville (particularly *The Old Régime and the Revolution*), and Herbert Spencer (especially his essays for the *Westminster Review* founded by Bentham). However, his sociological sympathies were formed above all by the ethnographic, statistical, and politically charged studies of his friend, co-author, and activist collaborator Friedrich Engels, whose 1845 study *The Condition of the Working Class in England* provided him with a model for the empirical work and political project he undertook in *Capital*.

The Reading Room floor plan may help us to imagine the scene of Marx encountering his predecessors and contemporaries while writing the notes, articles, and letters that would become *Capital*. Its great dome thus became the setting for his struggle to comprehend the major events of modern history—from the French and industrial revolutions to the world markets and colonial empires in his own day. We might extend this picture to include the core sociologists of the next generation (Simmel, Durkheim, Weber) taking a place in the Reading Room nearby as they grapple with *The Communist Manifesto* and *Capital*, often under the influence of Engels's popularizations of 'Marxism' in *Socialism: Utopian and Scientific* and *The Origin of the Family, Private Property, and the State*. Other social scientists on the Continent and in the United States would also take up Marx's ideas while developing them in new directions, through studies of symbolic exchange (Mauss); economic psychology (Tarde); social groups

(Tönnies); power elites (Pareto); bourgeois culture (Sombart); modern ideology (Mannheim); conspicuous consumption (Veblen); urban culture (Park); race relations (Du Bois); gender inequalities (Gilman); social psychology (Cooley and Mead); and many others. The age of enlightenment reason and global revolution that Marx and Engels left their mark on came to an abrupt end with rise of the Third Reich and the outbreak of World War II, only to be revived and rethought by later critical theorists.

The following list highlights what I think are the most influential editions and translations of the classical sociologists writing between 1789 and 1939:

Works of First-Generation Classical Sociologists:	
Karl Marx	with Engels, *The Communist Manifesto* (1848/1872/1883/1888)
	A Contribution to the Critique of Political Economy (1859)
	Capital, Volume 1 (1867/1873/1875/1883/1887/1890)
Friedrich Engels	*The Condition of the Working Class in England* (1845)
	Socialism: Utopian and Scientific (1880)
	The Origin of the Family, Private Property, and the State (1884)
Alexis de Tocqueville	*Democracy in America* (1835–1840)
	The Old Régime and the Revolution (1856)
Harriet Martineau	*Illustrations of Political Economy* (1834)
	Society in America (1837)
Auguste Comte	*Course in Positive Philosophy* (1835)
	System of Positive Polity (1851–1854)
Herbert Spencer	*Principles of Biology* (1864)
	Principles of Sociology, 4 volumes (1874–1896)

Works of Second-Generation Classical Sociologists:	
Emile Durkheim	*On the Division of Social Labour* (1893/1902)
	Suicide: A Study in Sociology (1897)
	The Elementary Forms of Religious Life (1912)
Max Weber	*The Protestant Ethic and the Spirit of Capitalism* (1904–1905/1920)
	Science as a Vocation/Politics as a Vocation (1919)
	Economy and Society (1922)
Georg Simmel	*Philosophy of Money* (1900/1907)
	Sociology: Studies in the Forms of Association (1908)
	View of Life (1918)
Gabriel Tarde	*Monadology and Sociology* (1893)
	Psychological Economics (1902–1903)
Vilfredo Pareto	*The Rise and Fall of the Elites* (1901)
	Treatise in General Sociology (1916)
Marcel Mauss	with E. Durkheim, *Primitive Classification* (1902)

	Essay on the Gift (1925)
Werner Sombart	*Modern Capitalism* (1902)
	The Bourgeois (1913)
Ferdinand Tönnies	*Community and Society* (1887/1912)
	Custom (1909)
Charles Horton Cooley	*Human Nature and the Social Order* (1902)
	Social Organization (1909)
George Herbert Mead	*The Philosophy of the Present* (1932)
	Mind, Self, and Society (1934)
Charlotte Perkins Gilman	*Women and Economics* (1893)
	The Man-Made World, or, Our Androcentric Culture (1911)
Thorstein Veblen	*The Theory of the Leisure Class* (1899)
	The Engineers and the Price System (1923)
Robert Park	with E. Burgess, *Introduction to the Science of Sociology* (1921)
	with E. Burgess and R. D. McKenzie, *The City* (1925)
W. E. B. Du Bois	*The Souls of Black Folk* (1903)
	Black Reconstruction in America (1935)
Karl Mannheim	*Ideology and Utopia* (1929/1936)
	Man and Society in an Age of Reconstruction (1935/1940)

Works Cited and Consulted

Abbreviations Used:

C—Marx, Karl (1976). *Capital: A Critique of Political Economy, Volume 1.* Ben Fowkes trans. Ernest Mandel intro. London: Penguin Books.

CW—*The Collected Works of Karl Marx and Friedrich Engels 1844–1895.* 47 Volumes. New York: International Publishers. (Electronic Edition, Charlottesville, Virginia).

DL—Durkheim, Emile (2004). *The Division of Labor in Society.* W. D. Wells trans. Lewis Coser intro. New York: The Free Press.

F—Goethe, Johann Wolfgang von (1986). *Faust: Eine Tragödie.* Erster und Zweiter Teile. Stuttgart: Philipp Reclam Jun.

Goethe, Johann Wolfgang von (1976). *Faust: A Tragedy.* Walter Arndt trans., Cyrus Hamlin ed. New York: W. W. Norton & Company.

PE—Weber, Max (2009). *The Protestant Ethic and the Spirit of Capitalism, with Other Writings on the Rise of the West.* Fourth edition. Stephen Kalberg trans., intro. Oxford: Oxford University Press.

PM—Simmel, Georg (2004). *The Philosophy of Money.* Thomas Bottomore, David Frisby trans. London: Routledge.

Alexander, Jeffrey C. (1989). 'Rethinking Durkheim's Intellectual Development: On the Complex Origins of a Cultural Sociology'. In *Structure and Meaning: Rethinking Classical Sociology.* New York: Columbia University Press, Pp. 123–55.

T. Kemple, *Marx's Wager*, Marx, Engels, and Marxisms,
https://doi.org/10.1007/978-3-031-08065-4

Althusser, Louis (1971). *Lenin and Philosophy and Other Essays.* Ben Brewster, trans. New York: Monthly Review Press.

Althusser, Louis and Étienne Balibar (1970). *Reading Capital.* Ben Brewster trans. London: New Left Books.

Anderson, Kevin B. (2019). 'Five explicit and implicit notions of revolution in *Capital, Volume I*, as seen from a multilinear, peripheral angle'. In *Marx's Capital after 150 Years: Critique and Alternative to Capitalism.* Marcello Musto ed. London: Routledge, Pp. 197–207.

Anderson, Kevin B. (2010). *Marx at the Margins: On Nationalism, Ethnicity, and Non-Western Societies.* Chicago & London: The University of Chicago Press.

Anderson, Kevin B. (1983). 'The "Unknown" Marx's *Capital, Volume 1*: The French Edition of 1872–75, 100 Years Later.' *Review of Radical Political Economies* 15 94): 71–80.

Arendt, Hannah (1958). *The Human Condition.* Chicago, IL: University of Chicago Press.

Baehr, Peter (2019). *The Unmasking Style in Social Theory.* London: Routledge.

Barbour, Charles (2012). *The Marx-Machine: Politics, Polemics, Ideology.* Lanham, MD: Lexington Books.

Bennett, Jane (2010). *Vibrant Matter: A Political Ecology of Things.* Durham, SC: Duke University Press.

Berman, Marshall (1988) *All that is Solid Melts into Air: The Experience of Modernity.* New York: Penguin Books.

Bhambra, Gurminder K. and John Holmwood (2021). *Colonialism and Modern Social Theory.* Cambridge, UK: Polity Press.

Binswanger, Hans Christoph (2017). 'Nutzen und Nachteil der Alchemie für die Wirtschaft: Eine geldtheoretische Faust-Deutung'. In *Wie man ein Arschloch wird: Kapitalismus und Kolonisierung.* Carl Hegemann ed. Berlin: Alexanderverlag. Pp. 88–108.

Bottomore, Thomas (1981). 'A Marxist Consideration of Durkheim'. *Social Forces* 59(4): 902–17.

Bourdieu, Pierre (1998). *Practical Reason.* Stanford, CA : Stanford University Press.

Brain, Robert M. (2001). 'The Ontology of the Questionnaire: Max Weber on Measurement and Mass Investigation'. *Studies in History and Philosophy* 32(4): 647–84.

Burkett, Paul (2014). *Marx and Nature: A Red and Green Perspective.* Chicago: Haymarket Books.

Carver, Terrell (2018). *Marx.* Cambridge, UK: Polity Press.

Carver, Terrell (1998). *The Postmodern Marx.* University Park, PA: Penn State University Press.

Cleaver, Harry (1979). *Reading Capital Politically.* Brighton, UK: The Harvester Press.

Comte, Auguste (1975). *Auguste Comte and Positivism: The Essential Writings*. G. Lenzer ed. New York: Harper and Rowe.

Coulthard, Glenn Sean (2014). *Red Skin, White Masks: Rejecting the Colonial Politics of Recognition*. Minneapolis: University of Minnesota Press.

Daub, Adrian (2020). *What Tech Calls Thinking*. New York: Ferrar, Strauss, and Giroux.

Davies, William (2021). 'The Revenge of Sovereignty on Government? The Release of Neoliberal Politics on Economics Post-2008'. *Theory, Culture & Society* 38(6): 95–118.

Dean, Jodi (2020). 'Neofeudalism: The End of Capitalism?'. *Los Angeles Review of Books*. https://lareviewofbooks.org/article/neofeudalism-the-end-of-capitalism/

Dodd, Nigel (2014). *The Social Life of Money*. Princeton, NJ: Princeton University Press.

Du Bois, W. E. B. (1995). *W. E. B. Du Bois: A Reader*. David Levering Lewis ed. New York: Henry Hold and Company.

Durkheim, Emile (1995). *The Elementary Forms of Religious Life*. Karen E. Fields trans. New York: The Free Press.

Durkheim, Emile (1993). *Ethics and the Sociology of Morals*. R. T. Hall. Prometheus Books. Amherst, NY: Prometheus Books.

Durkheim, Emile (1982). *The Rules of Sociological Method*. W. D. Halls trans. New York: The Free Press.

Durkheim, Emile (1960). *Les formes élementaires de la vie religieuse*. Paris: Presses Universitaires de France.

Durkheim, Emile (1958). *Socialism and Saint Simon*. C. Sattler trans. London: Routledge and Kegan Paul.

Durkheim, Emile (1957). *Suicide*. J. A. Spaulding, G. Simpson trans. New York: The Free Press

Durkheim, Emile (1930). *De la division du travail social*. Paris: Presses Universitaires de France.

Durkheim, Emile and Marcel Mauss (1963). *Primitive Classification*. Rodney Needham trans. Chicago: The University of Chicago Press.

Eagleton, Terry (1990). *The Ideology of the Aesthetic*. Oxford, UK: Blackwell.

Elson, Diane (1979). 'The Value Theory of Labour'. In *Value: The Representation of Labour in Capitalism*. Atlantic Highlands, New Jersey: Humanities Press. Pp. 115–80.

Featherstone, Mark (2019). 'Ecologies of Indebtedness'. In *The Sociology of Debt*. M. Featherstone ed. Bristol, UK: Policy Press. Pp. 231–49.

Finn, Ed (2017). *What Algorithms Want: Imagination in the Age of Computing*. Cambridge, MA: The MIT Press.

Follert, Micheal (2019). 'Contractual Thought and Durkheim's Theory of the Social: A Reappraisal'. *Journal of Classical Sociology* 8(4): 447–66.

Foster, John Bellamy, R. Jamil Jonna, Brett Clark (2021). 'The Contagion of Capital: Financialized Capitalism, COVID-19, and the Great Divide'. *Monthly Review* 72 (8): https://monthlyreview.org/2021/01/01/the-contagion-of-capital/?fbclid=IwAR1f9Iw1uL7FFrAsew1rAuw00me-0yoXmKEJsaL7Einl0PL9Mp486g-Sqpo

Foster, John Bellamy, Brett Clark, Hannah Holleman (2020). 'Marx and the Indigenous'. *Monthly Review* February: 1–19.

Foster, John Bellamy (2000). *Marx's Ecology*. New York: Monthly Review Press.

Foster, John Bellamy (1999). 'Marx's Theory of Metabolic Rift: Classical Foundations for Environmental Sociology'. *American Journal of Sociology* 105(2): 366–405.

Foucault, Michel (2005). *The Hermeneutics of the Subject: Lectures at the Collège de France 1981–1982*. G. Burchell trans. New York: Picador.

Foucault, Michel (1978). *The History of Sexuality, Volume 1*. R. Hurley trans. New York: Vintage Books.

Foucault, Michel (1977). *Discipline and Punish: The Birth of the Prison*. A. Sheridan trans. New York: Random House.

Fracchia, Joseph (2022). *Bodies and Artifacts: Historical Materialism as Corporeal Semiotics*, Volumes I and II. Leiden, NL and Boston, MA: Brill Academic Publishers.

Fraser, Nancy (2020). 'What Should Socialism Mean in the 21st Century?' *Socialist Register* 56: 282–294.

Fraser, Nancy (2014). 'Behind Marx's Hidden Abode: For an Expanded Conception of Capitalism'. *New Left Review* 86: 55–72.

Fraser, Nancy (2005). 'Reframing Justice in a Globalizing World'. *New Left Review* 32: 69–88.

Fraser, Nancy, Rahel Jaeggi (2018). *Capitalism: A Conversation in Critical Theory*. Brian Milstein ed. Cambridge, UK: Polity Press.

Freedgood, Elaine (1995). 'Banishing Panic: Harriett Martineau and the Popularization of Political Economy'. *Victorian Studies* 39 (1): 33–53.

Freud, Sigmund (1976). *The Interpretation of Dreams*. J. Strachey trans., ed. London: Penguin Books.

Freud, Sigmund (1972). *Die Traumdeutung*. Frankfurt-am-Main: S. Fischer Verlag.

Freud, Sigmund (1965). *New Introductory Lectures on Psychoanalysis*. J. Strachey trans., ed. New York: W. W. Norton & Co.

Gane, Nicholas (2019). 'Debt, Usury, and the Ongoing Crises of Capitalism'. In *The Sociology of Debt*. M. Featherstone ed. Bristol, UK: Policy Press. Pp. 175–95.

Giddens, Anthony (1990). *The Consequences of Modernity*. Stanford, CA: Stanford University Press.

Giddens, Anthony (1984). *The Constitution of Society: Outline of the Theory of Structuration*. Cambridge, UK: Polity Press.

Gilman, Charlotte Perkins (1989). *The Yellow Wallpaper and Other Writings*. Lynne Sharon Schwartz ed. New York: Bantam Books.

Goethe, Johann Wolfgand von (1983). *Selected Poems*. Christopher Middleton ed. London: John Calder.

Harvey, David (2018). *Marx,* Capital *and the Madness of Economic Reason*. Oxford, UK: Oxford University Press.

Harvey, David (2003). *The New Imperialism*. Oxford, UK: Oxford University Press.

Habib, A. R. (2017). *Hegel and Empire: From Postcolonialism to Globalism*, Basingstoke, UK: Palgrave Macmillan.

Haug, Wolfgang Fritz (2017). 'On the Need for a New English Translation of Marx's *Capital*'. *Socialism and Democracy* 31 (1): 60–86.

Hegel, G. W. F. (1977). *Phenomenology of Spirit*. A. V. Miller trans. Oxford, UK: Oxford University Press.

Hegel, G. W. F. (1975). *Hegel's Logic. Part one of the Encyclopaedia of the Philosophical Sciences*. W. Wallace trans. Oxford, UK: Clarendon Press.

Heinrich, Michael (2016). '*Capital* after MEGA: Discontinuities, Interruptions, and New Beginnings'. *Crisis & Critique* 3(2): 92–138.

Hobbes, Thomas (1968). *Leviathan*. C. B. Macpherson ed. London: Penguin Books.

Hochschild, Arlie (2012). *The Managed Heart: The Commercialization of Human Feeling*. Berkeley, CA: The University of California Press.

Hoecker-Drysdale, Susan (1992). *Harriett Martineau: First Woman Sociologist*. New York: Berg.

Humphreys, Jordan (2020). 'Conventional Capitalism is Dying': COVID-19, Recession, and the Return of the State'. *Marxist Left Review* 18: https://marxistleftreview.org/articles/conventional-capitalism-is-dying-covid-19-recession-and-the-return-of-the-state/

Hyman, Stanley Edgar (1962). *The Tangled Bank: Darwin, Marx, Fraser, and Freud as Imaginative Writers*. New York: Atheneum.

Ince, Onur Ulas (2021). 'Deprovincializing Racial Capitalism: John Crawfurd and Settler Colonialism in India'. *American Political Science Review* (September 2017): 1–17.

Ince, Onur Ulas (2018). *Colonial Capitalism and the Dilemmas of Liberalism*. Oxford, UK: Oxford University Press.

Jameson, Fredric (2011). *Representing 'Capital'*. London: Verso Books.

Jungmann, Robert (2020). 'Kollektives Handeln und die neue Kollektive: eine praxistheoretische Heuristik'. *Zeitschrift für Soziologie* 49(1): 49–65.

Jarvikoski, Timo (1996). 'The Relation of Nature and Society in Marx and Durkheim'. *Acta Sociologica* 39(1): 73–86.

Kemple, Thomas (2018a). *Simmel*. Cambridge, UK: Polity Press.

Kemple, Thomas (2018b). 'Infinite Ends and the Tempo of Life: Notes on the Marx/Simmel Convergence/Divergence'. *Dissonância* (2)2: 137–66.

Kemple, Thomas (2017). 'Comte's Civic Comedy: Secular Religion and Modern Morality in the Age of Classical Sociology.' In *Anthem Companion to Auguste Comte.* A. Wernick ed. London, New York, Delhi: Anthem Press. Pp. 159–174.

Kemple, Thomas (2014). *Intellectual Work and the Spirit of Capitalism: Weber's Calling.* Basingstoke, UK: Palgrave Macmillan.

Kemple, Thomas (2011). 'The Spatial Sense of Empire: Encountering Strangers with Simmel, Tocqueville and Martineau'. *Journal of Classical Sociology* 11(4): 340–355.

Kemple, Thomas (2000). 'Post-Marx: Temporal Rhetoric and Textual Action in *The Communist Manifesto*'. *Rethinking Marxism* 12(2) 2000: 44–60.

Kemple, Thomas (1995). *Reading Marx Writing: Melodrama, the Market, and the 'Grundrisse'.* Stanford: Stanford University Press.

Khatib, Sami (2017). '"Sensuously Supra-Sensuous": The Aesthetics of Real Abstraction'. In *Aesthetic Marx.* S. Gandesha, J. Hartle eds. London: Bloomsbury. Pp. 49–72.

Lazzarato, Maurizio (2015). *Governing by Debt.* J. D. Jordan trans. Semiotext(e). South Pasadena, CA.

Lopez, José (2003). *Society and its Metaphors: Language, Social Theory, and Social Structure.* London: Continuum.

Lukács, Georg (1971). *History and Class Consciousness.* R. Livingstone trans. London: Merlin Press.

Lukács, Georg (1968). *Goethe and his Age.* R. Anchor trans. London: Merlin Press.

Lukes, Steven (1973). *Émile Durkheim: His Life and Work.* London: Penguin Books.

Mallett, Kandist (2020). 'The Coronavirus Pandemic Demonstrates the Failures of Capitalism'. *Teen Vogue*, March 24: https://www.teenvogue.com/story/coronavirus-pandemic-failures-capitalism/amp?__twitter_impression=true&fbclid=IwAR3_bBS0b7Gioq2LOD5ZuCy0kcH-vEvd29UP4kvWWGVpulXmkK_QFAx8R5gg

Martin, James (2015). 'The Rhetoric of the *Manifesto*'. In *The Cambridge Companion to the Communist Manifesto.* T. Carver ed. Cambridge, UK: Cambridge University Press, pp. 50–66.

Martineau, Harriet (2004). *Illustrations of Political Economy: Selected Tales.* D. A. Logan ed. Peterborough, ON: Broadview Press.

Marx, Karl and Friedrich Engels (2008). *Manifest der kommunistischen Partei.* S. M. Suares. Amsterdam: MetaLibri.

Marx, Karl (2003). *Das Kapital, Dritter Band. Marx Engels Werke* 25. Berlin: Dietz Verlag.

Marx, Karl (1989). *Le Capital.* M. J. Roy trans., entièrement révisée par l'auteur. *Marx Engels Gesamtausgabe* II/7 and Apparat. Berlin: Dietz Verlag.

Marx, Karl (1988). *Das Kapital, Erster Band.* 4th edition. *Marx Engels Werke* 23. Berlin: Dietz Verlag. (parallel English text online: https://content.csbs.utah.edu/~ehrbar/cap1.pdf).

Marx, Karl and Friedrich Engels (2004). *The Communist Manifesto.* L. M. Findlay trans., ed. Peterborough, ON: Broadview Press.

Mauss, Marcel (1967). *The Gift.* I. Cunnison trans. NY: W.W. Norton & Co. Inc.

McNally, David (2012). *Monsters of the Market: Zombies, Vampires, and Global Capitalism.* Chicago: Haymarket Books.

Mead, George Herbert (1956). *On Social Psychology.* A. Strauss ed. Chicago: The University of Chicago Press.

Musto, Marcello (2020). *The Last Years of Karl Marx: An Intellectual Biography.* Stanford, CA: Stanford University Press.

Musto, Marcello (2019). 'Introduction: The Unfinished Critique of *Capital*'. In *Marx's* Capital *after 150 Years: Critique and Alternative to Capitalism.* M. Musto ed. New York: Routledge. Pp. 1–35.

Nemorin, Selena (2018). *Biosurveillance in New Media Marketing: World, Discourse, Representation.* Basingstoke, UK: Palgrave Macmillan

Neocleous, Mark (2003). 'The Political Economy of the Dead: Marx's Vampires'. *History of Political Thought* 24(4): 668–84.

Nicolaus, Martin (1968). 'The Unknown Marx'. *New Left Review* I(48):: 41–67.

O'Neill, John (2020). *Writing the Body Politic: A John O'Neill Reader.* M. Featherstone, T. Kemple eds. London: Routledge.

O'Neill, John (2004). *Civic Capitalism: The State of Childhood.* Toronto, ON: University of Toronto Press.

Pinho, Rodrigo Maiolini Bebello (2021). 'The Originality of Marx's French Edition of *Capital*: An Historical Analysis'. *International Marxist Humanist.* 3 September: 1–45. https://imhojournal.org/articles/the-originality-of-marxs-french-edition-of-capital-an-historical-analysis/

Prawer, S. S. (1976). *Karl Marx and World Literature.* Oxford, UK: Oxford University Press.

Pyyhtinen, Olli (2014). *The Gift and its Paradoxes: Beyond Mauss.* Surrey, UK: Ashgate.

Ricoeur, Paul (1970). *Freud and Philosophy: An Essay on Interpretation.* D. Savage trans. New Haven: Yale University Press.

Roberts, William Clare (2017). *Marx's Inferno: The Political Theory of Capital.* Princeton University Press.

Rose, Gillian (1981/2009). *Hegel Contra Sociology.* London: Verso Books.

Said, Edward W. (1978). *Orientalism.* New York: Vintage Books.

Saito, Kohei (2017). *Karl Marx's Ecosocialism: Capital, Nature, and the Unfinished Critique of Political Economy.* New York: Monthly Review Press.

Sekine, Thomas (1984/1986). *The Dialectic of Capital: A Study of the Inner Logic of Capitalism*, Volumes 1/2. Tokyo: Yushindo.

Silva, Ludovico (1971). *El estilo literario de Marx.* Mexico: Siglo Veintiuno.

Simmel, Georg (2010). *The View of Life: Four Metaphysical Essays, with Journal Aphorisms.* J. A. Y. Andrews, D. Frisby trans. Chicago: Chicago University Press.

Simmel, Georg (1997). *Simmel on Culture*. D. Frisby, M. Featherstone eds. London: SAGE Publications.

Simmel, Georg (1989). *Philosophie des Geldes. Georg Simmel Gesamtausgabe* 16. D. Frisby, O. Rammstedt eds. Frankfrurt: Suhrkamp.

Smith, David N. (2021). 'Accumulation and its Discontents: Migration and Nativism in Marx's *Capital* and Late Manuscripts'. In *Rethinking Alternatives with Marx: Economy, Ecology, Migration*. M. Musto ed. Basingstoke, UK: Palgrave Macmillan. Pp. 151–215.

Smith, David N. (2017). 'Sharing Not Selling: Marx Against Value'. *Continental Thought & Theory* 1(4): 653–95.

Smith, David N., Phil Evans (2012). *Marx's Capital Illustrated*. Chicago: Haymarket Books.

Spencer, Herbert (1972). *On Social Evolution*. J. D. Y. Peel ed. Chicago: University of Chicago Press.

Spivak, Gayatri Chakravorty (1987). 'Scattered Speculations on the Question of Value'. In *In Other Words*. London: Methuen. Pp. 154–75.

Stallybrass, Peter (1998). 'Marx's Coat'. In *Border Fetishisms: Material Objects in Unstable Spaces*. P. Spyer ed. London: Routledge. Pp. 183–207.

Swedberg, Richard (1998). *Max Weber and the Idea of Economic Sociology*. Princeton, NJ: Princeton University Press.

de Tocqueville, Alexis (1955) *The Old Regime and the French Revolution*. S. Gilbert trans. Garden City, NY: Doubleday & Co.

Traverso, Enzo (2021). *Revolution: An Intellectual History*. London: Verso.

Varoufakis, Yanis, and Evgeny Morozov (2022). 'Yanis Varoufakis on Crypto & the Left, and Technofeudalism'. *The crypto syllabus*. https://the-crypto-syllabus.com/yanis-varoufakis-on-techno-feudalism/

Veblen, Torstein (1958). *The Portable Veblen*. M. Lerner ed. New York: The Viking Press.

Wallace, Robert, Alex Liebman, Louis Fernando Chaves, Rodrick Wallace (2020). 'COVID-19 and Circuits of Capital'. *Monthly Review* 72 (1): https://monthlyreview.org/2020/03/27/covid-19-and-circuits-of--capital/?fbclid=IwAR2IVdc_SvHnH9R6jdF5W3ycZUnZpgOm1JTtZ_LBOhdilUsQyNKyhy7bouI#en29backlink

Wallerstein, Immanuel (2004). *World-Systems Analysis: An Introduction*. Durham, NC: Duke University Press.

Weber, Marianne (1988). *Max Weber: A Biography*. H. Zohn trans. New Brunswick, NJ: Transaction Books.

Weber, Max (2019) *Economy and Society: A New Translation*. Keith Tribe trans. Cambridge, UK: Harvard University Press.

Weber, Max (2014). *Wirtschaft und Gesellschaft: Soziologie. Max Weber Gesamtausgabe Studienausgabe*. K. Borchardt, E. Hanke, W. Schluchter eds. Tübingen: J. C. B. Mohr (Paul Siebeck).

Weber, Max (2012). *Collected Methodological Writings.* H. H. Bruun trans. H. H. Bruun, S. Whimster eds. London: Routledge.
Weber, Max (2004). *The Vocation Lectures.* R. Livinstone trans. D. Owen, T. B. Strong eds. Indianapolis, IN: Hackett.
Weber, Max (1994). *Political Writings.* P. Lassman, R. Speirs trans, eds. Cambridge, UK: Cambridge University Press.
Weber, Max (1978). *Economy and Society, Volumes 1 and 2.* G. Roth, C. Wittich eds. Berkeley, CA: University of California Press.
Weber, Max (1971). *Max Weber: The Interpretation of Social Reality.* D. Hytch trans. New York: Charles Scribner's Sons.
Weber, Max (1920). *Gesammelte Aufsätze zur Religionssoziologie* I. Tübingen: J. C. B. Mohr (Paul Siebeck).
Whyte, Haydn (2017). 'Marx: The Philosophical Defense of History in the Metonymical Mode'. In *Aesthetic Marx.* S. Gandesha, J. Hartle eds. London: Bloomsbury. Pp. 111–50.
Wilson, H. T. (2004). *The Vocation of Reason: Studies in Critical Theory and Social Science in the Age of Max Weber.* T. Kemple ed. Leiden: Brill.
Wolff, Robert Paul (1988). *Moneybags Must Be So Lucky: On the Literary Structure of Capital.* Amherst: The University of Massachusetts Press.
Wright, Eric Olin (1997). *Class Counts: Comparative Studies in Class Analysis.* Cambridge, UK: Cambridge University Press.

Index[1]

[1] Note: Page numbers followed by 'n' refer to notes.

T. Kemple, *Marx's Wager*, Marx, Engels, and Marxisms,
https://doi.org/10.1007/978-3-031-08065-4

GPSR Compliance
The European Union's (EU) General Product Safety Regulation (GPSR) is a set of rules that requires consumer products to be safe and our obligations to ensure this.

If you have any concerns about our products, you can contact us on

ProductSafety@springernature.com

In case Publisher is established outside the EU, the EU authorized representative is:

Springer Nature Customer Service Center GmbH
Europaplatz 3
69115 Heidelberg, Germany

www.ingramcontent.com/pod-product-compliance
Ingram Content Group UK Ltd.
Pitfield, Milton Keynes, MK11 3LW, UK
UKHW020836290926
15470UKWH00004B/1378
* 9 7 8 3 0 3 1 0 8 0 6 4 7 *